BRANDEIS: Lawyer and Judge in the Modern State

LONDON: HUMPHREY MILFORD
OXFORD UNIVERSITY PRESS

BRANDEIS: Lawyer and Judge in the Modern State

BY

ALPHEUS THOMAS MASON

ASSOCIATE PROFESSOR OF POLITICS
PRINCETON UNIVERSITY

1933

PRINCETON: PRINCETON UNIVERSITY PRESS

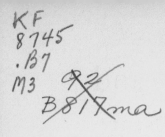

PRINTED AT THE PRINCETON UNIVERSITY PRESS
PRINCETON, NEW JERSEY, U.S.A.

PREFACE

THIS book considers chiefly the public-welfare activities, the ideology and constitutional principles of Mr. Justice Brandeis. No formal biography is attempted. When one observes how, in recent years, his work and his ideas have been vindicated, Brandeis emerges as a truly remarkable figure. Recent events have borne out his fears as well as his hopes. There is scarcely a phase of the recent economic and social débâcle that he did not foresee. In their effort to deal with it, the Roosevelt administrators have been guided, essentially, by the philosophy and by something of the spirit of Brandeis. The New Deal is a response, as the President himself has said, to the country's need for "bold, persistent experimentation."

It was almost inevitable that the statesmanship of economic and social recovery would require using the devices of so outstanding a "social inventor" as Mr. Brandeis. Nor is it surprising that certain of the objectives set by the present administration should be precisely those for which Brandeis has striven for more than a generation. The best evidence of the truth is that it shall come to prevail. Views he long expressed in dissent are now winning approval in law-making bodies, in the columns of the public press, and in the judgments of the Supreme Court itself. A political subordinate, whom he defended from the injustice of men in high places, has recently been reinstated in the department from which he was summarily dismissed because "he knew too much," thus correcting a wrong of twenty-five years standing. Rarely, if ever, has a gifted reformer been an eyewitness, as well as an effective participant, in so complete a realization of his own ideas.

In the preparation of this study, I have had the generous and helpful cooperation of colleagues and friends. The entire manuscript was read by the Chairman of my Department, Professor Edward S. Corwin, and several of his suggestions are incorporated in these pages. I am indebted to Mr. Paul A. Freund, secretary, 1932-33, to Mr. Justice Brandeis, for his penetrating comment and untiring kindness in the later stages of my work. Chapters two and five have profited by the historical knowledge and literary skill of Miss Margaret Sittler of the *Dictionary of American Biography*. Chapter two also had the advantage of a reading by Miss Alice H. Grady of Boston, formerly secretary to Mr. Brandeis, now deputy commissioner of Savings Bank Life Insurance, who was in intimate contact with, and a close student of, his public-welfare work. Chapter three embodies valuable suggestions, especially as to organization, made by Mr. Boris B. Shishkin, Economist, American Federation of Labor. Above all, I am under obligation to my colleague, Professor Walter Lincoln Whittlesey, who gave freely of his time and talent throughout the preparation of this book.

Certain of the material used herein appeared as articles in the *University of Pennsylvania Law Review* and the *American Political Science Review*. Such material, entirely rewritten, is presented here by permission of the editors. I wish also to acknowledge indebtedness to the Social Science Research Council for their grant-in-aid.

A. T. M.

Princeton, N.J.
September 18, 1933

CONTENTS

CHAPTER I

JUDGES RULE THE STATE

A S LONG ago as 1907, the present Chief Justice declared: "We are under a Constitution, but the Constitution is what the judges say it is. . . ."[1] The Supreme Court in deciding cases can rarely use the Constitution as a student uses his dictionary.[2] Since the ordinances of the Constitution do not establish and divide fields of black and white the problem of constitutional interpretation is not rule-of-thumb.[3] Certain main parts of our fundamental law are phrased in language so general as to leave almost everything to the discretion of the judges. What these provisions mean is, essentially, what the judges say they mean; and what the judges say will be determined by various forces. But any one decision will be more particularly influenced by whatever constitutional or judicial theories the

[1] Speech before the Elmira Chamber of Commerce, May 3, 1907, in *Addresses* (1908), p. 139.

[2] ". . . The provisions of the Constitution are not mathematical formulas having their essence in their form; they are organic living institutions transplanted from English soil. Their significance is vital not formal; it is to be gathered not simply by taking the words and a dictionary, but by considering their origin and the line of their growth." Language of Mr. Justice Holmes in Gompers v. United States, 233 U.S. 604, 610 (1914). See also E. S. Corwin, "Judicial Review," *Encyclopaedia of the Social Sciences*, Vol. VIII, p. 457 (1932); R. E. Cushman, "Due Process of Law," *ibid.*, Vol. V, p. 264 (1931).

[3] Justice Holmes dissenting in Springer v. Philippine Islands, 277 U.S. 189, 209, (1928).

Referring to the "due process" clause, Mr. Justice Holmes, dissenting in Baldwin v. Missouri, 281 U.S. 586 (1930) observed: ". . . We ought to remember the great caution shown by the Constitution in limiting the power of the States, and should be slow to construe the clause in the Fourteenth Amendment as committing to the Court, *with no guide but the Court's own discretion,* the validity of whatever laws the States may pass" (at 595). The italics are the author's.

members of the bench, individually, may then entertain.[4] Constitutional theory usually reflects the training, and also the economic and social background of the judge himself. The judge does not and cannot live in a vacuum. He is, and ought to be, influenced by the life about him.[5] The meaning of the Constitution, therefore, varies not only from age to age, but also from judge to judge, even though they sit on the same bench at the same time.

These truisms may explain the changing points of view which our basic law exhibits from generation to generation. During our earlier constitutional development, the relation of the states to the national government was expounded by John Marshall, and was shaped by his zeal for national power. After him this relation was interpreted largely by Chief Justice Taney and from the opposite position. Similarly, even in our own day, the relation of governmental power to individual rights has been expounded from diverse and conflicting points of view.

That an important phase of the judge's work is, and always has been, lawmaking, is not much questioned now.[6] The Con-

[4] "Under the constitutional system as developed in this country the political philosophy of the judges is a matter of vital importance." W. F. Dodd, "Social Legislation and the Courts," *Pol. Sci. Quart.*, Vol. XXVIII (1913), pp. 1, 3.

[5] "The moral code of each generation, this amalgam of custom and philosophy and many an intermediate grade of conduct and belief, supplies a norm or standard of behavior which struggles to make itself articulate in law. The sanction or source of obligation for moral rules, it has been said, is the pressure of society on the individual mind. The same pressure is ever at work in making the law declared by the courts. The State in commissioning its judges has commanded them to judge, but neither in constitution nor in statute has it formulated a code to define the manner of their judging." Benjamin N. Cardozo, *The Paradoxes of Legal Science* (1928), pp. 17-18.

"On social, economic and ethical questions, nature was always found to dictate the personal views of the individual jurist as they had been fixed and settled by education, association and, perhaps, class interest. On legal questions, nature was found to dictate for the most part the principles of law with which the individual jurist was familiar and under which he had grown up." Roscoe Pound, *The Spirit of the Common Law* (1921), pp. 95-6.

[6] "When a court decides a case upon grounds of public policy, the judges become, in effect, legislators. The question then involved is no longer one for lawyers only. It

stitution is not a congeries of wooden precepts shuffled about according to rules of mechanical logic.[7] If the Constitution is, as Woodrow Wilson once declared, "the vehicle of the nation's life," the Supreme Court makes it so.[8]

One is impressed, in recent discussions, by the general recognition these truths have received. "The Constitution . . . today," observed Senator Wagner in the debates on the nomination of Judge Parker, "is what the judges of the past have made it

seems fitting, therefore, to inquire whether this judicial legislation is sound." L. D. Brandeis, "Cutthroat Prices: The Competition that Kills," *Harper's Weekly,* November 15, 1913. Reprinted in *Business—A Profession* (1933), p. 243.

"Today, when all recognize, nay insist, that legal systems do and must grow, that legal principles are not absolute, but are relative to time and place, and that juridical idealism may go no further than the ideals of an epoch, the fiction [that the judges cannot make law] should be discarded." Roscoe Pound, "Courts and Legislation," *Am. Pol. Sci. Rev.,* Vol. VII (1913), pp. 361, 365. "I recognize without hesitation that judges do and must legislate, but they can do so only interstitially; they are confined from molar to molecular motions." Mr. Justice Holmes, So. Pac. Co. v. Jensen, 244 U.S. 205, 221 (1917). See also B. N. Cardozo, *The Nature of Judicial Process* (1928), Chap. III, and H. J. Laski, *Studies in Law and Politics* (1932), p. 202.

In the light of a recent address by Mr. Justice Butler of the United States Supreme Court, the statement that judicial lawmaking is now generally recognized, would seem to demand qualification:

"Judges may not put aside or stretch the law in order to decide according to their individual conceptions of right and wrong or to give effect to what in their view would best meet social and economic needs. They are bound to take the law as it is. They have to apply it impartially to the conditions, whether new or old, that are properly disclosed in controversies brought before them for decision. It is for others to determine whether new commercial, industrial or social conditions require amendment of the law. Courts may not substitute for fixed principles the changing popular conceptions of right or justice that from time to time may seem to merit approval. Interpretation cannot be made to serve in the place of legislation. When changes in the law are regularly accomplished the courts will give them effect according to their true meaning and intent." Address at the opening of the Civil Courts Building, June 21, 1930, St. Louis, Mo. For an able treatment of theories of law and of lawmaking, see J. Dickinson, "The Law Behind Law" (1929), 29 *Col. L. Rev.,* 113, 285.

[7] "The application of the law is not and ought not to be a purely mechanical process. Laws are not ends in themselves; they are means toward the administration of justice." Roscoe Pound, "Courts and Legislation," *Am. Pol. Sci. Rev.,* Vol. VII (1913), pp. 361, 365. See also the words of Senator Wagner, 72 Cong. Rec. 8033 (1930).

[8] Woodrow Wilson, *Constitutional Government in the United States* (1908), pp. 157 ff.

and the Constitution of the future will be what the judges appointed in our day will make it."[9] Senator Brookhart used more extravagant language in 1930: "Marbury v. Madison . . . arrogated to the Supreme Court the supreme authority in this country. It subordinated the legislative and the executive to the judicial department. That is a power which is the real sovereign power in this country. . . ."[10] While one may not subscribe entirely to this statement, it embodies a certain element of truth. Professor E. S. Corwin asserts much the same proposition: "judicial review, from being an instrument for the application of the Constitution, tends to supplant it. *In other words, the discretion of the judges tends to supplant it.*"[11] Professor Felix Frankfurter put the same idea boldly when he declared that "the Supreme Court *is* the Constitution."[12]

The old idea that ours is "a government of laws and not of men" must be modified. Today we recognize that it is the judges themselves, rather than the letter of constitutional provision, that determines limits for the vague contour of our fundamental law. Together with the ever-increasing volume of social, economic and technical legislation upon which judges may have to pass, this view of constitutional principles emphasizes the importance of the judicial function. We can, in this manner, account for the debates in the Senate when the names of Charles Evans Hughes and Judge Parker were under consideration.[13]

[9] 72 Cong. Rec. 8033 (1930).

[10] 72 Cong. Rec. 3506 (1930).

[11] E. S. Corwin, *The Constitution and What It Means Today,* Preface to 4th ed. (1930), p. vii.

[12] Felix Frankfurter, "The United States Supreme Court Moulding the Constitution," *Current History,* May 1930. See also H. J. Laski, *Studies in Law and Politics* (1932), p. 163.

[13] *The New Republic* in 1916 discussing the Senate debates regarding the nomination of Mr. Brandeis made an accurate prophecy of the kind of discussion that took place in that house regarding Parker and Hughes: "There is no use shirking the facts. The Court has been dragged into politics, and if at some future time an appointment is made which is as conspicuously conservative as that of Mr. Brandeis was conspicuously liberal, it will not be surprising if the radicals, throwing off the self-

Admittedly men of integrity, their nominations were nevertheless challenged chiefly because of their economic and social
views, and in protest against "the building up of a judicial system
of law that is fast bringing economic slavery in this country."[14]
It was recognized that the qualities required in a good judge
are not those that make a good advocate.[15] Knowledge of law
is merely the lawyer's stock in trade, and only one consideration,
a lesser one at that, in determining a candidate's fitness for the
Supreme Court.[16] That the nominee has the necessary legal
equipment may ordinarily be taken for granted. In the Senate
debates of 1930, it was recalled that even John Marshall, as a
lawyer, had his superiors; that his supremacy lay not in
knowledge of law, but in recognition of, and penetrating insight
into, the problems that in his day faced a new and growing
country.

Furthermore, qualifications that fit a person for judicial
functions in one generation are not necessarily suitable for the
next. The qualities that equip one for the exercise of judicial
functions have been aptly described as those of "statecraft."[17]
That is to say, in addition to a knowledge of law, the judge
should know the conditions that confront his own generation.
The judges who, throughout its history, have achieved pre-
eminence on our Supreme Court have been thus equipped.

restraint they have shown this time, should follow the wretched example set by
Mr. Brandeis' conservative enemies." *The New Republic,* June 10, 1916.

[14] Sen. Dill, 72 Cong. Rec. 3642 (1930).

[15] This fact was appreciated by Thomas Hobbes as early as 1651.

"The abilities required in a good Interpreter of the Law, that is to say, in a good
Judge, are not the same with those of a good Advocate; namely, the study of the
Lawes." *Leviathan* (Everyman's ed.), Chap. xxvi, p. 149.

[16] ". . . The . . . Supreme Court, by its own will, has moved its activities into
the larger orbit of determining social and economic policies, and then imparting to
them the force of law. It has, in other words, brought itself to the place where
legal competence is only one—and perhaps not the most important—test of fitness for
service on that court." *The Baltimore Sun,* February 13, 1930. Quoted in 72 Cong. Rec.
3553 (1930).

[17] Felix Frankfurter, *The Public and Its Government* (1930), pp. 75 ff.

Certain issues of major importance will soon confront the Supreme Court. The judges must ultimately be concerned with constitutional questions raised by the vast project of establishing a more balanced, safeguarded, and directed national economy. Whatever we may come to mean, in the near future, by such phrases as "a planned system of industry and finance," "an ordered national economic life," "a socialized system of production and distribution," these constructive efforts will thenceforth set goals and limits for the work of the Supreme Court. New adjustments are to be made as to relations between capital and labor, agriculture and industry, creditors and debtors. These adjustments will, as we see it now, extend the functions of government and also those of the Court, far beyond any previously imagined possibilities.

More familiar questions still await solution. How far may the government go in the exercise of police and taxing powers, for the promotion of the general welfare? What should be a reasonable rate and what should constitute the rate-base for public utilities? What is the scope of legitimate action by employers and employees who seek to advance their own social and economic interests? How far may Congress and the state legislatures go in their efforts to strike a balance between the naturally unequal bargaining powers of employer and employee? Clearly such questions are not primarily legal, they are rather economic and social in their nature, and when the Supreme Court passes upon these questions it becomes, in a sense, the ultimate arbiter of state and national legislation.[18]

[18] Judges "are policy determining officers, because they have power to declare null and void 'on principles of constitutional law which are scarcely more than general moral precepts,' laws enacted by legislative authority. It is this function of declaring laws unconstitutional, especially as violative of broad and indefinable guarantees that 'no one shall be deprived of life, liberty or property without due process of law,' which has made the courts in this country essentially lawmaking bodies, determining in the end what legislative policies shall or shall not be adopted." W. F. Dodd, "Social Legislation and the Courts," *Pol. Sci. Quart.*, Vol. XXVIII (1913), pp. 1, 3. ". . . The Supreme Court of the United States is not only determining legal questions

That the judges must exercise some choice of public policy in dealing with these problems is scarcely debatable.[19] But the point deserving special emphasis here is not merely that judges pass upon vital public policy, but rather that by reason of their narrow legalistic training and from the specialized nature of present-day legal practice, they are ill-prepared to exercise this all-important function. In performing this task, they need training in the subject matter with which they deal—politics, economics, and social science—such as will enable them to appreciate and weigh the highly intricate economic and social factors involved. One can point to numerous instances in which the United States Supreme Court has already departed from anything related, save by the most tenuous thread, to a fixed body of law, and has engaged in the statecraft of economics. Judges are often bound to make a choice of public policy. The nature of many modern constitutional questions demands it, and by reason of the glaring gap in legal education they do it,

but it is likewise determining the great economic questions." Language of Senator Wheeler, 72 Cong. Rec. 3516 (1930). ". . . Under the Fourteenth Amendment the Supreme Court of the United States, as to most questions of a nature similar to the one which the Court passed upon in the railway case [United Rys., etc., v. West, 280 U.S. 234 (1930)], becomes really the economic dictator in the United States." Language of Senator Borah, 72 Cong. Rec. 3449 (1930). Mr. Justice Brandeis himself declares that the Court's application of the doctrine of due process as a test of reasonableness may in certain cases amount to an "exercise of the powers of a super-legislature—not the performance of the constitutional function of judicial review." Jay Burns Baking Co. v. Bryan, 264 U.S. 504, 534 (1924). For another expression of the same idea, see his dissenting opinion in New State Ice Co. v. Liebmann, 285 U.S. 262, 300 (1932).

19 "What is a fair return [on property devoted to a public use] cannot be settled by invoking decisions of this Court made years ago based upon conditions radically different from those which prevail today. The problem is one to be tested primarily by present-day conditions." Mr. Justice Sutherland, in United Railways and Electric Co. v. West, 280 U.S. 234, 249 (1930). "What will constitute a fair return in a given case is not capable of exact mathematical demonstration. It is a matter more or less of approximation about which conclusions may differ." ibid., 251. In other words it depends upon the viewpoint of those who are passing on it; it is according to the view of whether one is thinking most about property and the rights of property, or about human rights or the rights of individuals. Compare language of Senator Borah, 72 Cong. Rec. 3449 (1930).

as one writer declares, "confusedly, or ignorantly, and therefore without a full sense of responsibility for what they are doing."[20] "To realize that there is a new economic order and to realize it passionately," Professor Frankfurter recently observed, "is the central equipment of modern statesmanship."[21] These qualities of statesmanship are no less necessary for the modern judge.

Since 1920 the Supreme Court has overturned more legislation than in fifty years preceding. Even more significant for our purpose is the fact that, since 1921, thirty per cent of the statutes contested under the "due process" clause have been held invalid.[22] One or both of two reasons may account for this unfavorable attitude toward social legislation. The judges may not have been in sympathy with the economic or social theory underlying the legislation in question. Of course this consideration alone should not conclude the judgment of the Court regarding the constitutionality or unconstitutionality of legislation. "A Constitution," Mr. Justice Holmes tells us, "is not intended to embody a particular economic theory. . . . It is made for people of fundamentally differing views."[23] The truth is, however, that the judges have at times, whether consciously or unconsciously, read their own economic and social theories into the Constitution. This is the opinion of some who have observed the Court at close range.[24] Dean Pound expressed the

[20] George H. Sabine, "Pragmatic Approach to Political Science," *Am. Pol. Sci. Rev.,* Vol. XXIV (1930), pp. 877, 878.

[21] "Social Issues Before the Supreme Court," *Yale Review,* Vol. XXII (1933), pp. 476, 477.

[22] Felix Frankfurter, "The United States Supreme Court Moulding the Constitution," *Current History,* Vol. XXXII (1930); see also his book, *The Public and Its Government,* pp. 47 ff.

[23] Dissenting opinion in Lochner v. N.Y., 198 U.S. 45, 75-6 (1905).

[24] Speech of Mr. Justice Holmes delivered February 15, 1913, 62nd Cong., 3rd Sess., Sen. Doc. Vol. XXV, No. 1106, pp. 4-5. Mr. Brandeis wrote in 1916: "The Supreme Court of the United States . . . showed by its . . . decision in the Coppage Case the potency of mental prepossessions." L. D. Brandeis, "The Living Law" (1916), 10 *Ill. L. Rev.* 461, 467. See also the dissenting opinion of Mr. Justice Holmes in Baldwin v. Missouri, 281 U.S. 586 (1930), for a stronger exposition of

point boldly: "Judges, like the king and like the people, when they act upon absolute theories, are not easily confined by self-imposed limitations and may even wield absolute power in an arbitrary manner."[25]

Legislation may have been invalidated because of an antiquated manner of approach to the problem of constitutional interpretation. Too often judicial consideration of modern social and economic problems has remained merely rationalist or historical.[26] Emphasis upon certain abstract concepts, such as "liberty of contract" under eighteenth century conditions, has justified objection to not a few legislative measures. Many, if not most, of our constitutional issues today cannot be dealt with in this manner.[27] Whether membership in a trade union bears

the same thought: "As the decisions now stand, I see hardly any limit but the sky to the invalidating of those rights if they happen to strike a majority of this Court as for any reason undesirable. I cannot believe that the Amendment [14th] was intended to give us *carte blanche* to embody our economic or moral beliefs in its prohibitions." p. 595.

Mr. Justice Brewer openly expressed his fear: "The paternal theory of government is to me odious." Budd v. N.Y., 143 U.S. 517, 551 (1892). For other illustrations of the Court's fear of "isms" in one form or another, see Pollock v. F. L. and T. Co., 158 U.S. 601 (1895); S.C. v. U.S., 199 U.S. 437 (1905).

This subject is discusscsd at some length in J. Dickinson, *Administrative Justice and Supremacy of Law* (1927), pp. 340-1.

25 Roscoe Pound, *The Spirit of the Common Law* (1921), p. 108.

26 "Settled habits of juristic thought are characteristic of American legal science. Our legal scholarship is chiefly historical. Our professional thinking upon juristic subjects is almost wholly from the point of view of eighteenth century natural law." Roscoe Pound, "Courts and Legislation," *Am. Pol. Sci. Rev.,* Vol. VII (1913), pp. 361, 373.

27 "Our legal philosophy and our whole system of constitutional guaranties were developed to fit conditions when property was the most general interest of the community, and the highly individualistic philosophy of our law was one not unadapted to the conditions of this country in the early days. For at least a generation, however, we have been living in a state of social and industrial development to which the earlier individualistic philosophy does not fit itself, and the adjustment of legal principles and legal philosophy to these new conditions is a slow one." W. F. Dodd, "Social Legislation and the Courts," *Pol. Sci. Quart.,* Vol. XXVIII (1913), pp. 1, 3. "What he [the lawyer] really needs to see . . . are not such phantom abstractions but rather a wealth of other particular facts, equally concrete—historical facts, economic facts, social facts, psychological facts—stretching away to the boundaries of knowledge before the realm of ultimates begins ever to be reached. Only so can

a reasonable relation to the general welfare, whether a minimum wage for women may be justified on the ground of health and morals, whether five, six or eight per cent is a fair return on public utility property, cannot be decided out of mind alone. These, like so many questions in modern constitutional law, require knowledge of facts and compel judgment on policy.

During the frontier-agricultural era, a study of the English and American reports was about all that was needed to settle most constitutional questions. Social and economic background in making and applying legal concepts did not require much consideration until about 1850. In the present industrial age all this is changed. The judge can not confine his researches to the law library.[28] He must study the available social and economic data bearing on his particular question. Lacking mastery of such essential material judges become "less and less competent to formulate rules for new relations which require regulation. They have the experience of the past. But they do not have the facts of the present."[29]

Modes of juristic thought have not kept pace with changes in social and economic conditions. As one reads recent Supreme Court opinions he may well wonder how much longer judicial thinking and method will be dominated by what may be described as the sovereignty of concepts.[30] Certainly one cannot

decisions like those in the Ives and Lochner cases be avoided." J. Dickinson, *op. cit.,* p. 341.

[28] "We must look away from the piecemeal law books, the miscellaneous and disconnected statutes and legal maxims, the court decisions, to the life of men. . . . After all, it is not a purely intellectual process, this interpretation of experience, this translation of experience, into law." Woodrow Wilson, "The Law and the Facts," *Am. Pol. Sci. Rev.,* Vol. V (1911), pp. 6, 9. See also Felix Frankfurter, *op. cit.,* Chap. 1.

[29] Roscoe Pound, "Common Law and Legislation," (1907), 21 *Harv. L. Rev.* 383, 403. See also H. W. Biklé, "Judicial Determination of Questions of Fact Affecting the Constitutional Validity of Legislative Action" (1924), 38 *Harv. L. Rev.* 6, 21.

[30] ". . . It happens too often in our Anglo-American case law that through over-ambition of our courts to lay down universal rules our empirical method is replaced

as yet say of our own constitutional jurisprudence what the Dutch publicist, Hugo Krabbe, has said of jurisprudence generally:

> We are about to close the period of our history in which the leading rôle was played by a rationalism which saw in the intellect the only source for the knowledge of reality, which opposed dogmas and doctrines to reality, and which confined the latter in a rigid form of thought where logic alone was decisive. We are on the point of discarding everything in the field of law that is included under the ill-famed phrase, "a jurisprudence of concepts."[31]

General propositions, it has been observed, do not decide concrete cases. Decisions involving social and economic legislation depend, as Mr. Justice Holmes has said, on "a judgment or intuition more subtle than any articulate major premise."[32] It

in many portions of the legal system by a jurisprudence of conceptions." Roscoe Pound, "Courts and Legislation," *Am. Pol. Sci. Rev.*, Vol. VII (1913), p. 372.

[31] Hugo Krabbe, *The Modern Idea of the State* (1922), p. 194. See note 30 *supra*.

As recently as 1932 Mr. Justice Brandeis was moved to write in a dissenting opinion: "If the Act is to be stricken down, it must be on the ground that the Federal Constitution guarantees to the individual the absolute right to enter the ice business, however detrimental the exercise of that right may be to the public welfare." New State Ice Co. v. Liebmann, 285 U.S. 262 at 300.

[32] Dissenting opinion in Lochner v. N.Y., 198 U.S. 45 at 76: "In determining whether an act has a substantial and rational or reasonable relation to the enumerated matters, the court has in mind a background of 'fundamental principles' which are beyond the reach of any legislative power. What these are and how they affect the question of the substantial or reasonable relation of the act to the enumerated objects depends upon 'a judgment or intuition, more subtle than any articulate major premise.' They are indeed the inarticulate major premise itself." A. M. Kales, " 'Due Process,' the Inarticulate Major Premise and Adamson Act" (1916), 26 *Yale L. J.* 519, 526.

"Considerations of public policy . . . underlie American constitutional law, but whether they are *inarticulate* is another matter. Usually they purport to be highly articulate in such terms as 'freedom of contract,' 'judicial independence,' 'freedom of commerce,' 'police power,' and the like. Unfortunately, not only are such phrases often vague and jejeune, but the values which they connote are frequently more or less contradictory. So the question arises whether the Court's employment of them may not conceal more than it reveals—whether, in other words, they may not serve, with or without the conscious intention of their users, as instruments for converting the unstated preferences and biases of individual judges into law." E. S. Corwin, "Judicial Review in Action" (1926), 74 *U. of Pa. L. Rev.* 639, 663.

follows that besides the dialectic training of his professional
studies, the judge has need of an understanding of social and
economic facts and a knowledge of the methods of ascertaining
them. Otherwise, "judicial lawmaking for sheer lack of means
to get at the real situation, operates unjustly and inequitably
in a complex social organization."[33] What is needed is proof
based on experience, social facts, and statistics, of whether the
legislation questioned does or does not bear reasonable relation
to the general welfare, and is or is not inimical to fundamental
rights which the Court must protect.[34] Abstract regard in law
for rights guaranteed by the Constitution may blind the judge
to the fact that unjust social and economic conditions render
those rights meaningless in life. Freedom of contract must be
protected, but it begins only where there is equality of bargaining power—a condition for which legislation must strive. Equal
protection of the law must be afforded, but the law should be
applied differently where conditions differ. The judge has the

[33] Roscoe Pound, "Common Law and Legislation" (1907), 21 *Harv. L. Rev.*,
383, 404.

[34] "If the lawyer should turn to economic history and statistics, which are perhaps
the most inductive branches of social science, he would find a change in method
sharply marked. The contrast between the mental characteristics exercised, on the
one hand, in stating legal principles neatly and clearly and applying them convincingly
to a given or assumed state of facts, and those exercised, on the other hand, in the
patient investigation of the facts as they have been and are is of the widest."
Walter F. Willcox, "The Need of Social Statistics as An Aid to the Courts" (1913),
47 *Am. L. Rev.* 259, 260.
    "In the immediate past the social facts required for the exercise of the judicial
function of lawmaking have been arrived at by means which may fairly be called
mechanical. It is not one of the least problems of the sociological jurist to discover
a rational mode of advising the Court of facts of which it is supposed to take judicial
notice." Roscoe Pound, "Legislation as a Social Function" (1913), 7 *Pub. Am. Soc. Society*, 148, 161. "How long we shall continue to blunder along without the aid of un-
partisan and authoritative scientific assistance in the administration of justice, no one
knows; but all fair persons not conventionalized by provincial legal habits of mind
ought, I should think, unite to effect some such advance." Judge Learned Hand
in Parke-Davis and Co. v. Mulford and Co., 189 Fed. 95, 115 (C.C.S.D.N.Y. 1911).
Quoted by Felix Frankfurter, "Hours of Labor and Realism in Constitutional Law"
(1916), 29 *Harv. L. Rev.*, 353, 373. See also Wilson Gee, *Research in the Social
Sciences* (1929), especially Chap. VI.

responsibility of recognizing that if law is to serve human needs, the legislature must deal with changing circumstances on the basis not of abstractions but of reality. "Judges are apt to be naïf, simple-minded men." They "need education in the obvious —to learn to transcend [their] own convictions and to leave room for much that [they] hold dear to be done away with short of revolution by the orderly change of law."[35] Considera tions such as these may have stimulated Judge Oliver Wendell Holmes to say in 1897:

> For the rational study of the law the black-letter man may be the man of the present, but the man of the future is the man of statistics and the master of economics. It is revolting to have no better reason for a rule of law than that so it was laid down in the time of Henry IV. It is still more revolting if the grounds upon which it was laid down have vanished long since, and the rule simply persists from blind imitation of the past.[36]
>
> The true science of the law does not consist mainly in a theological working out of dogma or a logical development as in mathematics, or only in a study of it as an anthropological document from the outside; an even more important part consists in the establishment of its postulates from within upon accurately measured social desires instead of tradition.[37]

Even this skill is not enough to qualify a man for the exercise of judicial functions in our own time. If the justification of a rule of law be that it helps bring about desired social ends, "it is no less necessary that those who make and develop the law should have those ends articulately in their minds."[38] And this obviously cannot be true unless that mental content is shaped by the personal experience and social environment of the law-moulder himself.

[35] Language of Mr. Justice Holmes, 62nd Cong., 3rd Sess., Sen. Doc., Vol. XXV, No. 1106, p. 5.
[36] O. W. Holmes, *Collected Legal Papers* (1897), p. 187.
[37] *ibid.* (1899), pp. 225-6. There remains the question of how "social desires" are to be "accurately measured."
[38] *ibid.* (1899), pp. 238-9.

CHAPTER II

THE PEOPLE'S ATTORNEY

THE passion for freedom is in the Brandeis blood. Born of a family long eminent for liberal sympathies and of a race whose history bears tragic evidence of a bitter struggle for social justice, Louis D. Brandeis inherited more than a goodly share of those capacities and bents which were, in later years, to distinguish his career.[1] His parents, Adolf Brandeis and Frederika Dembitz, came to America from Bohemia along with the " 'Forty-eighters"—a group whose political genius was heightened by the turmoil of European revolution.[2] On his mother's

[1] A complete biography of Mr. Brandeis is yet to be written. The following titles deal with certain aspects of his life and work: Josephine Goldmark, *Pilgrims of '48* (1930), especially valuable for family background and traditions; Jacob De Haas, *Louis D. Brandeis* (1929), a biographical sketch with special reference to his contribution to Jewish and Zionist history; Felix Frankfurter, ed., *Mr. Justice Brandeis* (1932), a collection of essays published on the seventy-fifth birthday of Mr. Justice Brandeis; Alfred Lief, *The Social and Economic Views of Mr. Justice Brandeis* (1930), collected from judicial opinions, speeches, articles and testimony, with introductory notes.

The following articles furnish valuable biographical sketches: Ernest Poole, "Brandeis, A Remarkable Record of Unselfish Work Done in the Public Interest," *The American Magazine,* February 1911; Elizabeth Glendower Evans, "Mr. Justice Brandeis, The People's Tribune," *The Survey,* October 29, 1931; Hamilton Holt, "Just the Man for Judge," *The Independent,* February 7, 1916; Livy S. Richard, "Up from Aristocracy," *The Independent,* July 27, 1914; Edgar Clifton Bross, "An Analysis of Louis D. Brandeis," *Eastern and Western Review,* August 1916; William Hard, "Brandeis," *The Outlook,* May 31, 1916; Bert Ford, "Boyhood of Brandeis, An Early View of the Man," an interview with Miss Alice H. Grady, *Boston American,* June 4, 1916; "Brandeis, Teacher of Business Economy," *Public Ledger,* December 4, 1910; Frederick W. Coburn, "Who Is this Man Brandeis?" *Human Life,* February 1911; Edward A. Filene, "Brandeis, the Man and Zionist Leader," *The Boston Post,* July 4, 1915; Philip J. Halvosa, "Louis D. Brandeis Pays Partners for His Service to People," *Boston American,* September 29, 1912.

[2] The romantic story of this migration is admirably told by Josephine Goldmark, a daughter of one of the young immigrants, in her book, *Pilgrims of '48* (1930). This

side, too, the active liberal tradition held, as her father had participated in the Polish uprising of 1830. When civil war broke out in the country of their adoption, the sympathies of the elder Brandeis and his brother-in-law, Lewis Dembitz, were enlisted strongly in the Union cause. One of Louis' early memories is helping his mother carry food and coffee to an encampment of Northern soldiers.[3]

The Brandeis family settled in Louisville, Kentucky, where Louis was born November 13, 1856. His father, meanwhile, had prospered in the grain business, and Louis spent his early years in an atmosphere of comfort and culture. The Brandeis home became a noted gathering place for persons of talent, especially musicians. Young Brandeis received his early education in the public schools of Louisville. He survived this process, as his report cards indicate, with such able grace as must have earned him many a nod of approval from his elders.[4] At the age of sixteen, he went with his family to Europe where he registered in the *Annen-realschule* in Dresden. For two years the rigid formalism and stiff, almost military, discipline of the academic routine which made German pre-university education a model of effectiveness, weighed down the spirit of young Brandeis. His general attitude was epitomized in an incident which he relates with some feeling. On one occasion he returned to the school late at night and discovering that he had forgotten his keys, whistled loudly enough to waken his roommate. For this annoying but necessary gesture he was taken to task by a stern *Schultz-mann*. "This made me sick," writes Mr. Brandeis. "In Kentucky you could whistle. . . . I wanted to go back to America and I wanted to study law. My uncle, the abolitionist, was a lawyer,

volume presents a vivid description of the Old World culture which characterized the members of the group and tells the story of the hardships they encountered during their early years in America.

³ Josephine Goldmark, *op. cit.,* p. 284.

⁴ In most of his studies he made a grade of "6," i.e., "without fault."

and to me nothing else seemed really worth while."[5] And back to America he came, to fulfil a desire which had constantly grown more insistent, and to escape the "Verbotenism" he hated.

The family fortune had been depleted by Civil War and Reconstruction, and when young Brandeis entered Harvard Law School, September 27, 1875, he had to earn his living by tutoring fellow students. He completed the course in two years, and made a record as yet unequalled, despite the fact that it was little precedented for an eighteen-year-old to enter Harvard Law "uncolleged"—genius or no genius. The rule regarding age was suspended to allow his degree. He stayed on another year for graduate work and in 1878 with about three hundred dollars saved began to practise law in St. Louis. After eight months he was attracted to the more congenial atmosphere of Boston, where he practised law with his friend and fellow student, Samuel D. Warren, Jr.[6]

Brandeis began his legal career ambitious only to become an honored member of his profession. His early practice was varied and lucrative, and he had his share of corporation business. It was inevitable, however, that with his inclinations, actual legal experience would raise questions not stimulating to the average lawyer. He constantly seized opportunities to go more deeply into the issues involved than strictly legalistic and procedural aspects would demand. Indeed his law practice became a lab-

[5] Josephine Goldmark, *op. cit.,* p. 286.

It should not be inferred that the years in Germany had only a negative effect. A friend writes me: "I have heard him say that although he did well in his studies theretofore, it was not until he went to Dresden that he really learned to think. He said that in preparing an essay on a subject about which he had known nothing, it dawned on him that ideas could be evolved by reflecting on your material. This was a new discovery for him."

[6] The association between these two graduates of the Harvard Law School continued until Mr. Warren's death in 1910, although the partnership was dissolved in 1889 when Mr. Warren took over the management of the paper manufacturing business established by his father. The law firm then became Brandeis, Dunbar and Nutter. F. W. Coburn, "Who Is This Man Brandeis?" *Human Life,* February 1911.

oratory for social and economic study. He first saw labor as such
and became vitally interested in the trade union as an agency
for promoting general welfare, when an employer called on him
to adjust a wage controversy. His client's almost incredible
ignorance as to the elementary economic facts of his own relation to his employees drew the following shaft from Brandeis:

> You say your factory cannot continue to pay the wages the
> employees now earn. But you don't tell me what those earnings are.
> How much do they lose through irregularities in their work? You
> don't know? Do you undertake to manage this business and to say
> what wages it can afford to pay while you are ignorant of facts such
> as these? Are not these the very things you should know, and should
> have seen that your men knew too, before you went into this fight?[7]

Mr. Brandeis' interest in scientific management was likewise
stimulated in the "laboratory" while he was counsel and business
advisor to W. H. McElwain, a prominent and eminently successful manufacturer, one of the pioneers in applying these principles. His activities in connection with the New Haven Railroad
gave him first-hand opportunity to study the Money Trust. He
came before the Interstate Commerce Commission in 1910, to
represent a body of shippers, equipped with exceptional and
practical knowledge of railroading gained during the years
1895-1902, when he was counsel for the Wisconsin Central
Railroad.

By 1890, Brandeis was a prominent member of the Boston
bar. The most alluring rewards of the profession were already his
when, about 1891, he decided to enlist in the battle for social
justice. The circumstances which tempted him thus to "rise"
from aristocracy to democracy, the motives which impelled him
to assume the rôle of "people's attorney," are understandable
only in terms of his social philosophy. "I have only one life to
live," Brandeis told an interviewer in 1911, "and it's short

[7] Related by E. G. Evans, "Mr. Justice Brandeis, The People's Tribune," *The Survey*,
October 29, 1931, p. 140.

enough. Why waste it on things that I don't want most? And I
don't want money or property most. I want to be free."[8] As
attorney for the people, he found that he best fulfilled his own
nature. It was more than social sentiment and a sense of fair
play which convinced him that the way of freedom for others
was also the way of freedom for himself. Aiming at essentials,
by no means a materialist, he committed himself to champion
the cause of the community.

Brandeis has consistently showed profound dislike for the
things of this world that are too much with us, the cumbering
incidentals that engross man's thought and care, and slay his
independence. "My luxury," he said, "is to invest my surplus
effort beyond that required for the proper support of my family,
in the pleasure of taking up a problem and helping solve it, for
the people, without compensation."[9] Sensitive both to the aspira-
tions and the conflicts of the world about him, Brandeis has
always shown congenital inability to stand aloof from issues and
controversies of the living present. He prefers to participate; he
is bound, so it seems, to choose his side. He is compelled to move
in an intellectual and emotional atmosphere much more electric
than suffices most lawyers. This fact goes far to explain his career
both as lawyer and as judge.

"I think it was the affair at Homestead," Brandeis told Livy S.
Richard in 1914, "which first set me thinking seriously about the
labor problem. It took the shock of that battle, where organized
capital hired a private army to shoot at organized labor for
resisting an arbitrary cut in wages, to turn my mind definitely
toward a searching study of the relations of labor to industry."[10]
This riot which lined up in battle array the opposing forces of
capital and labor was instrumental also in his making a fresh

[8] Ernest Poole, "Brandeis, A Remarkable Record . . . ," *The American Magazine*,
February 1911, p. 492.
[9] "Brandeis, Teacher of Business Economy," *Public Ledger*, December 4, 1910.
[10] L. S. Richard, "Up from Aristocracy," *The Independent*, July 27, 1914, p. 130.

approach to the relations of business and law. About this time he was asked to give a course of lectures on Business Law at the Massachusetts Institute of Technology. The lectures as originally prepared were of the traditional sort tracing the evolution of the common law in its relation to industry and commerce. But after the pitched battle between Pinkertons and steel workers, this theoretical treatment seemed much too remote. "I saw at once," Brandeis relates, "that the common law, built up under simpler conditions of living, gave an inadequate basis for the adjustment of the complex relations of the modern factory system. I threw away my notes and approached my theme from new angles. Those talks at Tech marked an epoch in my own career."[11] "That was the beginning of my work on economic subjects."[12]

In his effort to find the causes of obvious social afflictions and to devise remedies, he, along with certain other thinkers, was impressed by the social and economic aspects of our industrial revolution as presented in Lloyd's *Wealth Against Commonwealth*. He told his friends of its profound influence upon his thought;[13] he referred to it frequently in hearings before official investigating bodies; he found in Lloyd's pages an affirmation of his own ideas.

The attitude of fellow-lawyers and judges toward the new economic and social set-up did not escape the scrutiny of Mr. Brandeis. While political, as well as economic and social, science noted these revolutionary changes, "legal science—the unwritten or judge-made laws as distinguished from legislation —was largely deaf and blind to them."[14] He was irked by the

11 *ibid*. His *Notes on Business Law* in two volumes were published by the Massachusetts Institute of Technology. The first volume deals especially with the "Legal Limits of Business Combinations" (1892-94). The second volume treats of "The Legal Relation of Capital and Labor" (1895-96).
12 F. W. Coburn, "Who Is This Man Brandeis?," *Human Life*, February 1911.
13 Hamilton Holt, "Just the Man for Judge," *The Independent*, February 7, 1916.
14 L. D. Brandeis, "The Living Law" (1916), 10 *Ill. L. Rev.* 461, 464.

fact that courts ignored social needs and set up additional barriers besides enlarging the scope of judicial review so as to thwart
legislative efforts at alleviation. "They applied complacently,"
he wrote in 1916, "eighteenth century conceptions of the liberty
of the individual and of the sacredness of private property. . . .
Where statutes giving expression to the new social spirit were
clearly constitutional, judges, imbued with the relentless spirit
of individualism, often construed them away."[15]

Small wonder then that respect for law, for lawyers, and for
judges was waning; small wonder that there arose during the
first decade of the twentieth century a demand for recall of
judges, of judicial decisions, for amending the Constitution and
even for its abolition! Dissatisfaction with the law as administered was clear evidence that "it had not kept pace with the
rapid development of our political, economic, and social ideals."[16]
The reason, according to Brandeis, was that, "the judge came
to the bench unequipped with the necessary knowledge of economic and social science, and his judgment suffered likewise
through lack of equipment in the lawyers who presented the
cases to him."[17] Until this was remedied, legal justice could never
assist in carrying out the dictates of contemporary concepts of
social justice.

This "legal lag" is as old as the profession itself—an evil
inherent in the very process by which law comes into being. But
many a fervent complaint has been wrung from those who
watch with anxious eyes the slow progress of social experiment.
It was not heaven-born inspiration alone which made the phy-
sician Luke put these words into the mouth of a pioneer in
social justice: "Woe unto you, lawyers! for ye have taken away
the key of knowledge: ye entered not in yourselves, and them

15 L. D. Brandeis, "The Living Law" (1916), 10 *Ill. L. Rev.* 461, 464.
16 *ibid.,* p. 463.
17 *ibid.,* p. 470.

that were entering in ye hindered."[18] While the Reformation
was sweeping Germany clear of outworn creeds, the humanist-
jurist Ulrich Zäsius observed: "All sciences have put off their
dirty clothes, only jurisprudence remains in rags." Goethe, writing in another period of rapid transformation, used language
which Brandeis considered an accurate diagnosis of the twentieth century challenge to our law:

> Customs and laws, in every place
> Like a disease, an heirloom dread,
> Still trace their curse from race to race,
> And furtively abroad they spread.
> To nonsense, reason's self they turn;
> Beneficence becomes a pest;
> Woe unto thee, thou art a grandson born!
> As for the law, born with us, unexpressed
> That law, alas, none careth to discern.[19]

Brandeis urged that judges be better fitted for their tasks. He
quoted with approval the words of Professor Charles R. Henderson: "One can hardly escape the conclusion that a lawyer
who has not studied economics and sociology is very apt to
become a public enemy."[20] Broad experience, such as was gained
formerly by general legal practice and participation in public
life, is no longer common. Intense specialization must continue,
but he would "correct its distorting effects by broader education
—by study undertaken preparatory to practice—and continued
by lawyer and judge throughout life: study of economics and
sociology and politics which embody the facts and present the
problems of today."[21] There was little or no merit, he thought,
in the view of those who insist that the Constitution has been
made obsolete by new and unforeseen demands. Rather it was
by reason of ignorance of modern industrial life that judges so

[18] *Luke* xi: 52.
[19] Quoted by Brandeis, *op. cit.*, p. 463.
[20] *ibid.*, p. 470.
[21] *ibid.*

frequently erected constitutional barriers to economic and social progress.

The most effective cure for the profession's chronic ills, according to Brandeis, would be to shift the emphasis traditionally laid on corporate practice. Let the much-acclaimed "corporation lawyer" become the "people's advocate."

> Instead of holding a position of independence, between the wealthy and the people, prepared to curb the excesses of either, able lawyers have, to a large extent, allowed themselves to become adjuncts of great corporations and have neglected the obligation to use their powers for the protection of the people. We hear much of the "corporation lawyer," and far too little of the "people's lawyer." The great opportunity of the American bar is and will be to stand again as it did in the past, ready to protect also the interests of the people.[22]

These words of practical idealism, spoken in 1905, crystallized a desire which had prompted Brandeis years before to turn his efforts to new fields. As many men of public spirit have done, he first tried charity. He served on his district relief committee in Boston and visited applicants personally. In 1894, he acted as counsel in a movement to reform certain relief institutions, and took the initiative in a searching investigation of Boston's public charities. He interested himself particularly in the paupers' home on Long Island in Massachusetts Bay. Brandeis did not attack the character of those in charge; they had, he thought, two essential virtues—integrity and economy, but he pointed out certain shortcomings of policy. Their chief error was to devote all their energy to caring for the pauper, while neglecting opportunities to study means of prevention and cure which would ultimately be the greater social contribution. The sensitive nature of the man responded also to the needs of individuals who suffered from the whole system, and Brandeis' social wisdom flowed in direct and warm human sympathy.

[22] From an address delivered May 4, 1905, before the Harvard Ethical Society. Reprinted in L. D. Brandeis, *Business—A Profession* (1933), pp. 329, 337.

These people are not machines . . . these are human beings . . . they
. . . have emotions, feelings and interests. . . . They should have enter-
tainments, they may be literary, they may be musical, they may perhaps be of a class hardly worthy to be called either. The slightest
thing may interest them. They may be delighted with the flowers
which we who are used to them would cast aside. They may be
delighted with a chromo which we who have better knowledge of
art would turn down. But these people are human beings, and each
one of them, and all of them, can be raised and raised only by holding
up before them that which is higher and that which is better than
they.[23]

Brandeis urged public-spirited Bostonians to keep these institutions in touch with the outer world, believing that "unless
you bring the outer life, the outer sunshine, into the darkness
of the lives of these unfortunates, you can never expect to get
that moral growth to which this institution should ever strive
to bring its inmates. These are the main considerations. All else
is subsidiary."[24]

Early in the century Brandeis waged vigorous warfare against
bribery and corruption in Boston, where, as he said, "misgovern-
ment has reached the danger point."[25] In dispensing public
patronage and in granting public franchises, abuses were most
flagrant. He aroused and crystallized public opinion, "lest the
great heritage of an honorable, glorious past, handed down to
us by our fathers," be corrupted and besmirched by dishonest
office holders.[26] What the situation demanded was discriminating, intelligent public opinion, not merely "periodic, spasmodic
indignation at wrong."[27] So he helped organize the Good Government Association which devoted itself to safeguarding the public
interests of Boston. In 1903 this organization was merged in the

[23] *Report of the Committee of the Whole Board of Aldermen on the Care and Management of Public Institutions* (1894), Vol. III, pp. 3631-2.
[24] *ibid.*, p. 3634.
[25] *The Boston Herald*, April 9, 1903.
[26] *ibid.*
[27] *The Boston Post*, March 19, 1903.

Public Franchise League with activities including the Capitol on Beacon Hill as well as City Hall.

The economic-financial importance of franchises in public streets first began to attract public attention in the 1890's. Exasperated and indignant reformers suddenly wakened to find that many valuable city rights had been given away by the ignorance, carelessness or corruption of legislators and councilmen. The city had lost not only ample revenue, but also means of securing adequate facilities for public service. Largely through the tireless energy of the Public Franchise League, with Brandeis as counsel, Massachusetts is today in a more advantageous position as to the development and control of street railways than many of her sister states.[28] The Massachusetts system was developed according to three main rules: revocable franchises, no stock-watering, effective franchise rates. The first two were secured chiefly through the efforts of Mr. Brandeis.

From 1896 to 1911, he appeared frequently before the Massachusetts legislature to prevent letting franchises and leases to railways and other public utilities for long periods of years. He spoke at a public hearing in 1897 to protest against the gift of a franchise to the Boston Elevated Railroad Company.[29] In this he stood almost alone, without support from fellow citizens or the press. Not until 1900 was public interest of sufficient vitality to organize the Public Franchise League. After contests in the

[28] L. D. Brandeis, "The Experience of Massachusetts in Street Railways," *Municipal Affairs*, February 1903. See also "The Massachusetts System of Dealing with Public Franchises," address of L. D. Brandeis at Cooper Union, New York City, February 24, 1905 (typed manuscript); "Compensation for the Use of Streets," address of L. D. Brandeis delivered before the Good Government League of Cambridge, *Cambridge Chronicle*, April 9, 1904.

[29] See pamphlet by L. D. Brandeis, *Subway Controversy. Shall the Boston Elevated Railway Company Be the Servant or the Master of the People?* issued by the Associated Board of Trade and the Public Franchise League from the final hearings, April 14, 1902. *Comments on the Financial Condition of the Boston Elevated Railway Company*, submitted by L. D. Brandeis on behalf of the Boston Associated Board of Trade to the Committee on Metropolitan Affairs, August 26, 1902.

legislatures of 1900, 1901, and 1902, the company was obliged to yield to the demands of the people substantially at every point, and finally had to assent to the passage of an act which provided for the construction of one or more subways by the city. These were to be leased to the Elevated Railways Company, not for ninety-nine years, but for a term not exceeding twenty-five years. Brandeis thus balked the scheme of the traction trust to grab Boston's subway and other traffic systems by leases in perpetuity, and at the same time proved the wisdom of municipal control of transportation systems.

Stock-watering conspiracies by local public service corporations provided another issue on which Brandeis waged battle as counsel for the people. In 1905, he appeared for the State Board of Trade before the public lighting committee of the Massachusetts legislature, to oppose such an intrigue. He sponsored an act providing that the total debt of the consolidating companies (in this case gas and light) shall not, by reason of such consolidation, be increased. This protects the investor as well as the consumer:

> The law against stock-watering rests upon the fact that, in order to determine what a reasonable compensation is and to limit the return on capital to a reasonable compensation, it is essential that there should be before the public a knowledge of the capital originally invested in the enterprise. The devious devices of stock-watering have the inevitable effect of concealing that fact from the public, and by virtue of that concealment tempt the owners of the property to make unreasonable exactions from the public.[30]

For years the Boston gas business had been a storm center for greedy speculators. The struggle had evolved a decided public opinion in favor of municipal ownership and operation of gas plants. Certain members of the Public Franchise League held

[30] *Consolidation of Gas Companies and of Electric Light Companies.* Argument of Louis D. Brandeis on behalf of Massachusetts State Board of Trade before the Legislative Committee on Public Lighting, March 9, 1905, Boston: Geo. H. Ellis Co.

this view, but Brandeis himself doubted whether municipal ownership was the best solution. Instead he expounded the doctrine of technically measured efficiency and service. His influence helped obtain legislation to combine gas companies on the unique principle of the "sliding scale," which has since been generally recognized as securing the best conditions under private ownership. This principle permits profit sharing between the utility and the consumer—practically a mutual or bilateral bonus for efficiency, i.e., the dividend to the stockholder rises as the selling price to the consumer is reduced. The Boston company was allowed a seven per cent return on a fixed total of capital, as long as it sold gas at ninety cents a thousand feet. When, by increased efficiency, the price of gas was lowered five cents per thousand, the dividend rate might be raised one per cent.[31] The system worked admirably. The net result has been a reduced price of gas to the public and increased dividends to the stockholders.

It was Brandeis who exposed the plot of a Wall Street clique to monopolize the transportation system of New England by merging the New Haven and the Boston and Maine Railroads. Prior to 1906, the Morgan-controlled New Haven was known to have steadily engrossed transportation in Connecticut. It had swallowed five hundred miles of trolley lines in that state and, in 1906, acquired over one-third of the Boston and Maine's stock preparatory to merger. Meanwhile, public feeling rose high; the Anti-Merger League was formed with Brandeis as counsel. He engaged in a series of warm debates and wrote numerous searching articles on the financial status of both these roads.[32] Finally, he published a large pamphlet of facts and figures such as only

[31] L. D. Brandeis, "How Boston Solved the Gas Problem," *The American Review of Reviews*, November 1907. Reprinted in *Business—A Profession*, p. 99.

[32] *The Boston Morning Herald*, December 20, 1907. *New England Transportation Monopoly* (*The Proposed Merger*), an address delivered by L. D. Brandeis before the New England Dry Goods Association, February 11, 1908. Published by the Massachusetts Anti-Merger League. Reprinted in *Business—A Profession*, p. 262.

an expert could extract from the muddied sources.[33] Brandeis' analysis showed that the New Haven, because of excessive expansion at excessive prices, could not possibly absorb and develop the railroads of northern New England. His advice was unheeded, his warnings derided, and his motives impugned. Soon after Governor Eben S. Draper assumed office in January 1909, the New Haven was empowered (Chapter 519 of the acts of 1909) to acquire through a holding company all the stock of the Boston and Maine. As Brandeis had predicted difficulties resulted; rates were increased and service demoralized.[34] Complaints became so numerous and bitter that the Interstate Commerce Commission ordered an investigation, and Charles A. Prouty's report was a vindication of the League's counsel. What Brandeis prophesied years before not only became a matter of public record but of public knowledge.

This New Haven episode led him to investigate "the money trust" in its broader aspects. In 1911, "bigness" was considered necessary for efficiency. Big railroad systems, big industrial trusts, big public service companies and, as servant-masters of these, big banks and big trust companies. J. P. Morgan and Company, in their letter to the Pujo Committee, urged the needs of "Big Business" as justifying financial concentration. The elder Morgan declared that "cooperation" is simply a result of the necessity for handling great transactions; that "the country

[33] *Financial Condition of New York, New Haven and Hartford Railroad Company and of the Boston and Maine Railroad,* Boston, 1907.

[34] "Demoralized and curtailed freight service, antiquated equipment, frequent wrecks, discontented employees, heavy depreciation in the market value of the securities, and huge borrowings on short-time notes at high interest are the accumulated evidences of that deterioration in our transportation system which has been in process during the past eight years of aggressive monopolization." L. D. Brandeis, "The New England Railroad Situation," *The Boston Journal,* December 13, 1912. Reprinted as part of the Record in Senate Hearings on Interstate Commerce, Corporations, Persons, and Firms engaged in Interstate Commerce, 62nd Cong., S. Res. 98, Vol. III (1912), p. 15. See also L. D. Brandeis, "Banker Management: "Why It Has Failed: A Lesson from the New Haven," *Harper's Weekly,* August 16, 1913.

obviously requires not only the larger individual banks, but demands also that those banks shall cooperate to perform efficiently the country's business," and that "a step backward along this line would mean a halt in industrial progress that would affect every wage-earner from the Atlantic to the Pacific."[35]

Brandeis has never shared the Morgan view. He objects to "bigness" in industry not only because it is inefficient, not only because it crushes competition, but also because the social and political objections to combination are overwhelming, especially when the banker acts as a sort of inside copartner in such aggressive expansion. Brandeis first exposed the dangers inherent in tying up banks, railroads and industries in one mass of power capable of wielding tyrannical authority. He long ago criticized the huge tolls taken by bankers, syndicates, and exploitative underwriters such as formed the United States Steel Corporation, and those who control today the avenues of capital for the investing public. Twenty years ago or more he sounded a warning which, if heeded, might have forestalled some present difficulties. When bankers first began to tighten their clutch on the country's industrial life, he made violent protest and urged "publicity" as an immediate antidote.

In no field did Brandeis demonstrate his analytical power, his superb mastery of fact and detail, more effectively than in surgical exposure of insurance abuses.[36] As unpaid counsel for a group of New England policyholders of the Equitable Life Assurance Society, he revealed that nearly half of the tremendous assets of American life insurance were concentrated in three Wall Street companies, and that under unscientific and wasteful management excessive insurance costs were saddled on the investors. The principles he advocated for the reorganization of

[35] Quoted by L. D. Brandeis in *Other People's Money* (1932), p. 162.

[36] *Life Insurance: The Abuses and the Remedies,* an address delivered before the Commercial Club of Boston, October 26, 1905. Published by the Policy-Holders Protective Committee. Reprinted in *Business—A Profession* (1933), p. 15.

such insurance companies were embodied in the Armstrong bill in New York state, largely at the insistence of Charles Evans Hughes, counsel for the Armstrong Committee. Valuable as was this investigation, no remedy was offered by the committee for what Brandeis considered the greatest of life insurance wrongs —so-called "industrial insurance."[37] His deep concern for the working man led him to investigate in detail this sort of insurance in Massachusetts, and the facts disclosed were startling.

In a fifteen-year period ending December 31, 1905, the workmen of Massachusetts had paid to industrial life insurance companies $61,294,887 in premiums and had received in death benefit, endowment or surrender value, a total of $21,819,606. The insurance reserve outstanding from premiums held by insurance companies did not exceed $9,838,000. What had happened to thirty million dollars? This sum, one-half the whole amount paid by workmen as premiums, had been absorbed in "conducting the business," and in paying dividends to stockholders. It was evident to Brandeis that this business was not carried on for the benefit of the policyholder. The bitter need and the helpless financial inexperience of wage-earners were exploited by and for "insiders."

To end this waste and to curb these abuses, Brandeis urged that such insurance be made part of the service rendered by mutual savings banks. Years of experience had demonstrated the ability of these institutions to administer vast accumulations of assets with effectiveness. Moreover a huge clientèle was established in their lists of depositors who numbered about three-quarters of the population of the state. Why should not these institutions organize insurance departments and offer wage-earners the same safe and efficient service as was given their savings accounts? The idea, he thought, could be given practical

[37] L. D. Brandeis, "The Greatest Life Insurance Wrong," *The Independent*, December 20, 1906.

application. So he sponsored the Savings Bank Insurance Plan, lecturing frequently and writing articles in its behalf. A bill of his own drafting was presented to the Massachusetts legislature and, after a battle against the financial lobby kept by the old-line companies, he secured enactment of the bill on June 26, 1907. But this victory was not enough. He organized and financed a campaign to tell the people exactly how the system worked to their advantage. Until raised to the Supreme Court in 1916, he acted as foster-father to the system, and to this day follows its growth with interest and enthusiasm.[38]

During the twenty-odd years of its existence in Massachusetts, Savings Bank Insurance has grown enormously. At the end of the first year, 1908, there were 282 policies in force and the amount of insurance was $114,953. On July 31, 1933, the amount of insurance in force had mounted to $92,354,970, representing 102,488 policies. The anticipated low net cost of this insurance has been more than secured. It is estimated that the average net cost is about twenty-six per cent less than that of commercial life insurance companies on ordinary policies, and about fifty per cent less than their average net cost on weekly premium policies. In an effort to compete with the new system the premiums of the old-line weekly premium companies were reduced on an average by twenty per cent within five years after the introduction of Savings Bank Insurance and the people of Massachusetts and elsewhere were saved millions of dollars annually.

[38] For a description of the system, see *Business—A Profession*, pp. 160-205. See also L. D. Brandeis, "Massachusetts' Substitute for Old Age Pensions," *The Independent*, July 16, 1908; Alice H. Grady, *Brief Survey of the Massachusetts System of Savings Bank Life Insurance and Old Age Annuities*, November 30, 1932, State House, Boston; Alice H. Grady, "The Romance, Development of Savings Bank Life Insurance in Massachusetts," address delivered before the New Century Club of Boston, November 29, 1932; Alice H. Grady, "The Sacrifice of the Thrifty," address delivered before Massachusetts State Branch of the American Federation of Labor at Worcester, Mass., August 1, 1932.

This constructive economic statecraft has the quality of permanence. It has been subjected to every sort of test. It has passed through a great war and an epidemic. It has withstood the continuous opposition of strong financial groups, who feel that their personal interests are harmfully affected. Not even the industrial depression, which threw four hundred thousand Massachusetts workers out of employment, has stopped its steady growth. During the critical years 1930 and 1931, Savings Bank Insurance made a net gain of 34.58 per cent over the amount of insurance in force on October 31, 1929, whereas, during the same period, commercial life insurance companies in Massachusetts increased their business only 6.83 per cent. As continued experience has demonstrated the soundness and safety and feasibility of this plan, employers have been coming to its support in constantly increasing numbers for the benefit of their employees, and it has grown not only in volume of business in force, but the rate of increase has itself been accelerated.

There may be differences of opinion as to some of Brandeis' devices for economic and social betterment, but the value of Savings Bank Insurance has been abundantly proved. Of all his contributions to social justice there is none in which he takes such personal pride as in his Savings Bank Insurance Plan. One wonders that the plan has been adopted nowhere else. The wasteful system against which such headway is being made in Massachusetts exists today in most of our states. With a tried and tested plan working before our very eyes, the insurer still is permitted to exploit the insured.

No other field has so long engaged the attention and interest of Brandeis as that of industrial relations. After acting as arbitrator and conciliator in a number of disputes in the New England cotton mills and elsewhere, he was asked, July 1910, to arbitrate a dispute in the most sweated and anarchistic of industries, the New York City garment trade.[39] Here was a strike involving over seventy thousand employees, and a business of one hundred and eighty million dollars annually—a business whose morale was degenerating into racketeering.

All attempts to bring employer and employees together had failed. The strike had gone on for weeks. Millions of dollars were tied up; thousands of hands were idle; hundreds of shops closed; riots and evictions occurred daily. Over on the East Side suffering was intense. Finally, Meyer Bloomfield and A. Lincoln Filene of Boston came down to New York and brought Brandeis' offer to attempt a settlement. For a time even his subtle efforts seemed ineffective. The sore spot proved to be the "closed shop." This bogey issue was cautiously avoided until lesser differences could be settled. Brandeis finally introduced the forbidden subject under a compromise plan of his own making— "the preferential union shop." The agreement finally reached embodied the core of his plan which proposed a shop where union standards as to working conditions, hours of labor and rates of wages would prevail, and where union men would be preferred. But under this plan it is recognized that since there are differences in skill among workers, employers shall have freedom to choose as between one union man and another, and while giving preference to the union men, shall not be held to any list or bound to follow any prescribed order. Brandeis explained that his idea was based on the assumption that the union would be so strengthened as in the course of time to have

[39] For a detailed account of "the great revolt" of 1910, see Lewis L. Lorwin, *The Women's Garment Workers* (1924), Chap. XXII, and J. B. McPherson, "The New York Cloak Makers' Strike," *Journal of Political Economy*, 1911, Vol. XIX, p. 153. For good newspaper accounts see John E. Lathrop, "Brandeis in Rôle of Peacemaker," *The Oregon Sunday Journal*, December 4, 1910, and Philip Davis, "A New Cure for Strikes," *Boston Evening Transcript*, August 24, 1910. See also address of L. D. Brandeis, *American Cloak and Suit Review*, February 15, 1911.

practically all, if not all, of the operatives in the shops as its members.[40]

The signing of the protocol on September 2, 1910, marked the beginning of a new period of constructive experimentation in collective bargaining. The protocol differed from the usual trade agreements in that it was intended to be a permanent "treaty of peace." It created an institution, entirely new in industrial history, known as the Joint Board of Sanitary Control. It provided for permanent bodies of conciliation and arbitration. A Committee on Grievances was established to consider minor differences arising between the manufacturers and their employees. Important disputes were to be submitted to a permanent Board of Arbitration, whose decisions were final and conclusive. The provision for membership on this board was unusual in that "the public" was recognized as a party interested and shared equal representation with the manufacturers and unions.

Brandeis did more than settle one particular dispute. He helped to build an effective system of industrial government. For six years prior to his elevation to the Supreme Court, he served as chairman of the arbitration board and enjoyed to a remarkable degree the confidence both of employers and employees. In appraising his work as chairman of the arbitration board, Dr. Lewis L. Lorwin writes:

> The protocol raised industrial relations in the industry to a plane of correctness and of mutual respect in procedure. Brandeis set the example of great dignity and suavity at the sessions of the Board of Arbitration, and his air of judicial calm and correctness deeply impressed both sides. The engagement of special statisticians, economists, and industrial experts to carry out technical investigations of conditions

[40] For the full text of the agreement, see *The Survey*, September 17, 1910. See also Henry Moskowitz, "An Experiment in Democratic Industrial Control," *La Follette's Weekly*, April 19, 1913.

Many, if not all, of Brandeis' objectives are embodied in codes recently submitted by unions and manufacturers in the garment industry. *The New York Times*, July 14 and 20, 1933.

in the industry gave an added touch of seriousness and authoritative-
ness to industrial proceedings.[41]

Brandeis' work had come to nation-wide attention as early as
1897, when he appeared in Washington before the Ways and
Means Committee hearings on the Dingley Tariff bill, to speak
in behalf of American consumers, even now a neglected class.
He found no congenial atmosphere then; his ideas were heard
with impatience and ridicule. Amidst jeers and laughter, the
spokesman for seventy million consumers was able to persist in
his plea only ten minutes when he was abruptly cut off. The
Ways and Means Committee were there to listen but when one
spoke of common interests as transcending those of any priv-
ileged class, to them he uttered nonsense. The attitude of the
committee toward this argument was shown by the Pittsburgh
corporation attorney, John Dalzell, a congressman from the
most corrupt, contented, and tariff-coddled of our common-
wealths: "Oh, let him run down!"[42]

Most widely noted and most important politically was
Brandeis' investigation of the famous Ballinger controversy of
1910. This case involved coal filings and entries on 240 square
miles of Alaskan lands and the efforts of a Morgan-Guggenheim
syndicate and other corporations to acquire these valuable tracts
by means of "dummy" entrymen in violation of law. Louis R.
Glavis, chief of the field division of the Interior Department,
exposed this conspiracy; he discussed it with his chief, Richard A.
Ballinger, Secretary of the Interior, and suggested that an opinion
be sought from George W. Wickersham, Attorney General. A
letter to Wickersham was prepared, but Ballinger, who had

[41] Lorwin, *The Women's Garment Workers* (1924), p. 317. For an official study,
see C. H. Winslow, "Conciliation, Arbitration and Sanitation in the Cloak, Suit and
Skirt Industry in New York City," *Bulletin of the U.S. Bureau of Labor Statistics*, No. 98,
and "Industrial Court of the Cloak, Suit, and Skirt Industry of New York City," *ibid.*,
No. 144.
[42] *The Boston Herald*, January 12, 1897.

himself been an attorney for some of these coal land applicants, ruled that the question be settled in his own department.

A part of the lands in question were in the national Alaskan forest reserve and thus under the jurisdiction of Gifford Pinchot, Chief Forester. Pinchot considered the matter of sufficient importance to bring to the attention of President Taft. Thereupon Glavis went to Beverly, Mass., and made a full and direct report to the President, who, in turn, submitted this report to Secretary Ballinger and requested that he and the solicitor of his department, Oscar W. Lawler, prepare an opinion for the President's signature! This was done and the President signed a report addressed to Ballinger praising the Secretary in highest terms and directing him to dismiss Glavis for insubordination.

A Congressional probe into the whole affair was undertaken when Congress met in December 1909.[43] Brandeis represented Glavis. His task was a difficult one, for the whole administration was set against the investigation. To his requests for records there were evasions, delays and denials. Still he persisted in his effort to get at the truth. The result was the most shocking disclosure of misconduct in high places, involving a serious charge against the Attorney General and also the President. But for Brandeis the case had deeper meaning:

> We are not dealing here with a question of the conservation of natural resources merely; it is the conservation and development of the individual; it is the conservation of democracy; it is the conservation of manhood. That is what this fight into which Glavis entered most unwillingly means.[44]

[43] The Congressional joint committee of twelve voted seven (all Republicans) to five (four Democrats and one Progressive) to sustain Ballinger. Shortly thereafter Ballinger was succeeded by Walter L. Fisher. Before the end of the Taft administration Fisher reversed his predecessor and cancelled all Alaskan coal entries and filings, completely sustaining Glavis. Soon after the present Secretary of the Interior, Harold L. Ickes, was appointed, he made Glavis chief of the Division of Investigation of the Interior Department, and President F. D. Roosevelt restored him to his former civil service status.

[44] Investigation of the Department of Interior and of the Bureau of Forestry. Argu-

In this same year the railroads, east of the Mississippi and north of the Ohio and Potomac Rivers, filed new tariffs with the Interstate Commerce Commission, providing for large advances in freight rates. To determine the reasonableness of the proposed rates, the commission ordered an investigation, and Brandeis acted as counsel for the Traffic Committee of the Trade Organizations of the Atlantic Seaboard. In this capacity he demonstrated a knowledge of the economics of railroading extremely rare among lawyers.[45]

Answering the contention of the railroads that possible economies in operation had been exhausted, Brandeis spoke in terms of scientific management. He argued that the railroads had thus far realized economies from levelling grades, eliminating curves, introducing larger cars and engines—in short, from improvements in plant. They had left practically untouched the greater efficiency to be gained by the new science of management—a science which in other industries was already being developed with amazing results—a science by which the efficiency of the individual workman was often more than doubled, a scheme which resulted in increased compensation to the worker as well as increased profit to the employer. In terms of dollars and cents, he estimated that at least $1,000,000 a day could be saved by scientific railroad management. "This investigation," Brandeis concluded, "has developed clearly that the railroads to meet any existing needs should look not without, but within. If their net income is insufficient, the proper remedy is not higher rates resulting in higher costs and lessened business, but scientific

ment and brief of L. D. Brandeis in behalf of L. R. Glavis, 61st Congress, 3rd Sess., Sen. Doc., Vol. XLII, p. 4923 (1911). See, in this connection, Norman Hapgood's excellent chapter in *The Changing Years* (1930), pp. 186-91.

[45] Argument of L. D. Brandeis, counsel for Traffic Committee of the Trade Organizations of the Atlantic Seaboard, 61st Cong., 3rd Sess., Sen. Doc., Vol. LIII, p. 5251 (1911).

management, resulting in lower costs, in higher wages and increased business."[46]

That his argument in the case was effective is evidenced by the fact that the Interstate Commerce Commission refused to grant the proposed increase in rates. But the influence of his ideas on scientific management spread far beyond these bounds. "By a single stroke," as one engineer put it, "Brandeis created a greater advance in scientific management than would otherwise have come in the next quarter of a century."[47]

Brandeis later appeared before the Interstate Commerce Commission in a new capacity. When the eastern roads applied in 1913 for permission to increase freight rates five per cent horizontally, the commission requested his assistance and asked that he "undertake the task of seeing that all sides and angles of the case are presented of record without advocating any particular theory for its disposition." He was instructed, however, "to emphasize any aspect of the case which in your judgment, after an examination of the whole situation, may require emphasis."[48] This appointment immediately aroused comment, and some criticism especially in Wall Street circles. There was speculation as to the exact capacity in which Brandeis would serve the commission, indeed, it was questioned whether it was legitimate that

[46] L. D. Brandeis, *Scientific Management and the Railroads* (1911), p. 91, being part of a brief submitted to the Interstate Commerce Commission in 1910.

[47] Quoted by Ernest Poole in foreword to Brandeis, *Business—a Profession* (1933), p. xlviii. For an appraisal of Brandeis' principles of scientific management, see W. J. Cunningham, "Scientific Management in the Operation of Railroads," *Quarterly Journal of Economics,* May 1911, Vol. XXV, p. 539; Harry A. Bullock, "Higher Railroad Rates vs. Scientific Management," reprinted from articles appearing in *The Boston Transcript,* November 12, 19, and 21, 1910. See also B. A. Franklin, "An Efficiency Experiment Station for Railroads," *The Engineering Magazine,* October 1911; F. L. Hutchins, "The Railroad Problem; Rates, Unit Costs, and Efficiency," *ibid.,* January 1912.

[48] Brief of Louis D. Brandeis, special counsel for the Interstate Commerce Commission, Five Per Cent Rate Case (1913-14). The functions of special counsel as stated in the commission's letter of August 15, 1913, to Brandeis, are reprinted in note 1, p. 6, of the brief.

he serve at all. An official statement was made to the effect that Brandeis was not to be regarded as counsel for the commission, nor was it intended that he represent the shippers or any other special interests. Finally so much mystery was attached to his employment by the commission that Chairman E. E. Clark felt obliged to make public this statement:

> Mr. Brandeis is not employed as an advocate for any special interests, but is employed to assist the commission in analysis of the big general question which underlies this proposal by the railroads. We see no reason why anyone should assume that his employment can disadvantageously affect any interest.[49]

In other words, Mr. Brandeis was retained to get all the pertinent facts, favorable or unfavorable. Reports that he was engaged to represent only the opponents of the rate advances were entirely erroneous. The confidence which the commission vested in Brandeis' ability to see all sides of such matters was entirely justified. He conceded that railroad revenues, on the whole, were insufficient, but insisted that they might be raised by economies in management and especially by abolishing special privileges then granted to favored shippers at great cost to the roads. Arguing that the general horizontal increase proposed should be denied, Brandeis closed his brief by saying:

> Though a general need of greater revenues be shown, it seems clear that it should be provided in ways other than through the tariffs filed. The alleged horizontal increase would intensify existing injustice and discrimination in rates. It would give additional revenues where relief is not needed, and would fail to give adequate revenues to carriers who are most in need of relief. It would burden some traffic already extremely remunerative to the carriers and exempt from contribution other which is unremunerative. The prosperous coal-carrying roads would have their revenues largely increased. Other roads, less prosperous, having a large passenger traffic, would get a much smaller addition to their revenues.[50]

49 *The New York Times,* November 27, 1913.
50 Brief of L. D. Brandeis, Five Per Cent Rate Case, p. 192.

At the same time, it was admitted that higher freight rates seemed to be required in the Central Freight Association territory, and that relief could not be had "without a readjustment of the rate schedule."[51] For this admission he was severely criticized by Clifford Thorne, railroad commissioner for the state of Iowa and counsel for various groups of shippers. Much stress was laid upon it in the hearings on Brandeis' nomination for the Supreme Court.[52] The contention was that even though his studies had convinced him that the railroads needed more money, he should not have made the admission. Mr. Thorne's criticism not only loses sight of the commission's purpose in retaining Brandeis but also fails utterly to appreciate the scrupulous flexibility of a mind no less conscious of the needs of the roads than of the rights of the public.

Brandeis, true to his ancestry and training, has, as we have seen, served the public in whatever crusade the general welfare might enlist him. He battled for enlightened preventive relief for the delinquent, dependent and defective; for control of public utilities, insurance for insured—especially workers; for effective industrial government; to conserve both resources and men, and to curb arbitrary financial monopoly. Thus the true lawyer, from time immemorial, has preferred to fight his courtroom campaigns for the needier client, for the supplicant in greater danger of injustice from arbitrary power. The labors of "the people's attorney" had early led him to see that his imperilled client was not so much an individual or a corporation but rather our entire community, that we are all endangered by the emergence of an economic oligarchy in a political democracy.

[51] ibid., p. 193.

[52] Hearings before the Sub-Committee of the Senate Committee on the Judiciary on the Nomination of Louis D. Brandeis to be an Associate Justice of the Supreme Court of the United States, 64th Cong., 1st Sess., Vol. I, pp. 20 ff. (1916).

CHAPTER III

THE CHALLENGE OF CORPORATE AGGREGATES TO SOCIAL INTELLIGENCE

R ESEARCH in mechanical, chemical, and electrical science has raised vast new problems for human affairs.[1] Discovery and invention lessened drudgery, but new dangers to liberty appeared with the factory system and increased with the growth of business corporations. Large aggregates replaced small privately owned concerns; control of the instruments of production passed from workman to employer; personal relations between the proprietor and his help became impersonal. The individual contract of service lost force as the employer became an economic power, and the employee a commodity. To protect the workers' interest, group relations of employees to deal with employers became common practice, collective bargaining a common doctrine. These changes call for ever-increasing governmental regulation which becomes more and more difficult to plan and to establish. Nevertheless the Roosevelt administration is using the resources of government to correct maladjustments of capital and labor, agriculture and industry, creditors and debtors.

Few contributions in social research compare with those of Steinmetz, Michelson, Millikan, and Pasteur.[2] Even elementary

[1] For an exhaustive examination of this subject, see *Recent Economic Changes in the United States*, 2 vols. (1929), especially the concluding chapter, "A Maze of Economic Changes and a Clue," by Wesley C. Mitchell, Vol. II, pp. 841-911.

President's Research Committee on Social Trends, 2 vols. (1933). For a detailed review of the latter study, see *The New York Times*, section 2, January 2, 1933.

[2] Some noteworthy studies have been made recently in an attempt to grapple with our social and economic ills. Among the best are: Norman Thomas, *America's Way Out: A Program for Democracy* (1931); Sumner H. Slichter, *Modern Economic*

social questions are still unsolved. Can machine production, which floods our markets with unsold goods, be restricted? If so, how? Why are men hungry in the midst of plenty? Why are factories closed when multitudes are undernourished, under-clothed, and clamoring for jobs? Should unemployment be left to supply and demand, or are unemployment insurance and dole to be established by law? Why, amid labor-saving devices, is there little leisure for workers? How can men promote human welfare save as accessory to profit, property, and vested interest? How can production and distribution be so framed that all have more of the good things of life, less poverty, misery, and distress? With few conveniences and labor-saving devices our parents were more contented, peaceful, and secure than we.

Keenly aware of the new industrial era's complexities, Brandeis broadcast its challenge to our social and economic intelligence: "The reason why," he said in 1911, "we have not made more progress in social matters is that these problems have not been tackled by the practical men of high ability, like those who have worked on industrial inventions and enterprises. We need *social inventions,* each of many able men adding his work

Society (1931); Paul H. Douglas and Aaron Director, *The Problem of Unemployment* (1931); Stuart Chase, *The Nemesis of American Business and Other Essays* (1931); Wallace B. Donham, *Business Adrift* (1931); John A. Hobson, *Poverty in Plenty* (1931); Harry W. Laidler, *Concentration of Control in American Industry* (1931).

Among the books published in 1932 and 1933, the following are especially significant: Charles A. Beard, ed., *America Faces the Future* (1932); Adolf A. Berle, Jr., and Gardiner C. Means, *The Modern Corporation and Private Property* (1932); Arthur Dahlberg, *Jobs, Machines and Capitalism* (1932); Harry W. Laidler, *Socialist Planning and a Socialist Program* (1932); George H. Soule, *A Planned Society* (1932); Sir Arthur Salter, *Recovery, The Second Effort* (1932); G. D. H. Cole, *A Guide Through World Chaos* (1932); Lawrence Dennis, *Is Capitalism Doomed?* (1932); John Strachey, *The Coming Struggle for Power* (1933); Franklin D. Roosevelt, *Looking Forward* (1933); Max Lowenthal, *The Investor Pays* (1933). The periodical literature dealing with various aspects of the problems raised by the depression is voluminous and important.

The League for Industrial Democracy has just published a bibliography on social reconstruction which purports to confine the titles to those which involve "pioneer thinking."

until the invention is perfected."[3] "When men begin to think as hard, as intensely, about their social problems as they have thought about automobiles, aeroplanes, and wireless telegraphy, nothing will be socially impossible. Many things which have seemed inevitable will be seen to have been quite unnecessary."[4]

It requires long and rigid training, as well as creative thought, to bend our economic and social system to the service of human needs. But once that effort is made, success must follow. That Brandeis himself did not shirk the responsibility involved, has already been shown.[5] There is hardly a phase of social, economic or industrial life to which he has not turned his hand—labor, trusts, railroads, insurance, and finance—these are but part. To deal with such matters he formulated definite social and economic policies of precise method and wide application, deserving close study. We have noted his fear of monopolized public utilities, and his concern for both employees and consumers. He insisted that utility relations be squared with prudent investment, effective capitalization, scientific management, and fair earnings; the latter shared with consumers and employees under the sliding-scale principle.

The pivotal point in the Brandeisian analysis of our economic and social ills is the power of the business corporation in our modern life. Despite the Sherman Act, competition has ceased to be a conspicuous factor in industry. In 1919 more than twenty thousand manufacturing establishments were not conducted independently but formed part of some industrial corporation.[6] The reach and grip of this golden net over every limb of our economic body is indicated by the fact that in 1930 two hundred non-banking corporations controlled total assets of

[3] Recorded by Ernest Poole from an interview with Mr. Brandeis, *The American Magazine*, February 1911.
[4] "An Unusual Man of Law," *The New York Times Annalist*, January 27, 1913.
[5] See Chap. II, *supra*.
[6] James G. Smith, ed., *Facing the Facts* (1932), p. 188.

$81,000,000,000, or half of all such corporate wealth in the United States; that total assets of all non-banking corporations of the nation then amounted to $165,000,000,000, almost half the total estimated national wealth.[7] These enormous capital resources have vested the corporation with unprecedented economic power and made it the keystone of the country's economic structure. While the number of stockholders had mounted to 1932 by leaps and bounds, control was increasingly held by a minority, sometimes by management which owned no appreciable amount of stock. The economic security of millions of men and women today is at the mercy of corporate organization.

Autocratic power is held by a few "inside" managers who point with pride to the fiction of formal power diffused among a mass of "outside" investors. It was supposed that this increased size of business compelled increased business efficiency. Increased efficiency, "expected economies from combination,"[8] have figured prominently in promoters' prospectuses along with praises of all corporate "bigness." But Brandeis long ago refuted this as the real motive for combination. There was, first, the desire "to avoid what those interested deemed destructive or, at least, very annoying competition."[9] Second, an "extremely effective cause was the desire of promoters and bankers for huge commissions," and, above all, the craving for higher prices.[10]

[7] Adolf A. Berle, Jr., and Gardiner C. Means, *The Modern Corporation and Private Property*, pp. 28-31. See also William Z. Ripley, "Our Corporate Revolution and Its Perils," *The New York Times*, July 24, 1932; Harry W. Laidler, *Concentration of Control in American Industry* (1931).

[8] Hearings before the Senate Committee on Interstate Commerce. Control of Corporations, Persons, and Firms engaged in Interstate Commerce, 62nd Cong., 2nd Sess., Vol. III, p. 2788 (1912). Reprinted as part of the record from articles appearing in *Collier's Weekly* for September 14 and 21, 1912.

[9] *ibid.*, Vol. I, p. 1171.

[10] *ibid.* Mr. Brandeis points out that J. P. Morgan and Company took $62,500,000 in cash values for their services as promoters in the formation of the United States Steel Corporation. *ibid.*, Vol. III, p. 2790. The amount of bankers' commissions in connection with the organization of the Steel Trust was $150,000,000 in securities. *ibid.*, Vol. I, p. 1171.

The purpose of combination was frequently not efficiency at all but to preserve inefficiency—"the desire to capitalize failures." Steel men saw that competition with Andrew Carnegie was impossible, so they capitalized their inability to compete with him and bribed Carnegie to go out of business that their own less efficient concerns might not be destroyed.[11] There is, then, Brandeis holds, no necessary connection between "bigness" and efficiency but rather the opposite. The core of his argument is that:

> When . . . you increase your business to a very great extent, and the multitude of problems increase with its growth, you will find, in the first place, that the man at the head has a diminishing knowledge of the facts and, in the second place, a diminishing opportunity of exercising a careful judgment upon them. Furthermore—and this is one of the most important grounds of inefficiency of large institutions—there develops a centrifugal force greater than the centripetal force. Demoralization sets in; a condition of lessened efficiency presents itself. . . . These are disadvantages that attend bigness.[12]

The gravest objection to large business aggregates is that their so-called organization of absentee stockholding and remote directorships prevents the directors from knowing what goes on. They cannot pass intelligent judgment on problems arising in the business because they do not know the facts of the business. Long before interlocking directorates had flowered so that Samuel Insull could serve on more than eighty boards, Richard B. Mellon on nearly fifty, Percy A. Rockefeller on sixty-eight, Albert H. Wiggin on about fifty, Charles E. Mitchell on thirty-two, etc., etc.,[13] Mr. Brandeis gave warning:

[11] The bribe paid to eliminate Carnegie's efficiency was "at least $250,000,000. . . . It was paid to save the huge paper values which George W. Perkins and others had recently created by combining into eight grossly overcapitalized corporations a large part of the steel mills of America." *ibid.,* Vol. III, p. 2789.

[12] *ibid.,* Vol. I, pp. 1147-48.

[13] See, in this connection, Harry W. Laidler, *Concentration of Control in American Industry,* pp. 441-2.

Nobody can form a judgment that is worth having without a fairly detailed and intimate knowledge of the facts, and the circumstances of these gentlemen, largely bankers of importance, with a multitude of different associations and occupations—the fact that those men cannot know the facts is conclusive to my mind against a system by which the same men are directors in many different companies. I doubt whether anybody who is himself engaged in any important business has time to be a director in more than one large corporation. If he seeks to know about the affairs of that one corporation as much as he should know, not only in the interest of the stockholders, but in the interest of the community, he will have a field for study that will certainly occupy all the time that he has.[14]

Since this statement was made many facts have appeared to confirm its truth. Some of the persons named above have figured in Senate investigations[15] and legal proceedings that prove the Justice's point.

Perhaps the most insidious influence of corporate aggregates results from their money power. The problem, in Brandeis' opinion, had by 1911 reached such proportions as "to baffle the best minds of the country."[16]

This advent of trusts, the mobilizing of that huge capital, was like pouring oil into the rising flame of the Money Trust. All that property theretofore locally owned and controlled in the different parts of the country has now become subject to the money kings of Wall Street, and with the advent of each new trust, with its unconscionable promoters and underwriters' charges, and the daily tribute of the stock exchange commissions, the power is further augmented.[17]

[14] Statement before the Commission on Industrial Relations, 64th Cong., 1st Sess., Sen. Doc., Vol. XXVI, p. 7661 (1915). See also L. D. Brandeis, "Interlocking Directorates," *Annals of American Academy of Political and Social Science,* Vol. LVII, January 1915, p. 45; Hearings before the Committee on the Judiciary, Trust Legislation, 63rd Cong., 2nd Sess., Pt. 22, February 25, 1914.

[15] Hearings before a Sub-Committee of the Committee on Banking and Currency, 72nd Cong., 2nd Sess., Sen. Res. 84 and Sen. Res. 239, February 21-28, March 1 and 2, 1933.

[16] Hearings before the Senate Committee on Interstate Commerce, 62nd Cong., 2nd Sess., Vol. I, p. 1156 (1911).

[17] *ibid.*

. . . The wealth of the Astors does not endanger political or industrial liberty. . . . It lacks significance largely because its owners have
only the income from their own wealth. The Astor wealth is static.
The wealth of the Morgan associates is dynamic. The power and the
growth of power of our financial oligarchs comes from wielding the
savings and quick capital of others. . . . The fetters which bind the
people are forged from the people's own gold.[18]

"Financial oligarchy," as he characterized it, takes the golden
eggs laid by someone's else goose. The situation is all the more
tragic because of the position of trust in which bankers stand to
the investing public. Small investors, especially women, rarely
ascertain facts on which to base judgment as to securities offered
for sale. Investors need, and are entitled to have, Brandeis insists,
the banker's advice and—advice which is obviously unbiased.
This is not possible where the banker, as a factor in the corporation's management, participates in the creation of the
securities which he sells to the investor for his own profit. With
penetrating insight, Brandeis early pointed out the peril of thus
merging banker, business man, manufacturer, and promoter,
and calling the sum "banker." These activities of miscellany are
entirely alien to legitimate banking:

> It is not the proper function of the banker to construct, purchase,
> or operate railroads or to engage in industrial enterprises. The proper
> function of the banker is to give to or to withhold credit from other
> concerns; to purchase or to refuse to purchase securities from other
> concerns; and to sell securities to other customers. The proper exercise
> of this function demands that the banker should be wholly detached
> from the concern whose credit or securities are under consideration.[19]

This divorce should occur if for no other reason than the strain
which such a combination of functions imposes on human
nature:

[18] L. D. Brandeis, "Breaking the Money Trust," *Harper's Weekly*, November 22,
1913.
[19] "The Failure of Banker-Management," *Harper's Weekly*, August 16, 1913.
Reprinted in *Other People's Money* (1932), p. 198.

. . . Banker-management contravenes the fundamental laws of human limitations: *First,* that no one can serve two masters; *second,* that a man can not at the same time do many things well. We must break the Money Trust or the Money Trust will break us.[20]

Brandeis threw out these challenges by 1914. It took over fifteen years of the "new era," and the collapse of our banking system, to drive home to the American public the true significance of the facts he revealed. Not until the Banking Act of 1933[21] was any effort made to divorce commercial and investment banking. Under this new legislation national and member banks must, within one year, divest themselves of their securities affiliates. Also, after one year, it shall be unlawful for any securities company to engage in banking. This hits directly at private banking houses, like J. P. Morgan and Company, that have been exercising both functions.

The Securities Act of 1933[22] seeks to protect the investor against another common evil—that of deceptive and fraudulent securities. As with its English prototype, the government, under this legislation, does not tell a man what risks he shall take with his money, but it does require that he be fully informed as to the facts. Brandeis long ago saw the need for such publicity. His ideas now find embodiment in legislation. As early as 1913 he urged that the investor be informed as to the securities offered him for sale:

[20] L. D. Brandeis, "The Inefficiency of the Oligarchs," *Harper's Weekly,* January 17, 1914, p. 18.

[21] P. L. No. 66, 73rd Cong., sec. 21.

[22] P. L. No. 22, 73rd Cong.

After signing this bill, President Roosevelt issued the following statement: "Events have made it abundantly clear that the merchandising of securities is really traffic in the economic and social welfare of our people. Such traffic demands the utmost good faith and fair dealing on the part of those engaged in it. . . . To that end this bill requires the publicity necessary for sound investment." *The New York Times,* May 28, 1933.

In other words, the basic policy of the Act is that of informing investors of the facts concerning securities to be offered for sale in interstate and foreign commerce and providing protection against fraud and misrepresentation.

Compel bankers when issuing securities to make public the commissions or profits they are receiving. Let every circular letter, prospectus or advertisement of a bond or stock show clearly what the banker received for his middleman services, and what the bonds and stocks net the issuing corporation. That is knowledge to which both the existing security holder and the prospective purchaser are fairly entitled. If the banker's compensation is reasonable, considering the skill and risk involved, there can be no objection to making it known.[23]

Recent events bear eloquent testimony to the views Mr. Brandeis has long held: that financial oligarchy is the most serious menace to freedom in modern society; that the line of greatest advance lies in the direction of financier control. Twenty years ago he said:

Break the control so exercised by the investment bankers over railroad, public service and industrial corporations, over banks, life insurance and trust companies, and a long step will have been taken toward attainment of the New Freedom.[24]

While some progress has been made, the "New Freedom" is yet to be attained. There is reason for believing that it may soon be had as part of the "New Deal," and to some extent as a result of the demotion, or degradation, of the bankers.

Even if it be true that as an engine of production a large unit is more efficient than a small one, Brandeis is convinced that the social and political ills inherent in huge economic-financial power far outweigh any possible advantages of efficiency. Consider first the effect of massed corporate employing power on the workers. Brandeis instances the United States Steel Corporation:

While this corporation is the greatest example of combination, the most conspicuous instance of combination of capital in the world, it has . . . undertaken, and undertaken successfully, to deny the right of combination to the workingmen, and these horrible condi-

23 "What Publicity Can Do," *Harper's Weekly*, December 20, 1913. Reprinted in *Other People's Money* (1932), pp. 101-2.

24 "The Endless Chain. Interlocking Directorates," *Harper's Weekly*, December 6, 1913. Reprinted in *Other People's Money* (1932), p. 51.

tions of labor, which are a disgrace to America, considering the wealth which has surrounded and flowed out of this industry, are the result of having killed or eliminated from the steel industry unionism. All the power of capital and all the ability and intelligence of the men who wield and who serve the capital have been used to make practically slaves of these operatives, because it does not mean merely in respect to the way in which they have lived, but the very worst part of all this is the repression. It is a condition of repression, of slavery in the real sense of the word, which is alien to American conditions.[25]

The above labor problem will be mitigated by anything which improves the economic, physical and social conditions of labor. It is absolutely essential that men be properly housed, clothed, and fed, that they enjoy advantages for education and recreation. "We cannot reach our goal without those things. But we may have all those things and have a nation of slaves."[26] "Men must have industrial liberty as well as good wages."[27] The mental needs of the workingmen are of equal importance.

We must bear in mind all the time that however much we may desire material improvement and must desire it for the comfort of the individual, that the United States is a democracy, and that we must have, above all things, men. It is the development of manhood to which any industrial and social system should be directed. We Americans are committed not only to social justice in the sense of avoiding things which bring suffering and harm, like unjust distribution of wealth; but we are committed primarily to democracy. The social justice for which we are striving is an incident of our democracy, not the main end. It is rather the result of democracy—perhaps its finest expression—but it rests upon democracy, which implies the rule by the people. And therefore the end for which we must strive is the attainment of rule by the people, and that involves industrial democracy as well as political democracy.[28]

[25] Statement before the House Committee Hearings on Investigation of the United States Steel Corporation, p. 2856, January 30, 1912.

[26] Statement before the Commission on Industrial Relations, 64th Cong., 1st Sess., Sen. Doc., Vol. XXVI, p. 7663 (1915).

[27] ibid.

[28] ibid., pp. 7659-60.

While there are many causes contributing to unrest, the one which Brandeis considers fundamental is the inevitable conflict between our political liberalism and our industrial absolutism.

> We are as free politically, perhaps, as free as it is possible for us to be. Every male has his voice and vote; and the law has endeavored to enable, and has succeeded practically, in enabling him to exercise his political franchise without fear. He therefore has his part; and certainly can secure an adequate part in the government of the country in all of its political relations. . . .[29]

In the industrial realm, the position of the ordinary worker is exactly reversed. The individual employee has no effective voice or vote.[30] No real solution, nor even an approximation, can be reached "as long as there exists in this country any juxtaposition of political democracy and industrial absolutism."[31]

Modern industrial society appears to Brandeis as a "contest between those who have and those who have not."[32] The day of the entrepreneur is past. No longer does the individual look forward to becoming independent in his own shop or on his own land. The United States is largely a nation of employees, and the most significant consequence of our industrial revolution has been to fix for most men this status of employeeship. When Brandeis was testifying before the House Committee which investigated the United States Steel Corporation, his attention was centered not so much on hours of labor, standards of wages, and the like, but on the more fundamental question whether or not the position accorded labor was consistent with the American ideal of democracy.

> . . . The question here is not so much the question whether the number of cents per hour that this miserable creature receives is a

[29] Statement before the Commission on Industrial Relations, 64th Cong., 1st Sess., Sen. Doc., Vol. XXVI, p. 7659 (1915).

[30] *ibid.*

[31] *ibid.*, Vol. XIX, p. 1005 (1914). Herein one finds an extended and excellent statement of Brandeis' position.

[32] Ernest Poole, *op. cit.*, p. 492.

little more or a little less. Whether it is enough, none of us are competent to determine. What we are competent to determine, sitting right here, as American citizens, is whether any men in the United States, be they directors of the Steel Corporation or anyone else, are entitled and can safely determine the conditions under which a large portion of the American [workmen] shall live; whether it is not absolutely essential to fairness, for results in an American democracy, to say that the great mass of working people should have an opportunity to combine, and by their collective bargaining secure for themselves what may be a fair return for their labor. There is the fundamental question, and there is the question which is at the bottom of this situation. The denial of that right of collective bargaining is an explanation of the miserable condition of the workingmen in the steel industry.[33]

Huge profits and numerous advantages had, it is true, resulted from improved processes of steel-making but, from a social point of view, these gains had been largely dissipated. The employers had appropriated for themselves the greater part of the profit instead of raising the general standard of working conditions. The result was that a new kind of despotism, economic absolutism, replaced what was formerly political and social absolutism. Theoretically free, the American workman was actually a neglected and exploited serf. The inconsistency and injustice of this situation is patent enough and cannot long continue. The words of Mr. Brandeis express deep conviction:

The people are beginning to doubt whether in the long run democracy and absolutism can coexist in the same community; beginning to doubt whether there is a justification for the great inequalities in the distribution of wealth, for the rapid creation of fortunes, more mysterious than the deeds of Aladdin's lamp. The people have begun to think; and they show evidences on all sides of a tendency to act.[34]

[33] Statement before the House Committee Hearings on Investigation of the United States Steel Corporation, pp. 2857-8, January 30, 1912.
[34] L. D. Brandeis, *Business—A Profession* (1933), p. 342.

Brandeis was concerned lest this movement for popular rights take the form of violence. He was therefore driven to seek immediate remedies. Realizing that profits from the machine had already been largely absorbed by the wasteful speculations of capital, he looked elsewhere for potential benefits to employees, and so sponsored his well known principles of scientific management.[35] The application of these principles, he believed, could effect economies in production comparable to those realized in the transition from hand to machine labor. The purpose of scientific management is not merely to conserve human effort but also to secure greater profit, a large part of which, Brandeis argues, should go to the workers. "Those who do the work shall get in some fair proportion what they produce. The share to which capital as such is entitled is small. All the rest should go to those, high and low, who do the work."[36]

Labor can get its just due, as the general welfare requires, largely by organized effort. Therefore Brandeis favors unionism and collective bargaining. Industrial peace and prosperity are not to be attained by weakening trade unions. He is convinced that conditions in American industry would have been intolerable without the active intervention of the few labor organizations we have. "They have been largely instrumental in securing reasonable hours of labor and proper conditions of work; in raising materially the scale of wages, and in protecting women and children from industrial oppression."[37] And these contributions of trade unions have not been in the interest of workers alone, but for all of us, "since the conditions under which so

[35] For a detailed statement of these principles as they apply to labor see *ibid.*, pp. 37-71. See also L. D. Brandeis, *Scientific Management and the Railroads* (1911); F. B. Gilbreth, *Primer of Scientific Management* (1914), introduction by Louis D. Brandeis.

[36] Hearings before the Senate Committee on Interstate Commerce, 62nd Cong., 2nd Sess., Vol. I, p. 1152 (1911).

[37] L. D. Brandeis, *Business—A Profession* (1933), p. 88. See also Mr. Brandeis' statement before the Commission on Industrial Relations, 64th Cong., 1st Sess., Sen. Doc., Vol. XXVI, pp. 7671 *ff.* (1915).

large a part of our fellow citizens work and live will determine, in great measure, the future of our country for good or for evil."[38]

The interests of wage-earners cannot, however, be cared for by unions alone. Nor is sporadic, emotional charity to be depended upon. The community, more particularly the employers, must bear the burden of supporting needy wage-earners in some other way. Workmen's compensation legislation had already made clear the need for a comprehensive system extending protection to wage-earners against financial dependence. The tenor of Brandeis' argument may be gleaned from the following:

> Everybody recognizes the fire insurance premium as a current expense. And yet the chance of loss by fire is very slight as compared with the chance of loss of earnings by sickness, accident or premature death. Every intelligent manufacturer makes in some form a regular charge for depreciation of machinery and plant. And yet the depreciation of man through invalidity and superannuation is no less certain, and frequently more severe, than the depreciation of machinery. Every intelligent manufacturer recognizes rent, interest, and taxes as current daily charges which continue although his plant is shut down or operates at less than full capacity. The manufacturer makes allowance for this in calculating the cost of production as an extra charge to be met from the earnings of active days. But the cost to the employer of carrying an unused plant is not as great relatively as the cost to the employee of carrying himself and family while unemployed. The manufacturer who fails to recognize fire insurance, depreciation, interest, and taxes as current charges of the business treads the path of bankruptcy. And that nation does the like which fails to recognize and provide against the economic, social and political conditions which impose upon the workingman so large a degree of financial dependence.[39]

Irregular employment, Brandeis feels, is not only the worst but also the ever-present labor menace. Even in prosperous periods, American workers are subject to forced idleness and

[38] *ibid.*
[39] L. D. Brandeis, *Business—A Profession* (1933), pp. 60-1.

lost earnings for probably ten to twenty per cent of their time.[40]
Industry has developed thus chaotically because irregular employment is accepted as inevitable and as entirely outside the
responsibilities of management. "It is no more inevitable than
insistence upon payment for a great many of the overhead
charges in a business, whether the business is in daily operation
or is not."[41] There is bound to be unemployment but it is for
the most part remediable, and he insists should be prevented as
a matter not only of justice but also of business. In 1914, he urged
that regular employment be made a specific demand of society
and of the labor unions, on the ground that "the conception of
day labor is entirely unsocial and is entirely uneconomical; it is
distinctly contrary to the whole conception of scientific management, because it involves such waste as you can find in any
possible department of industry."[42]

Under scientific management, it can be shown that spotty
employment tends to disappear; wherever existing it should be
subject to compensation as is the "inevitable" accident. Brandeis
firmly believes that "when we once get to the point where
workingmen are paid throughout the year, as the officers of a
corporation are paid throughout the year ... everyone will recognize that a business can not be run profitably unless you keep
it running, because if you have to pay, whether your men are
working or not, your men will work."[43]

Toward the achievement of industrial freedom which Brandeis
seeks, both trade unions and government have contributed
greatly. There are distinct limits, however, to what either can
do. The trade union has furnished collective bargaining which
is an advance, but only a first step. The government has im-

[40] L. D. Brandeis, *Business—A Profession* (1933), pp. 6-7.
[41] Statement before the Commission on Industrial Relations, 64th Cong., 1st Sess.,
Sen. Doc., Vol. XIX, pp. 995-6 (1914).
[42] *ibid.*, p. 995.
[43] *ibid.*

proved by legislation the material conditions of the workers. Even if it had been successful in doing more, that still would not be enough. No remedy is adequate which does not devolve upon workers a responsibility for the conduct of the business. Some of Brandeis' observations suggest that he might sympathize with guild socialist theory:

> . . . The end for which we must strive is the attainment of rule by the people, and that involves industrial democracy as well as political democracy. That means that the problems of a trade should be no longer the problems of the employer alone. The problems of his business, and it is not the employer's business alone, are the problems of all in it. The union cannot shift upon the employer the responsibility for conditions, nor can the employer insist upon determining, according to his will, the conditions which shall exist. The problems which exist are the problems of the trade; they are the problems of employer and the employee. . . . There must be a division not only of profits, but a division also of responsibilities.[44]

Brandeis rejects schemes frequently offered in the name of industrial democracy. The discretionary pension system which the United States Steel management proudly trumpeted as toward democratization of their industry, he characterized as but one more chain shackling the workers to the corporation. It robbed the worker of "that little liberty which under present industrial conditions remains to him."[45] Under pretense of "discretionary pensions" men entering employment won no vested rights save by long service and conduct pleasing to the management. A better name for this device, he said, would be "pensioned peonage."[46]

Both employer and employee should contribute to a just pension system, each having absolute and inalienable right to the

[44] Statement before the Commission on Industrial Relations, 64th Cong., 1st Sess., Sen. Doc., Vol. XXVI, pp. 7659-60 (1915).

[45] Hearings before the Committee on Investigation of the United States Steel Corporation, p. 2865, January 30, 1912.

[46] ibid. See, in this connection, Business—A Profession (1933), pp. 71-99.

money he has put in.[47] That fund should be administered not by the corporation as an act of discriminating and interested charity, but as a judicial joint exercise of right and equity, the employees having equal voice on the fund's board of directors. Acting for Boston and Maine Railroad employees, Brandeis secured on May 29, 1909, the enactment of a bill embodying these views by the Massachusetts legislature.[48]

Employee stock ownership is even less calculated to improve the condition of labor. The panorama of scores of thousands of employees holding company stock, all partners along with J. P. Morgan and Company, and the National City Company, does not arouse any enthusiasm in Mr. Brandeis. He is confident that such a system is dangerous to the community as well as to the workers:

> The wide distribution of stock, instead of being a blessing, constitutes, to my mind, one of the gravest dangers to the community. It is absentee landlordism of the worst kind. . . . Such a wide distribution of the stock dissipates altogether the responsibility of stockholders, particularly of those with five shares, ten shares, fifteen shares, or fifty shares. They recognize that they have no influence in a corporation of hundreds of millions of dollars capital. Consequently they consider it immaterial whatever they do, or omit to do; the net result is that the men who are in control it becomes almost impossible to dislodge, unless there should be such a scandal in the

[47] "From the point of view of the workingman, the expense of providing old-age pensions is a part of the daily cost of living. He should contribute while able to work to a fund which will sustain him when he ceases to earn. From the point of view of the employer, the expense of providing old-age pensions is a part of the current expense of his business. He should pay as he goes the accruing cost of retiring employees who will become superannuated. . . . Every pension system should be contributory and cooperative; that is, the cost should be borne partly by the employer and partly by the employee, and preferably in equal shares." L. D. Brandeis, "Our New Peonage: Discretionary Pensions," *The Independent*, July 25, 1912.

[48] Under the Boston and Maine bill the employee acquires a large right to the pension. If he ceases to be an employee of the company, he loses the pension proper, but he has paid to him an amount equal at least to the amount of his contributions. For a detailed description of this measure, see *ibid.*, p. 191.

corporation as to make it clearly necessary for the people on the outside to combine for self-protection.[49]

A recent controversy in the Bethlehem Steel Corporation illustrates the truth of this statement. The salient points are: first, that these masses of hired-man owners are the most hushed of "silent partners" and, second, that they cannot unite effectively with non-company owners for any purpose whatever. Nor do profit sharings or bonus payments, however liberal, meet the situation, since these mean merely dividing certain profits of the business. Such division may do harm or good depending on how it is applied.[50] To win industrial democracy much more than the division of profits is necessary. There must be division also of responsibility. "The employees must have the opportunity of participating in the decisions as to what shall be their condition and how the business shall be run."[51] Industrial democracy means that the worker has "not only a voice but a vote; not merely a right to be heard, but a position through which labor may participate in management."[52] "This participation in and eventual control of industry," Brandeis contends, is "essential for obtaining justice in distributing the fruits of industry."[53]

[49] Statement before the Commission on Industrial Relations, 64th Cong., 1st Sess., Sen. Doc., Vol. XXVI, p. 7661 (1915).

[50] ibid., p. 7660. George W. Perkins pointed with pride to the profit-sharing system of the United States Steel Corporation under which twelve million dollars had been distributed during the ten years that scheme was in operation. But Brandeis pointed out that the benefits conferred upon the employees were inconsequential. The average share of profit due each employee during this period was six dollars a year, or fifty cents per month. The rest went to the management. Report of the Senate Committee on Interstate Commerce, 62nd Cong., 2nd Sess., Vol. I, p. 1151 (1911).

Brandeis' ideas on profit-sharing were in operation in the Dennison Manufacturing Co. The Dennison idea was to give to capital a liberal return of eight per cent which Brandeis thought was perhaps too liberal and to give to those who do the work all the rest of the profit in addition to their fixed salaries and wages. ibid., p. 1152.

[51] Statement before the Commission on Industrial Relations, 64th Cong., 1st Sess., Sen. Doc., Vol. XXVI, p. 7660 (1915).

[52] ibid., p. 7664.

[53] Letter to Robert W. Bruère, February 25, 1922.

Such revolutionary change in industrial control and management should be voluntary, not compulsory. The need is education; the task is to develop institutions of industrial government to deal with current problems in each trade. There must be created, according to Brandeis, a relation of employer and employee similar to that which existed in the garment trade of New York City under the protocol of September 2, 1910. In the garment industry institutions were established for joint responsibility and control. It was something in the nature of constitutional government, the problems of the trade being settled in parliamentary and juridical fashion. Under this scheme, "representatives of employers and employees come together to determine the problems of the trade in precisely the same way that members of the legislatures and the judges of the courts come together to decide the matters" for city, state or nation.[54] As a result of the experiment, representatives of employer and employee in the garment industry came to realize that trade problems did not pertain strictly to one side or the other, that no satisfactory solution could be had either by shifting or engrossing responsibility. Labor learned that in sharing such responsibility it must suffer the consequences along with the employer. "But the right to assist in making the decisions, the right of making their own mistakes, if mistakes there must be, is a privilege which should not be denied to labor. We must insist upon labor sharing the responsibilities for the result of the business."[55]

There is no evidence that Brandeis entertains any illusions as to cure-all trade unions. Strong advocate that he is of collective bargaining, no one is more conscious of the abuses that have attended this movement. The acts of trade unions are "in many instances acts to be condemned, acts to be opposed, acts to be

[54] Statement before the Commission on Industrial Relations, 64th Cong., 1st Sess., Sen. Doc., Vol. XXVI, p. 7665 (1915).
[55] *ibid.*, p. 7660.

suppressed."[56] Some of the aims of labor are not shared by him. He is definitely opposed to the "closed shop" as tending toward monopoly.[57] He has always urged the incorporation of trade unions, and has never sympathized with the objections of Gompers, Green, and other labor leaders to this idea.[58] "The plea of trades unions for immunity, be it from injunction or from liability for damages, is as fallacious as the plea of the lynchers."[59] He encourages the formation of unions, but would hold them responsible for using well what power is entrusted to them. There is nothing to be gained by substituting the tyranny of labor for the tyranny of capital. Indeed he stresses the need for employers' associations to protect and safeguard the interest of capital, the best results being attained by strong organization on both sides, bargaining collectively.[60] From six years' experience as chairman of the Arbitration Board of the New York Garment Trade, Brandeis concludes that the problems of industry can best be solved, without government aid, once there is full understanding of the facts by both employer and em-

[56] Statement of Brandeis before the House Committee Hearings on Investigation of the United States Steel Corporation, p. 2862, January 30, 1912. See also his statement before the Committee on Industrial Relations, 64th Congress, 1st Sess., Sen. Doc., Vol. XXVI, p. 7671 (1915).

[57] "The 'closed shop' seems to me opposed to our ideas of liberty as presenting a monopoly of labor which might become as objectionable a monopoly as that of capital." Strauss Magazine Theatre Program, March 31, 1913. See also Report of the Senate Committee on Interstate Commerce, 62nd Cong., 2nd Sess., Vol. I, p. 1180 (1911).

[58] "Should Trade Unions Be Incorporated? Joint debate between Gompers and Brandeis," The Boston Post, December 5, 1902. See also Business—A Profession (1933), pp. 88 ff.

[59] L. D. Brandeis, Business—A Profession (1933), p. 26.

[60] ". . . The laboring men and the employers are undoubtedly both very much better off when those conditions exist, where they can come together, the unions on the one hand and the employers' associations on the other, both strong and effective organizations, come together and determine the basis on which men will work." Report of the Committee on Interstate Commerce, 62nd Cong., 2nd Sess., Vol. I, p. 1183 (1911).

ployee.[61] Therefore he favors investigation and conciliation as against compulsory arbitration of industrial controversies.[62]

By what process can the industrial democracy which Brandeis seeks be achieved? One thing is certain, it will not come by gift, for "all of our human experience shows that no one with absolute power can be trusted to give it up even in part.[63] . . . This is as true now as during the days of political absolutism. The "New Freedom" must be won by those who desire it—that is, by the group whose interests are most concerned. If those who wield economic power are blind to the demands and needs of economic interests other than their own, that is only proof "that the employing organization is larger than is consistent with the public interest. . . . And the State must in some way come to the aid of the workingmen if democratization is to be secured."[64] The "New Deal" is apparently based upon this logic.

What Brandeis has in mind, however, is not primarily legislation as to hours, wages, and conditions of labor. He does not mince words as to the goal set for government regulation, regardless of group interests concerned. He has "grave doubt as to how much can be accomplished by legislation unless it be to set a limit upon the size of corporate units."[65] "Many dangers to

[61] ". . . Most of the difficulties between employers and employees . . . can be adjusted by discussion rather than by arbitration, and . . . up to the present time in the more serious disputes persons other than a state board, the officially appointed individuals, have been more effective in securing the proper adjustment than the constituted officials." *ibid.*, p. 1251.

[62] See "Brandeis on the Labor Problem," an interview by Treadwell Cleveland, Jr., in *La Follette's Weekly*, May 24, 1913.

It is interesting to note that he joined Chief Justice Taft in overthrowing a section of the Kansas Industrial Court Act (Wolff Packing Co. v. Court of Industrial Relations, 262 U.S. 522, 1923), thus approving an opinion which is one of the most conservative utterances that has come from the court in recent years.

[63] Statement before the Commission on Industrial Relations, 64th Cong., 1st Sess., Sen. Doc., Vol. XXVI, p. 7662 (1915).

[64] *ibid.*

[65] *ibid.*, p. 7663.

democracy . . . are inherent in these huge aggregations."[66] "The objections to despotism and monopoly are fundamental in human nature. They rest upon the innate and ineradicable selfishness of man. They rest upon the fact that absolute power inevitably leads to abuse. They rest upon the fact that progress flows only from struggle."[67] "Concentration of power has been shown to be dangerous in a democracy, even though that power may be used beneficently."[68]

It follows that, unless we eradicate monopoly and tyrannical corporate aggregates, unrest will not only continue but grow worse. Trusts and monopolies are wrong economically, socially and politically. They make for inefficiency, discourage inventions,[69] oppress and enslave labor, and exert a corrupting influence on government.[70] "Its benighting and benumbing effect extends as well to the small and seemingly independent business man, to the vast army of professional men and others directly dependent upon 'Big Business.' "[71] Nor have trusts, as is sometimes supposed, benefited consumers by giving them lower prices. "So far as prices have been reduced, it has been in spite

[66] Hearings before the Committee on Investigation of the United States Steel Corporation, p. 2872, January 30, 1912.

[67] Statement before the Committee on Interstate Commerce, 62nd Cong., 2nd Sess., Vol. III, p. 19, an article reprinted as a part of the record from *The Boston Journal*, December 13, 1912.

[68] Statement before the Commission on Industrial Relations, 64th Cong., 1st Sess., Sen. Doc., Vol. XXVI, p. 7663 (1915).

[69] "Men have not made inventions in business, men have not made economies in business, to any great extent because they wanted to. They have made them because they had to, and the proposition that 'necessity is the mother of inventions' is just as true today in the time of the trusts, in the era of the trusts, as it was hundreds of years before." Statement before the Senate Committee on Interstate Commerce, 62nd Cong., 2nd Sess., Vol. I, p. 1208 (1911).

[70] "As a part of this very desire to control everything, not content to stop with the control of the market, and extending to the control of their employees, they [the trusts, such as United States Steel] proceed to the control of the political organizations in the communities in which they live." Hearings before the Committee on Investigation of the United States Steel Corporation, p. 2861, January 30, 1912.

[71] L. D. Brandeis, *Other People's Money* (1932), p. 49.

of the trusts."[72] No amount of prosperity, stock-market booming or statistical hosannas can atone for the backwardness of business, the shrinkage of purchasing power, the mummifying of the state and the multiplication of "yes-men," since these make the business man a tyrant and the workingman a serf.

Brandeis' objection to trusts and corporate bigness does not extend to all forms of capitalist organization. It is "perfectly possible that a state of affairs might arise under which it might be necessary, in order to preserve competition, to allow some kind of trade agreements."[73] He has long held that unless business competitors are able to organize they may be forced into cutthroat competition, hurting both capital and labor, into piratical price-cutting, of which there has been so much, especially during these years of depression, and finally into monopolistic combination. When under the anti-trust laws the Supreme Court in 1911 denied the right of the manufacturer of a trade-marked article to maintain an established price, he was outstanding among lawyers who protested.[74] He saw that such con-

[72] Statement before the Senate Committee on Interstate Commerce, 62nd Cong., 2nd Sess., Vol. I, p. 1157. The Commissioner of Corporations found, for example, that whereas seven-tenths of a cent a gallon would have been a fair profit, the Standard Oil trust had raised its profit from year to year until it reached 8.4 cents a gallon— twelve times what the commissioner found to be a fair profit. *ibid*.

[73] *ibid.*, p. 1250.

[74] Dr. Miles Medical Co. v. Park & Sons Co., 220 U.S. 409 (1911). This decision followed the precedent set in Bobbs-Merrill Co. v. Strauss (denying the right of a copyright owner to fix the resale price of his goods), 210 U.S. 339 (1908). See also Bauer v. O'Donnell, 229 U.S. 1 (1913), which applies the same doctrine to patented articles.

"I believe the Supreme Court," Brandeis declared, "made an error in business judgment when it held that a man could not fix the price at which a particular article which he manufactured should be sold. It is the common law of the land and has so been recognized by court decisions not only in this country but in foreign countries as well." *The New York World*, June 10, 1915.

"Regulation is essential to the preservation and development of competition, just as it is necessary to the preservation and best development of liberty. We have long curbed physically the strong, to protect those physically weaker. . . . Similarly the right to competition must be limited in order to preserve it. For excesses of competition lead to monopoly, as excesses of liberty lead to absolutism. . . . There are wastes of

struction of the Sherman law worked injustice upon the manufacturer; worse still, it encouraged what the Sherman Act was
intended to prevent—consolidation and monopoly.

The great corporation with ample capital, a perfected organization
and a large volume of business, can establish its own agencies or
sell direct to the consumer, and is in no danger of having its business
destroyed by price-cutting among retailers. But the prohibition of
price-maintenance imposes upon the small independent producers
a serious handicap. Some avenue of escape must be sought by them;
and it may be found in combination.[75]

To correct this Supreme Court "error in business judgment,"
Brandeis drafted the Stevens bill (H.R. 13305) to permit independent producers of standardized goods to fix by contract the
resale price of their product. He felt such legislation necessary to
protect the many who wished to sell at a legitimate profit, from
the few who would sell well known goods at cost or less, making
up their loss on sales of other merchandise. He appeared in
committee hearings to support the measure but it failed of enactment.[76] In this matter, as always, Brandeis emphasized "knowledge" as "the first essential of wise and just action." Without it
"we shall not be able to deal intelligently with the problem of
the extent to which trade agreements among competitors should
be permitted." As a means of gaining this knowledge, "we
should secure uniform accounting." He subscribes to the observation of the great Colbert: "Accountancy—that is government."[77]

competition which do not develop, but kill. These the law can and should eliminate, by
regulating competition." L. D. Brandeis, "Shall We Abandon the Policy of Competition?" (1912), 18 Case and Comment, pp. 494-5.

See also Mr. Brandeis' statement before the Senate Committee on Interstate Commerce, 62nd Cong., 2nd Sess., Vol. III, p. 1169, "The Living Law" (1916), 10 Ill. Law
Rev. 461, 468, and L. D. Brandeis, Business—A Profession (1933), pp. 243 ff.

[75] L. D. Brandeis, Business—A Profession (1933), pp. 259-60. See also Brandeis'
statement before the House Committee on the Judiciary. Trust Legislation, January
26, 1912, pp. 13 ff.

[76] Hearings before the House Committee on Interstate and Foreign Commerce,
Regulation of Prices, 64th Cong., 1st Sess., p. 198, January 9, 1915.

[77] Statement at the Hearings of the House Committee on Interstate and Foreign
Commerce, 63rd Cong., 2nd Sess., p. 5, January 30, 1914.

Brandeis has always favored "regulated competition" as opposed to "regulated monopoly," and doing so has shown the evils of degenerate competition.[78] He has insisted also on increasing cooperation among those in a particular industry. "The functions of government," he said in 1914, "should not be limited to the enactment of wise rules of action, and the providing of efficient judicial machinery, by which those guilty of breaking the law may be punished, and those injured, secure compensation. . . . We need the inspector and the policeman even more than we need the prosecuting attorney, and we need for the enforcement of the Sherman law and regulation of competition, an administrative board with broad powers."[79] Above all, he urged government publicity of current business information since "the methods of destructive competition will not bear the light of day. The mere substitution of knowledge for ignorance —of publicity for secrecy—will go far toward preventing monopoly." And, beyond all this, "The inequality between the great corporations, with huge resources, and the small competitor and others is such that equality before the law will no longer be secured merely by supplying adequate machinery

[78] "Some people believed that trusts and monopolies in private business were inevitable and perhaps desirable and that the remedy to be applied should be a 'regulation of monopoly.' A far larger number of Americans became convinced that trusts and monopolies in private business were neither inevitable nor desirable, and that they were in fact largely a result of unrestricted, unfair, and oppressive competition. They therefore proposed as a remedy the 'regulation of competition.'" Hearings before House Committee on Interstate and Foreign Commerce, Regulation of Prices, 64th Cong., 1st Sess., p. 198, January 9, 1915.

See "Constructive Cooperation vs. Cut-throat Competition," address of L. D. Brandeis before the National Rivers and Harbors Congress, Washington, D.C., December 9, 1914 (Mimeograph copy); L. D. Brandeis, "The Solution of the Trust Problem," *Harper's Weekly*, November 8, 1913. See also Charles G. Ross, "The Philosophy of Justice Brandeis, Credited with Fathering Woodrow Wilson's Theory of Regulated Competition," *St. Louis Post-Dispatch*, June 19, 1927.

[79] Statement at the Hearings of the House Committee on Interstate and Foreign Commerce, 63rd Cong., 2nd Sess., p. 4, January 30, 1914.

for enforcing the law. To prevent oppression and injustice, the government must be prepared to lend its aid."[80]

These observations of twenty years ago are now embodied in the National Industrial Recovery Act.[81] Neither Brandeis nor the Roosevelt administration has favored government ownership or operation of industry, as socialists and communists propose. The above act does not even provide, except as regards recalcitrants, that government impose its own codes upon industry, but places upon business the obligation of putting its house in order. The various trades are not only permitted but urged to frame and adopt their own codes. If they get government approval, particularly as to labor and the consumer, such codes become mandatory on the whole industry.

President Roosevelt's account of the act stresses those features which embody Brandeis' philosophy.[82] It provides, the President states, for a great cooperative movement throughout all industry in order to obtain wide reemployment, shorten the working week, pay decent wages for this shorter week, and prevent unfair competition. Employers cannot do this singly or even in organized groups, because such action increases costs, and makes for cutthroat underselling by selfish competitors. The public interest can be served only with aid from government. Under this new legislation some of the safeguards of the anti-trust acts are admittedly relaxed. Indeed, a chief purpose is to repair for industry some of the damage caused by what Brandeis considered an erroneous Supreme Court decision twenty years ago.

Yet Brandeis has never pinned entire faith on government control. The mind of the bureaucrat, no less than banker or business man, is limited as to what it can comprehend. He holds

[80] *ibid.*
[81] P. L. No. 67, 73rd Cong. See especially sec. 7.
[82] For a complete statement, see *The Evening Star,* Washington, D.C., June 17, 1933.

that the obligation rests not upon government but upon each
economic group to see to it "that the higher standards of that
organization are lived up to by its members. . . . There is no
possible way of bringing about justice in the protection of classes,
except the assumption by the class of the obligation of making
the members of that class conform to proper moral standards."[83]
Government should at most declare certain minimum standards.
Beyond these each class must work out for itself codes of conduct
higher than the legal requirements. This, too, according to
official pronouncements, will be the policy followed in administering the National Industrial Recovery Act.[84]

The years of depression have proved conclusively that modern
industrial economy does not coordinate itself. One of our ablest
publicists has observed that "at a thousand vital points the system
has become rigid through contracts, gentleman's agreements,
virtual monopolies, trade union rules, legislation and other
devices for interfering with the law of supply and demand."[85]

[83] Statement before the Commission on Industrial Relations, 64th Cong., 1st Sess.,
Sen. Doc., Vol. XXVI, p. 7677 (1915).

[84] It is interesting to note, in this connection, the recent announcement of the new
chairman of the board of the Chase National Bank, Winthrop W. Aldrich, to the
effect that the Chase bank would not only divorce its securities affiliate, but that he
favored far-reaching measures designed to sever the "intimate connection" which
now exists "between commercial banking and investment banking." "It is impossible," Mr. Aldrich declared, "to consider the events which took place during the
past ten years without being forced to the conclusion that the intimate connection
between commercial banking and investment banking almost inevitably leads to
abuses." New York Herald Tribune, March 9, 1933.
This is as it should be. The responsibility for higher moral standards rests primarily
upon the bankers themselves. They can produce results which legislation, however
carefully framed, is powerless to bring about. Mr. Brandeis reached this conclusion
more than twenty years ago, but it was not until Mr. Aldrich spoke that the head
of any great banking house subscribed to any such proposition.

[85] Walter Lippmann, "Planning and Human Nature," New York Herald Tribune,
June 22, 1933. This excellent article is devoted to pointing out the error of Dr.
Benjamin M. Anderson, Jr., who apparently believes that "our present system relies
upon the unconscious automatic functioning of the markets; that there is coordination
of the multitudinous elements . . . through the markets." B. M. Anderson, Jr., "A

The failure of Adam Smith to furnish a formula adequate for the government of modern industry does not, however, hold us to a centralized and controlled system of economy according to the principles of Lenin. A middle course long urged by Brandeis appears as a guiding principle in the National Industrial Recovery legislation. Most significant, perhaps, for this experiment is the scarcity of prohibitions and commands. So far as there is an element of Leninist autocracy in the act, it is as it subdues the industrial buccaneer, the unscrupulous price-cutter, the exploiter of labor.

When Brandeis was appearing before the Industrial Commission in 1914 and 1915 there was, as now, much talk of "overproduction." Even the Roosevelt administration today seems to have fallen into this fallacy.[86] But Mr. Brandeis saw the issue more clearly. Overproduction, he holds, is not the difficulty. While there are hungry mouths and naked bodies there cannot be any overproduction. The problem as he saw it then was and is now one of "underconsumption, or maladjustment in distribution."[87] "There is plenty of consumptive power but not enough ability to buy things."[88] He knew it might benefit certain interests to restrict production, "but the benefit to labor as a whole would be immensely advanced by increasing production."[89]

Planned Economy and a Planned Price Level." Reprinted from *The Chase Economic Bulletin*, Vol. XIII, No. 3, June 9, 1933.

Dr. Anderson is also in error as to the extent of government regulation which the National Industrial Recovery Act contemplates. Commenting on the act, Dr. Anderson naïvely observed: ". . . there is required a central brain of such vast power that no human being who has yet lived, or can be expected to live, can supply it."

[86] I refer to such proposals as those for plowing under growing cotton, also the recent malthusian project of the Agricultural Adjustment Corporation for reducing "overproduction" of pork products by birth control among swine.

[87] Statement before the Commission on Industrial Relations, 64th Cong., 1st Sess., Sen. Doc., Vol. XXVI, p. 7666 (1915).

[88] *ibid.,* Sen. Doc., Vol. XIX, p. 997 (1914).

[89] Statement before the Commission on Industrial Relations, 64th Cong., 1st Sess., Sen. Doc., Vol. XXVI, p. 7666 (1915).

Surveying the problems of our troubled world in 1915, Brandeis insisted that the basic need was for a changed point of view. "We ought to develop enlightened unselfishness, as a substitute for the old, so-called, enlightened selfishness; and enlightened unselfishness would give us all a great deal more than we have."[90] Such a change is necessary whether the problem be labor or trusts. As Brandeis pointed out years ago in words peculiarly applicable to this hour of Wall Street "revival":

> . . . If I were to answer that question as to what ought to be regarded as a fair profit, I should say that no particular return ought to be regarded; and that if a man were going to invest in a manufacturing concern he ought to invest in men, and not bricks and mortar.[91]
>
> The trust problem can never be settled right for the American people by looking at it through the spectacles of bonds and stocks. You must study it through the spectacles of people's rights and people's interests; must consider the effect upon the development of the American democracy. When you do that you will realize the extraordinary perils to our institutions which attend the trusts; you will realize the danger of letting the people learn that our sacred Constitution protects not only vested rights but vested wrongs. The situation is a very serious one; unless wise legislation is enacted we shall have as a result of that social unrest a condition which will be more serious than that produced by the fall of a few points in stock-exchange quotations.[92]

When economic, social, and political affairs were somewhat less baffling than today, Brandeis made a diagnosis of the ills from which society is suffering and suggested remedies to aid recovery. He went further, even, and said that unless society radically alters its point of view and habits of life, that which

[90] Statement before the Commission on Industrial Relations, 64th Cong., 1st Sess., Sen. Doc., Vol. XXVI, pp. 7666-7 (1915).

[91] Statement before the Senate Committee on Interstate Commerce, 62nd Cong., 2nd Sess., Vol. I, p. 1246 (1911).

[92] ibid., p. 1166.

appears a lingering disease may terminate fatally. These convictions, growing through the years, give Brandeis honorable rank in our progressive thought, and lend special significance to the place he occupies on the bench today. The prophet has indeed come into honor in his own country and in his own time.

CHAPTER IV

BRANDEIS: SENSE, SANITY, IDEALISM

I N THE fight for the "New Freedom," there was room for such an extraordinary galaxy of progressives as Bryan, La Follette, Roosevelt, Steffens, and Wilson.[1] Their differing talents lent variety and vitality to the struggle. But, far more essential for results, was the unspectacular, expert, creative skill to adapt and remould old ideas and accepted principles in the service of the changing times. For this Brandeis was particularly fitted. His equipment and contribution, as contrasted with those of the crusaders of 1912, were distinctive and of earlier origin.

None of the other great progressives was a first-class lawyer of actual experience with big law practice in "the trust belt." The aid of a first-rate legal mind, when outstanding legal ability had become conventionally an adjunct of great corporate aggregates, was worth more to the cause of liberalism than the entire menagerie of publicists, politicos, muckrakers, and mob-rousers. And Brandeis was more than a lawyer, ready on occasion to parry deceptive assertions as to rate differentials or to criticise accounting systems incompetent to separate transit and terminal charges.[2] He was thoroughly grounded in modern business technicalities as well as in legal intricacies and court circumlocutions. At the same time, he could cut loose of all technical detail and urge that the roads had no moral right to raise rates, nor business to cut wages, until scientific management had been tried to reduce costs and expenses. Such brains as his were

[1] For a brilliant survey of the rise and decay of the progressive mind in America, see John Chamberlain, *Farewell to Reform* (1932).

[2] See especially Brandeis' brief as special counsel for the Interstate Commerce Commission, Five Per Cent Case, pp. 103 ff.

extremely rare among those who "battled at Armageddon" under the liberal banners of 1912. While Bull Moose gospeleers were trumpeting generalities, vagaries and invective, Brandeis showed genius for detail, for facts and figures, for the masonry of constructive conviction.

Like Henry Demarest Lloyd he drew his materials from primary sources and knew whereof he spoke, but unlike Lloyd and others, he had had authoritative contact with the problems of his and our day. Thus when Brandeis told the Interstate Commerce Commission that the railroads by scientific management could save a million dollars a day, it was no mere advertising advocate's flourish. Reaching this conclusion after long and exact study, he put experts on the stand to prove it. While Bryan and his fellows denounced the "money trust" with vague heat, arguing furiously that we must not be enslaved by the Morgans, Rothschilds, and other demons of high finance, Brandeis, relying chiefly on the Pujo investigation materials and on his own first-hand study of Morgan's New Haven Railroad, made accurate diagnosis of the concentrated perversion of credit. He unerringly pointed out the stupid knavishness of bankers and analyzed their holding companies and interlocking directorates, all to support his devastating attack on money-power "competition," and then published the results in a book which is today a classic of American economics. There is no idle prattle in these pages about the divine origin and power of capitalism. Much less is the author betrayed into the follies of socialists and communists. *Other People's Money* (a new edition of which has recently appeared)[3] is neither a muckraking exposé nor a crusading sermon, but a learned and painstaking analysis of irresponsible banking control in business. It sounded a warning to

[3] Published by Frederick A. Stokes Co. (1932). The first edition of this book was published in 1914. For a brief but appreciative review of the new edition, see *The American Mercury*, February 1933, p. xxiv.

which our latest financial tragedy gives back a grim gigantic echo.

Brandeis' passion for public service he holds in common with most progressives, but none have equalled his genius for practising it. His insistence on translating his ideas into realities, his fruitful intellectual inventiveness in devising schemes of detail for this translation into life, is what distinguishes him. He is well called a "social inventor," for certainly no man of our generation has been so successful in framing social and legal devices for solving our hard American problems. His "sliding scale system" for public utilities resulted in cheaper gas prices and in sounder security values; for railway regulation he applied the principles of scientific management; in his study of trusts and corporations he destroyed the common delusion that efficiency results from "bigness"; for industrial disputes he devised and applied the "preferential union shop" principle; he insisted that business must maintain regular employment for workers, and pointed out the basic economic and social wastes of unemployment. Finding Massachusetts wage-earners burdened by a greedy and obsolete system of industrial life insurance, a most unconscionable system of heavy costs and uncompensated lapses, Brandeis urged wage-earners' life insurance at cost by means of savings banks.

Events have usually vindicated Brandeis' judgment. Three years before the Metropolitan Traction Company of New York went into receivership, he explained in a Cooper Union speech how the frenzied finance of that company was bound to fail. Two years before the crash of the New Haven Railroad he made a like prophecy. There was no magic about it, for the financial failure of the New Haven Railroad was neither accidental nor exceptional. "It was the natural result," he wrote, "of confusing the functions of banker and business man."[4] These trying years since 1929 drag out the long proof of how right he was in 1923 when he suggested that within a decade the price level might fall to that of 1914.

Perhaps a single mind could tackle many, if not all, of these lions in the path of what may become our industrial civilization. But it is extraordinary that one man should have formulated constructive proposals for their conquest. The city public service corporation, railroads, banks, insurance companies, inflated industrials, the evil mass of their interlocked interests, the paralysis of long hours, low wages and unemployment, had all been dealt with by him before 1912. And during the campaign of that year his was the most powerful intellect helping Woodrow Wilson expound the principles of democracy in our present industrial-financial era.[5]

The Brandeis method has been to arouse interest so the public will save itself by right action. His consideration of any problem has usually three stages: (1) Thorough investigation by and with experts, (2) Public education by both press and platform, (3) Legislative measures securing such changes in economic and social relations as the facts demand.

Whatever the abuse or the device that engages Brandeis' attention, the human aspect of it is his ultimate and governing concern. "Always and everywhere, the intellectual, moral and spiritual development of those concerned will remain an essential—and the main factor—in real betterment."[6] Facts and figures are the tools with which he works, but are merely tools to serve human ends, human needs. Accounting, in his hands, becomes a sort of social science measuring process. Old-age pen-

[4] L. D. Brandeis, "Banker-Management. Why It Has Failed: A Lesson from the New Haven," *Harper's Weekly*, August 16, 1913. Reprinted in *Other People's Money* (1932), pp. 189, 196.

[5] James Kerney, *The Political Education of Woodrow Wilson* (1926), p. 284.

[6] Letter to Robert W. Bruère, February 25, 1922. Compare "Mr. Justice Brandeis," *The New Republic*, November 18, 1931.

sions are a depreciation charge reserved to meet the inevitable wearing out of the individual human factors. He places on business the responsibility of winning for the worker his fruitful economic freedom. The worth of the individual is his constant theme; the object of his concern is so to transform present-day institutions as to free individuals for their own more abundant life. Thus he reinterprets democratic ideals in terms of our day.

Brandeis' career aroused bitterest antagonism. He has often been maligned and sometimes purposely misunderstood. In the course of the fight over his nomination for the Supreme Court he was denounced as "a radical, a theorist, impractical, with strong socialistic tendencies."[7] Neither radicals nor conservatives found him acceptable. Radicals call him conservative; conservatives damn him for an anarchist-radical. No such labels fit. Brandeis is rather an individualist democrat of the Jeffersonian type.[8] He professes no rigid philosophy unless the democratic ideal be so styled.[9] He stresses individual liberty, freedom and initiative. The development of the individual is "both a necessary means and the end sought."[10] He believes so strongly in private property that he wants to see it more equitably diffused among the masses of men. He values private capital so highly that he would make it available to the independent entrepreneur, rather

[7] "A 'People's Lawyer' for the Supreme Court," *The Literary Digest*, February 12, 1916, p. 362. One finds herein interesting newspaper comments on Brandeis' nomination.

[8] "Brandeis is an individualist. He is an extreme individualist. That is the very heart of his philosophy. The notion that he is a socialist is frantically absurd. He would be fired from any good socialist local as soon as he had opened his mouth." William Hard in the *Public Ledger*, May 16, 1916. See also "Brandeis, the Conservative or a 'Dangerous Radical,'" William Hard, *ibid.*, May 12, 1916.

[9] Answering the question as to whether he has a complete philosophy of life, Mr. Brandeis replied: "I have many opinions, but I am not a doctrinaire. My habit of mind has been to move from one problem to another, giving to each, while it is before me, my undivided study. I am a Democrat, but I have laid most stress on the little 'd.' Give men a free field. Provide equality of opportunity and we attain the New Freedom." L. S. Richard, "Up from Aristocracy," *The Independent*, July 27, 1914.

[10] Letter to Robert W. Bruère, February 25, 1922.

than have it monopolized and controlled by a money trust. He has such respect for profits that he desires to enlarge them by scientific management so the share of labor (purchasing power itself) may be increased. He thinks of private enterprise not only as an instrument of private gain but also as a means of raising the individual to creative personality.

Concentrated wealth, not wealth as such, is decried; not only because this concentration thwarts the liberty and independence of the entrepreneur, but also because it plays into the hands of the socialists. "Socialism," he thinks, "has been developed largely by the power of the individual trusts. What is more, they have pointed the way to the Socialists."[11] He realizes, as did Karl Marx, that concentration of wealth in a few hands may be carried to a point where the expropriators themselves may inevitably and easily be expropriated.[12] He favors trade unions as "a strong bulwark against the great wave of socialism." They "stand out for individualism as against the great uprising of socialism on the one hand and of the accumulation of great fortunes on the other."[13] He firmly believes that "the greatest factors making for communism, socialism, or anarchy among a free people, are the excesses of capital. . . . Every act of injustice on the part of the rich will be met by another act or many acts of injustice, on the part of the people."[14] Lawyers, Brandeis insisted, must

[11] Statement before the Senate Committee on Interstate Commerce. Control of Corporations, Persons, and Firms Engaged in Interstate Commerce, 62nd Cong., 2nd Sess., Sen. Res. 98, Vol. I, p. 1258 (1911).

[12] "Just as Emperor Nero is said to have remarked in regard to his people that he wished that the Christians had but one neck that he might cut it off by a single blow of his sword, so they [Socialists] say here: 'Let these men gather these things together; they will soon have them all under one head, and by a single act we will take over the whole industry.' So Socialists say in regard to Morgan—Morgan, preeminently the great organizer and great combiner. They say: 'He is our best friend, because he is paving the way for us, and we will have only a slight amount of legislation after Mr. Morgan is through with his work.' " ibid.

[13] Daily Eastern Argus, April 19, 1905.

[14] Consolidation of Gas Companies and Electric Light Companies. Argument of Louis D. Brandeis on behalf of the Massachusetts State Board of Trade before the Legislative Committee on Public Lighting. George H. Ellis and Co., Boston (1905).

give adequate legal expression to the general aspiration lest the
people revolt against mounting inequalities in the distribution
of wealth.

> There is only one safe course . . . for us who want property rights
> protected and preserved; and that course is neither to seek nor to grant
> special privileges. Let us all stand equal before the law, and let the
> law be so just, so reasonable, so carefully drawn, that it protects alike
> the rights of all.[15]

In all public activities Mr. Brandeis has thought of himself
as a conservative, on the true theory that "the conservative classes
in the community are not those who wish to leave unrestricted
the power of wealth, but those who in economic relations are
working for justice to capital and the public alike."[16] Like the
arch-conservative, Edmund Burke, he understands that a constitution without means of change is without the means of its
own conservation.

The trouble Brandeis senses in our modern state is its lack of
social adjustment between political democracy and industrial
absolutism. For him "the greatest problem before the American
people in this generation [is] the problem of reconciling our
industrial system with the political democracy in which we
live."[17] As Rousseau, John Stuart Mill, and other libertarians
of the eighteenth and nineteenth centuries, feared the tyranny
and oppression of political power, so Brandeis fears for indi-

[15] *ibid.* "If I were a Communist," writes Bruce Bliven, "intent on increasing the
spirit of violent revolution in this country, I should move earth and hell to prevent
the functioning of men like Holmes and Brandeis. They are a safety valve for many
people who would otherwise find our prevailing economic system well-nigh intolerable.
They are the best friends capitalism has—and capitalism as usual hasn't got sense
enough to know it." *Forward,* January 11, 1931.

Dr. Lewis L. Lorwin (*The Woman's Garment Workers,* 1924) tells how Mr. Brandeis
as chairman of the Arbitration Board in the Garment Trade "insisted on the necessity
of an 'educational campaign' to wean the workers from the 'radical' ideas which they
had acquired as a result of a 'generation of miseducation,' " p. 485.

[16] Argument . . . on behalf of the Massachusetts State Board of Trade. . . . Note 14,
supra.

[17] *Filene Cooperation Association Echo,* May 1905.

vidual liberty in our new industrial society. Where they wished to protect the individual against the state, he looks ultimately to the state for protection against arbitrary industrial and financial force.

In the days of Andrew Jackson men fondly trusted that political liberty would ultimately breed economic equality. Prior to the full development of capitalism with its pyramided corporate control and microscopic divisions of labor, the pressing problem for liberals was one of erasing ancient political privilege and abuse. By removing these unjust inequalities they hoped to secure for the masses a chance to live more abundantly and, as individuals, more freely. Little did they anticipate the industrial situation that followed political revolution, and even less its consequent submerging pressure on the individual.

Since 1776 and Adam Smith's *Wealth of Nations,* our main doctrine in industry has been that self-interest secures the welfare both of the individual and of society. "Heralded as a final truth of 'science' this proves," as one acute observer has said, "to have been nothing higher than a temporary formula for a passing problem. It was a reflection in words of the policy of the day."[18] Perhaps it did not occur to eighteenth century individualists that the profit-seeking motive would ever emerge as socially dominant. At any rate, few, other than ex-President Hoover, have been bold enough to express the notion that all good arises from the efforts of the materially successful; for this is what Thomas Carlyle once characterized as pig-philosophy.

A century and a half of scientific change exceeding that of two thousand years previous, could not possibly have left unaltered either our theory of the Constitution, or the functioning of our government. The kind of system applicable to the agrarian age of Jefferson, is without meaning for industrial society today. The liberty that eighteenth century individualists

18 H. D. Lloyd, *Wealth Against Commonwealth* (1894), p. 494.

were so anxious to safeguard, turns out to be the liberty of
Al Capone and Sam Insull and Sunshine Charlie Mitchell, who
use national well-being to advance their own fortunes.

Brandeis sees keenly how the machine has revolutionized
economic and social relationships, and for this reason twentieth
century individualism does not mean for him, as for some ex-
tinguished Americans, merely the right to participate in a race
for private gain. We must become genuine individuals ourselves. Rather than merge self in our possessions and activities,
we must strive to become self-sufficient and independent. For
this the obstacles which capitalism has placed in the way of its
own functioning must be removed. If the government must
interfere more frequently and at more points today than formerly, as Brandeis believes it should, it is not because he values
individualism less; rather because we have passed to "a subtler
civilization," in which there are barriers for privilege and against
progress, not known in the agrarian era.

The older individualism assumed that every extension of
social control must be at the expense of individual liberty.
Brandeis realizes that now it is only through social control of
rights formerly considered natural, unalienable and immutable,
such as liberty of contract, that the individual can be free at
all. Just as the frontier individualist held by equality of political
rights, and of opportunity before the law, the right of every
man to make as much of himself in every way as he could, and
frowned on advantages not due to individual capacity and
accomplishment, so Brandeis today argues for individual freedom and for equality of opportunity. But where an orthodox
individualist such as Mr. Justice Sutherland sees the maintenance
of individualism as the dawn of a new society daily more like
Locke's simple Eden of the innate rights of man, Mr. Justice
Brandeis is impressed by our growing economic dependence
and interdependence, which cut us off from Locke and compel

us to go forward to a new order where individual rights and social relations are harmonized by the aid of government and law. Under the capitalist system, he long ago saw that production had become inextricably involved with government; that factory production means more rigid government.[19] All this, of course, is now commonplace at Washington.

Despite the shortcomings of our social, economic, and political situation as revealed by his study, Brandeis is no pessimist. He has implicit faith in our basic institutions and in their ability, wisely administered, to satisfy the requirements of a changing civilization. He listens impatiently even to those who doubt the capacity of our legal system to meet the demands of the times. "The law will catch up," he observes cheerfully. "It will adequately meet modern conditions."[20] Despite faults, he believes our country has boundless opportunities for the development and happiness of the ordinary man. Whether the existing order can meet the present demands made upon it, depends upon ourselves as individuals. If we cannot be men instead of yessers and go-getters; if we cannot show character as a result of opportunity; if employers as well as employees cannot stand firm when things go wrong and if each cannot meet his own responsibilities, then our system has failed.[21]

The way out of our present difficulties lies neither toward Fascism nor Socialism. He has shown profound distrust of absolute power in any hands whatever. "Neither our character nor our intelligence can long bear the strain of unrestricted power."[22] "I should not," he says, "rely upon the goodness of heart of anybody. . . . Nobody ought to be absolute; everybody ought to be protected from arbitrariness and wrong decisions

[19] Compare A. D. Lindsay, *Karl Marx's Capital* (1925), pp. 80, 103, 105.

[20] Frederick W. Coburn, "Who Is This Man Brandeis?" *Human Life,* February 9, 1911.

[21] Compare James Truslow Adams, "What of 'the American Dream'?" *The New York Times,* Sec. 6, March 14, 1933.

[22] *Civic Federation Review,* May 15, 1905.

by the representations of others who are being affected."[23] These
conclusions depend on the idea that human "nature may be
refined and bettered, perhaps not revolutionized."[24] The human
equation is as great, potentially, under one system as another:
"we need democracy at all times no matter what the system
is under which we work."[25]

Socialism tends to rob one of that self-reliance essential to
genuine individuality. The inherent worth of individual initiative is stimulated by private enterprise, therefore he supports
the capitalist system, but as someone has well said: "Mr. Brandeis
is endeavoring to find a way by which capitalism can be saved.
Perhaps he does so not so much out of a love for the capitalist
class as in response to some inherent inclination to preserve
the established order if possible."[26] This recalls Edmund Burke's
definition: "A disposition to preserve, and an ability to improve,
taken together, would be my standard of a statesman";[27] and
surely for Burke "a statesman" was essentially a conservative.
In reordering our economic and social life we should not lose
sight of the basic element in individualism. One must rely
primarily upon himself and upon the group of which he is a
member and not upon government, to bring about needed reforms. Brandeis believes that "the great developer is responsibility" and no remedy can be either helpful or hopeful which
does not take this into account. His purpose, in other words,
like that embodied in the policy of the present Roosevelt administration is not "to destroy individual initiative or to lessen
the opportunity for voluntary action but rather to establish those

[23] Statement before the Commission on Industrial Relations, 64th Cong., 1st Sess.,
Sen. Doc., Vol. XIX, p. 995 (1914).
[24] *ibid.*, p. 998.
[25] *ibid.*, p. 999.
[26] *Chicago Daily Socialist,* March 25, 1912.
[27] *Reflections on the French Revolution* (Everyman ed.), p. 153.

conditions in which initiative and enterprise can effectively flourish."[28]

Brandeis, then, is not a visionary destructor and projector who would tear down the old merely to build by schemes new and unfamiliar. Rather he seeks "betterment within the broad lines of established institutions."[29] He attacks no existing practice or principle unless able to replace it with something better. His one continuing problem is how best to adapt institutions and laws to meet the exigencies of our machine age, and yet retain the human-economic values of *laissez faire* and individualism. "Our objective is the making of men and women who shall be free—self-respecting members of a democracy—and who shall be worthy of respect."[30] The fundamental contribution of government toward this end must continue to be that of protection —not merely the protection that secures the individual against oppression by physical force. Today the individual needs to be safeguarded more particularly against those modern forces that exploit him, dwarf his personality, and tend to make him a thing.

The extent of government regulation cannot be settled by reference to a definite rule. Nevertheless Brandeis insists, as do all good individualists, that "No law limiting the liberty of contract ought to go beyond the necessity."[31] But recourse to reason, he thinks, is not enough: "There is no logic that is properly applicable to any of these [labor] laws except the logic of facts."[32] Experience and expediency thus play the decisive rôle in determining the need and scope of governmental regulation.

[28] Language of Henry Morgenthau, Jr., as reported by Russell Owen in *The New York Times*, May 22, 1933.

[29] Letter to Robert W. Bruère, February 25, 1922.

[30] *ibid.*

[31] Statement at the Hearings of the New York State Factory Investigating Commission, Vol. V (1915), p. 2893.

[32] *ibid.*

We should not regulate anything by law except where an evil
exists which the existing forces of unionism or otherwise, labor, are
unable to deal with. . . . It is desirable that people should be left with
the powers of free contract between one another except so far as
experience shows that existing forces will prevent contracts fair in
their results.[33]

Each man may develop himself so far, but only so far, as his doing
so will not interfere with the exercise of a like right by all others.
Thus liberty has come to mean the right to enjoy life, to acquire
property, to pursue happiness, in such manner that the exercise of
the right in each is consistent with the exercise of a like right by
every other of our fellow citizens. Liberty thus defined underlies
twentieth century democracy.[34]

These are propositions to which either John Stuart Mill, Mr.
Justice Sutherland or any other eighteenth century individualist,
could heartily subscribe. But Mr. Justice Brandeis' keen aware-
ness of the underlying facts of social and economic life leads
him to conclusions utterly unlike theirs as to what conditions
make it expedient for government to intervene.[35] For him
"liberty of contract means such liberty as it is not necessary to
curtail in the public interests."[36]

Brandeis has no illusions about democracy. He understands
that "democracy in any sphere is a serious undertaking. It sub-

[33] Statement before the Commission on Industrial Relations, 64th Cong., 1st Sess.,
Sen. Doc., Vol. XXVI, p. 7672 (1915).

[34] L. D. Brandeis, "An Essential of Lasting Peace," *Harper's Weekly*, March 13,
1915. Compare J. S. Mill's *Essay on Liberty* (Everyman ed.), pp. 72-3.

[35] Life and liberty as guaranteed by our Constitution should be interpreted, Brandeis
wrote in 1914, "according to demands of social justice and of democracy as the right
to *live*, and not merely to exist. In order to live men must have the opportunity of
developing their faculties; and they must live under conditions in which their faculties
may develop naturally and healthily. . . . Men and women must have leisure, which
the Athenians called 'freedom' or liberty. In the second place, the earnings of men
and women must be greater, so that they may live under conditions conducive to
health and to mental and moral development."
"Our American ideals cannot be attained unless an end is put to the misery due
to poverty." L. D. Brandeis, "Efficiency and Social Ideals," *The Independent*, November 30, 1914.

[36] Statement at the Hearings of the New York State Factory Investigating Commission, Vol. V, p. 2897 (1915).

stitutes self-restraint for external restraint. It is more difficult to maintain than to achieve."[37] So he sets high the educational standards it demands, for in a democracy, "The citizen should be able to comprehend among other things the many great and difficult problems of industry, commerce and finance, which with us necessarily become political questions."[38] It is conceded that "our great beneficent experiment in democracy will fail unless the people, our rulers, are developed in character and intelligence."[39] To this end government has a greater obligation than most individualists are disposed to allow, for it must do more than assume or cause to be assumed by others, the social and economic burdens incident to our industrial system.[40] "Improvements in material conditions are merely incidents of better conditions, valuable mainly as they may ever increase opportunities for development."[41] The essentials of American citizenship cannot, therefore, be satisfied by supplying workers' physical needs or wants: "It devolves upon the state . . . to fit its rulers for their task. It must provide not only facilities for development, but the opportunity of using them. It must not only provide opportunity, it must stimulate the desire to avail of it."[42]

Any teacher appreciates the task of one undertaking to stimulate desire on the part of others to "demand education." But Brandeis has an even deeper understanding of the human limits to the power of government to arouse intelligent interest in affairs of state:

> Democracy is only possible, industrial democracy, among people who think; among people who are above the average intelligence.

[37] Letter to Robert W. Bruère, February 25, 1922.
[38] L. D. Brandeis, *Business—A Profession* (1933), p. 32.
[39] *ibid.*, p. 29.
[40] L. D. Brandeis, "The Road to Social Efficiency," *The Outlook*, June 10, 1911. Reprinted in *Business—A Profession* (1933), p. 59.
[41] Letter to Robert W. Bruère, February 25, 1922.
[42] L. D. Brandeis, "True Americanism," *Harper's Weekly*, July 10, 1915. Reprinted in *Business—A Profession* (1933), pp. 364, 366-7.

And that thinking is not a heaven-born thing, that intelligence is not a thing that comes merely. It is a gift men make and women make for themselves. It is earned and it is earned by effort. . . . The brain is like the hand. It grows with using.[43]

Democracy for Brandeis, therefore, is in certain respects "an experiment noble in motive" and the conditions of its success are most exacting. The chief responsibilities of government herein are discharged once it has furnished opportunity and facilities for training in matters of citizenship. The individual must then rely chiefly upon himself.

There is much in Brandeis' thought and work to justify the conclusion that he is fundamentally an idealist, not always entirely objective, seldom without a social bias toward the questions that come before him. His vision is that of an ideal state wherein tyranny, political and industrial, is abolished.[44] He longs "for a truer democracy."[45] He well understands that to many this goal is not only remote but quite unattainable. But the skeptical are reminded:

> The civilized world [one hundred years ago] did not believe that it was possible that the people could rule themselves . . . they did not believe that it was possible to have government of the people, by the people, and for the people. America in the last century proved that democracy is a success.
>
> The civilized world today believes that in the industrial world self-government is impossible; that we must adhere to the system which we have known as the monarchical system, the system of master and servant, or, as now more politely called, employer and employee. It rests with this century and perhaps with America to

[43] *Filene Cooperative Association Echo,* May 1905.
[44] These conclusions, in part, are confirmed in the recollections of William G. McAdoo:
"Brandeis is a humanitarian; an idealist, but not a dreamer, for no man living has a firmer grasp of business or of economic actualities. He has an unusual capacity for looking at civilization objectively, as if he were not part of it, and reducing its activities and results to the common denominator of human welfare." W. G. McAdoo, *Crowded Years* (1931), p. 182.
[45] L. D. Brandeis, *Business—A Profession* (1933), p. 38.

prove that as we have in the political world shown what self-government can do, we are to pursue the same lines in the industrial world.[46]

The extraordinary success which many of his seemingly idealistic measures and devices have already won affords some justification for believing that his democratic ideal, in both its political and industrial aspects, may yet be realized. Certainly that ideal is both goal and inspiration to the forces of statesmanship now struggling to shape aright the course of the nation.

[46] *Filene Cooperative Association Echo,* May 1905.

CHAPTER V

BOURBON LAW IN THE INDUSTRIAL AGE

IN OUR generation no man has come to the Supreme Court so versed in problems peculiarly our own as Louis D. Brandeis. No other judge has understood so well our technical problems of economic and social import, many still unsolved; few have had such wide experience in action with these problems; none has devoted more time and toil to the study of economic behavior. Steeped in realities, Brandeis was trained for judgeship, not so much by books, not at all by judicial experience or office-holding, but rather by contact with affairs in matters of public interest. "As a whole," he said in 1911, "I have not got as much from books as I have from tackling concrete problems. I have generally run up against a problem, have painfully tried to think it out, with a measure of success, and have then read a book and found to my surprise that some other chap was before me."[1]

Brandeis, nevertheless, has kept abreast in legal and social science and to these fields has made noteworthy contributions.[2]

[1] Recorded by Ernest Poole from an interview, *The American Magazine,* February 1911.

[2] Among Brandeis' legal writings are the following: L. D. Brandeis, "Liability of Trust-Estates on Contracts Made for Their Benefit" (1881), 15 *Am. L. Rev.* 449; L. D. Brandeis (with Samuel D. Warren, Jr.), "The Watuppa Pond Cases" (1888), 2 *Harv. L. Rev.* 195; L. D. Brandeis (with Samuel D. Warren, Jr.), "The Law of Ponds" (1889), 3 *Harv. L. Rev.* 1; L. D. Brandeis (with Samuel D. Warren, Jr.), "The Right to Privacy" (1890), 4 *Harv. L. Rev.* 193.

In the latter article the authors suggested a new category in the law of torts, the right of privacy. Appraisal of the actual results of this contribution to legal analysis is the subject of a note, "The Right to Privacy Today," which appears in 43 *Harv. L. Rev.* 297 (December 1929). The note concludes that "the battle is still being waged over the original article, which remains a classic example of creative juristic activity through the medium of legal periodicals." For a more exhaustive study of the same

Unlike some members of his profession, he has profited by the work of the social scientist. From sociologists such as Charles R. Crane and Charles R. Henderson, economists such as Thorstein Veblen, and publicists such as Henry Demarest Lloyd, he has gained increased vitality of thought, new values and deeper perspectives. For Brandeis, law is not a thing divorced and set apart but an integral factor in our mental climate and social life. He has drawn inspiration from James Bradley Thayer (under whom he studied constitutional law), from Ernst Freund and other jurists accustomed to think of the law as existing not in watertight compartments but as inextricably related to our whole social and economic complexus. But it was the labor movement, the rise of trusts, and other such forces not peculiar to the law itself, that especially drove Brandeis on to creative leadership in reform.

To relate what Brandeis said, thought, or did on any occasion or at any particular time is not enough. His words, thoughts, and actions fall into proper perspective only when projected against the intricate pattern of his immediate background—a pattern which traced boldly a dominant design of legal opinion. One sees in clear relief the clash of group and class interests, how the courts intervened to repel and to curb within lines of economic orthodoxy the current forces bent on restricting the exploitative aims of capitalist enterprise. The life of his time impinging upon his nature shaped the weapons which he was to seize as he emerged, a daring and formidable combatant in the bitterest and most significant constitutional conflicts of our day.

The early years of Mr. Brandeis' practice (1878-1890) marked the end of an epoch; a new and revolutionary era in American

subject, see Rufus Lisle, "The Right of Privacy Today" (1931), 19 *Ky. L. Jour.* 101.

Mr. Brandeis' promise in legal research is evidenced by the fact that five years after his graduation from the Harvard Law School, he became a lecturer on evidence. Before the end of the year he was offered an assistant professorship. This was when Oliver Wendell Holmes became a judge on the Supreme Court of Massachusetts.

economic and social life had begun.[3] Free land had been largely absorbed, the frontier closed; agriculture had ceased to be the norm of American life. This new era spelled industrialism. The census of 1890 showed an enormous increase in manufactured articles since 1870, though manufacture had outstripped agriculture even earlier than that; the product had greatly increased in value, many more factory workers were employed. The drift from rural to urban regions was more pronounced; corporate forms of industrial organization were rapidly displacing copartnership. Railroad consolidation, even in its first stages, demonstrated such advantages to the roads and the public that combination became the order of the day. A like integration of small industrial and commercial enterprises took place more slowly from 1870-90, but the process was no less inevitable. While the whole pattern of American life was undergoing a fundamental change, promoters, exploiters, monopolists, and trust magnates pushed aggressively to places of power in American economic society.

Transition from the agricultural to the urban status reeked with abuses. Industrial combinations engaged in railroad malpractice which led to the Interstate Commerce Act of 1887. There were industrial pools as well as railway pools, and with similar results. Financiers who organized combinations took fabulous profits. Officers, speculating entirely in their own interest, bought and sold stocks of their own companies. An obvious alliance of business and politics became increasingly odious. Certain industrial corporations rivalled the railroads in controlling practical politics. Indeed, according to one observer, the Standard Oil Company "had done everything with the Pennsylvania legislature except refine it."[4]

[3] This period is admirably treated by Harry Thurston Peck, *Twenty Years of the Republic, 1885-1905* (1913); C. R. Lingley, *Since the Civil War* (1926); Charles A. and Mary R. Beard, *The Rise of American Civilization* (1930), Vol. II, especially Chaps. xxv, xxvii, xxx; John Chamberlain, *Farewell to Reform* (1932).

[4] H. D. Lloyd, "Story of a Great Monopoly," *Atlantic Monthly,* March 1881.

For certain fortunate individuals the efficacy of the "American way of life" (to use a phrase dear to Herbert Hoover) was never more effectively demonstrated than at that time, unless it was during the Coolidge era. For justification of the abuses that attended the rise of industrialism, oppression of the masses by powerful vested interests, exploitation of natural resources, ruthless competition, etc., etc., one had only to turn to the writings of *laissez faire* professors. Economic activity, they said, is governed by laws of its own; so long as government did not interfere with it (save against outsiders), these laws would work inevitably for universal human betterment. During an investigation of a coal combination in 1893, a Congressional committeeman declared it to be "a law of business for each proprietor to pursue his own interest. There is no hope for any of us, but the weakest must go first."[5] These ideas were modernized by William Graham Sumner, who argued fiercely for freedom of contract and other sacred prerogatives of the free man in a free society, the existence of which was assumed in these United States of America. Such was the golden (or brazen) rule of business, which, under the *laissez faire* philosophy of government and law that sustained it, weighted the economic scales heavily in favor of Armour, Harriman, Morgan, Rockefeller, and Schwab.

The rise of industrialism was accompanied by unprecedented disorder, "storm and stress." "The American way of life" proceeded apace but not without challenge. There were the Molly Maguires, the Haymarket Riots, the Panic of 1893, the Pullman Strike, the Chicago Stock Yards Strike, and Coxey's Army, to mention only a few. These were, however, merely symptoms of transition and any attempt to crystallize an underlying philosophy was almost unknown.

The 'seventies, 'eighties, and 'nineties saw movements emerge offering panaceas for the problems of the new era. Among these

[5] Quoted by H. D. Lloyd, *Wealth against Commonwealth* (1894), p. 495.

were Grangers, Greenbackers, Farmers' Alliance, Populists, Knights of Labor, a variety of socialist parties, the Henry Georgeites, the American Federation of Labor, and others. Publicists, trust-busters and muckrakers engaged in invective and vague talk of the "New Freedom," but few understood in any realistic way the economic, social, and political significance of the changes then taking place. One was Frederick J. Turner who on January 12, 1893, read before the American Historical Society his famous paper on "The Significance of the Frontier in American History."[6] Briefly he pointed out that with the passing of the frontier the westward movement ends; the heretofore mobile, land-seeking American is due to settle down but will not; instead he must and will press on in the frontier spirit and find other ways of meeting his needs despite a solidifying civilization.

Equally significant but from a different point of view was Henry Demarest Lloyd's *Wealth against Commonwealth,* published in 1894. Lloyd's appraisal of the new order is unique both in depth and in method of analysis. Paraphrasing the opening words of Rousseau's *Social Contract,* "Man is born free; and everywhere he is in chains," Lloyd said, "Nature is rich; but everywhere man, the heir of nature, is poor."[7] Unlike Rousseau's idealistic and contradictory treatise of 1762, Lloyd's study made a venture in realism in a world of realities. His book was quarried from official records, decisions of courts and special tribunals, such as the Interstate Commerce Commission, reports of committees of state legislatures and of Congress, oath-sworn testimony from legal proceedings and official inquiries with full and accurate references throughout. For grasp of the facts of

---

[6] Reprinted in F. J. Turner, *The Frontier in American History* (1921), Chap. 1.
[7] Lloyd, *Wealth against Commonwealth* (1894), p. 1.

the industrial situation then taking shape, this volume is without an equal.[8]

Wealth against Commonwealth appeared in 1894, but Lloyd had been investigating trusts for some years before. He had fired his first volley in 1881 in an attack on the Standard Oil monopoly.[9] This appeared in the *Atlantic Monthly* and caused that number of the Boston periodical to go through seven editions. In the growth of wealth and corporate control Lloyd saw new dangers to liberty. An industrial absolutism, he feared, was being erected in a political democracy. The period concerning which he wrote was to him but a passing phase in the "evolution of industrial Caesars," and he prophesied that "Corporate Caesars" must become the type of industrial tyrant. The "naked issue," according to Lloyd, was precipitated by a situation in which property was "becoming master instead of servant, property in many necessaries of life becoming monopoly of the necessaries of life."[10]

There arose, meanwhile, a growing demand for legislation to deal with the problems pressing for solution. As early as 1872, the labor reformers had condemned western capitalists for importing Chinese labor. In the same year both the Republican and Democratic parties opposed further grants of public land to corporations and monopolies. The Greenbackers, in 1880, and the Anti-Monopolists, Prohibitionists, and Democrats, in 1884,

---

[8] The following illustrate Lloyd's thesis, as well as his style:
"Liberty produces wealth, and wealth destroys liberty" (p. 2).
. . . Competition has killed competition, . . . corporations are grown greater than the state and have bred individuals greater than themselves . . ." (p. 494).
"Political government by the self-interest of the individual we call anarchy. It is one of the paradoxes of public opinion that the people of America, least tolerant of this theory of anarchy in political government, lead in practising it in industry" (p. 496).
"Politically we are civilized; industrially, not yet" (p. 496).
For a brilliant appraisal of Lloyd's study, see John Chamberlain, *Farewell to Reform*, pp. 48-54.
[9] "Story of a Great Monopoly," *Atlantic Monthly*, March 1881, p. 317.
[10] H. D. Lloyd, *Wealth against Commonwealth*, p. 494.

had denounced corporations and had called for government action to abolish or control their power. The Union Labor, Prohibitionist, and Republican parties in 1888, had urged legislation abolishing or regulating both trusts and monopolies.

Significant federal enactments were the Interstate Commerce Act of 1887, the Sherman Anti-Trust Act of 1890, and the Income Tax Law of 1894. Eight states had passed anti-trust laws by 1890 and several had enacted factory and granger legislation. Against such reforms arose the cry for unrestricted competition, the demand that government should not intrude, interfere, or undertake to regulate free business enterprise. The theoretical basis of such legislation did run counter to well established doctrines of the campus, the court, and the market-place. To shift from legislating for the few to legislating for the many, to transfer emphasis from the doctrine of *laissez faire* to a social philosophy which took cognizance of human welfare and social justice, seemed to sincere men to reverse the very currents which were sweeping the nation on to permanent prosperity.

Strangely enough, that emergence of industrialism which made Henry Demarest Lloyd demand a new theoretical approach to political and economic problems left American economic and legal theory unchanged. Then, as now in certain quarters, the philosophy of pioneer America was still held valid although the foundation of the theory had been seriously undermined. The disinclination of lawyers and judges to see the facts of social and economic life, and to seek ways whereby the law might be harmonized therewith, especially during 1890-1905, is indeed shocking. Rarely was the law viewed as purposing social justice, or utilized as an instrument in its service. One of the ablest and most respected lawyers was Joseph S. Choate, who had acted as counsel in the Income Tax Cases and successfully defended property interests. Invited in 1907 by the attorney-general of Oregon to join in defending the ten-hour law for women, he declined courteously, saying that he could see no reason why "a great husky Irish woman should not work in a laundry more than ten hours in one day, if her employer wished her to do so."[11] "As between persons *sui juris* what right has the legislature," one state court judge asked, "to assume that one class has the need of protection against another?"[12] As violating a theoretical concept of equality, legislation designed to give some economic self-determination to workers in industry, was regarded as paternalistic, arbitrary, and unconstitutional, belittling their intelligence and lowering their standing as free citizens.

Nor need it be supposed that such narrow individualism, such disregard of the facts of a changing social order, was confined to lawyers and state court judges. The alignment of the Supreme Court is demonstrated by three cases decided in the October term of 1894.[13] In the Sugar Trust Case,[14] the Sherman Anti-Trust Act was virtually emasculated. If a combination of manufacturers, which admittedly controlled ninety-eight per cent of the total output of sugar in the United States, did not come within the terms of the Sherman law, it was difficult indeed to conceive of any combination which did. Business was thus left free, at least for the time being, to make the most of its opportunities.

The Court undertook to correct in the Income Tax Cases[15] what it characterized as "a century of error," and in so doing placed large incomes beyond the reach of national taxation for almost twenty years. The judges who voted with the majority as well as those who expressed their views in dissent departed

---

[11] Communication of Florence Kelley, *The Survey*, May 13, 1916.

[12] State v. Haun, 61 Kan. 146, 162 (1899). For a good discussion of similar cases, see Roscoe Pound, "The End of Law as Developed in Legal Rules and Doctrines" (1914), 27 *Harv. L. Rev.* 195.

[13] For a penetrating analysis of these cases, see E. S. Corwin, "Social Planning Under the Constitution," *Am. Pol. Sci. Rev.*, February 1932, Vol. XXVI, p. 1.

[14] U.S. v. E. C. Knight, 156 U.S. 1 (1895).

[15] Pollock v. Farmers' Loan and Trust Co., 157 U.S. 429 (1895), and 158 U.S. 601 (1895).

notably from the objective and impersonal manner usual to that tribunal, and spoke in terms of marked feeling. Justice Field in particular was alarmed by legislation such as that laying taxes on incomes; he conjured up the spectre of socialism and regarded the income tax as "but the beginning" of an "assault upon capital" which was bound to continue "till our political contests will become a war of the poor against the rich; a war constantly growing in intensity and bitterness."[16] Certain judges in dissent were as much disturbed but for different reasons. Justice Harlan declared that the Court's decision dealt a severe blow to the safety and stability of American institutions:

> The practical effect of the decision today is to give to certain kinds of property a position of favoritism and advantage inconsistent with the fundamental principles of our social organization, and to invest them with power and influence that may be perilous to that portion of the American people upon whom rests the larger part of the burdens of the government, and who ought not to be subjected to the dominion of aggregated wealth any more than the property of the country should be at the mercy of the lawless.[17]

Justice Brown expressed himself with even greater feeling. He regarded the decision as a "confession of feebleness" which "may prove the first step toward the submergence of the liberties of the people in a sordid despotism of wealth."[18]

No case in that period brings out in such sharp relief the Court's attitude toward the issue so clearly stated by Lloyd, as does the decision in the Income Tax Cases. It is now generally agreed that the income tax decision was reached not by any legalistic reasoning, not on the basis of any economic theory as to the incidence of taxation, but by evoking "the spectre of Socialism,"[19] of "Communism on the march," by raising the fear

---

[16] 157 U.S. 429, at 607.
[17] 158 U.S. 601, at 685.
[18] ibid., at 695.
[19] Language of Justice Brown, ibid., at 695.

that unless this march was stopped then and there, taxes might soon be imposed by a "board of 'walking delegates.' "[20] Doubtless Justice Holmes, in 1913, had this decision in mind as he wrote:

> When twenty years ago a vague terror went over the earth and the word socialism began to be heard, I thought and still think that fear was translated into doctrines that had no proper place in the Constitution or the common law.[21]

During the same period it came to pass that if property was threatened with mob violence, there was available for its protection every resource of national executive and judicial power. Under the Court's decision in the Debs Case,[22] the executive enjoys the prerogative, without statutory authorization, to appeal to federal courts of equity and thus obtain an injunction to protect any widespread public interest of a proprietary nature under control of the national government. The serious constitutional question brought into prominence by the Pullman Strike of 1894 concerned, however, not so much the executive as the judiciary. "Government by injunction" came into general use for the first time. Thenceforth business men and employers increasingly sought protection from equity courts whenever their property or property rights were threatened by the activities of labor. The point has since been reached where, in such cases, the injunction is the most important instrument for the enforcement of law itself.[23]

[20] Language of Justice Field, 157 U.S. 429, at 607.

The most effective and frequently cited authority in this case was an excerpt from Coke on Littleton. Adam Smith, Turgot, and a few other eighteenth century writers, were accorded equal rank with the best English dictionaries in defining "direct tax." Two casual references to J. S. Mill and one to E. R. A. Seligman were made incidentally. These are all the references to economic writings contained in the 339 pages covered in the reports. See, in this connection, H. W. Humble, "Economics from a Legal Standpoint" (1908), 42 Am. L. Rev. 379, 382.

[21] Speech of Mr. Justice Holmes delivered February 15, 1913, 62nd Cong., 3rd Sess., Sen. Doc., Vol. XXV, No. 1106.

[22] In re Debs, 158 U.S. 564 (1895).

[23] See in this connection, E. E. Witte, The Government in Labor Disputes (1932), p. 183; Felix Frankfurter and N. Greene, The Labor Injunction (1930), pp. 105, 107, 125.

Meanwhile the scope of judicial review in cases arising under the "due process" clause of the Fourteenth Amendment, had been greatly expanded. Expressly denying, in the Slaughter-House Cases, any purpose to become "a perpetual censor upon all legislation of the states,"[24] and expressing doubt that the "due process" clause would ever arise except in cases involving the negro, the Court by 1900 no longer hesitated to apply this clause of the Fourteenth Amendment as a substantive limitation on legislative power, and the number of cases other than those involving the negro was constantly increasing.[25]

The attitude of the Court prior to 1890 was marked by extreme toleration of state acts dealing with economic and social conditions, as was clearly stated in the case of Powell v. Pennsylvania.[26] Facts presented by opposing counsel to show that the law did not really protect the public health, drew this statement from the Court:

> . . . As it does not appear upon the face of the statute, or from any facts of which the court must take judicial cognizance, that it infringes rights secured by the fundamental law, the legislative determination of those questions is conclusive upon the courts. It is not a part of their functions to conduct investigations of facts entering into questions of public policy merely, and to sustain or frustrate the legislative will, embodied in statutes, as they may happen to approve or disapprove its determination of such questions. . . . The legislature of Pennsylvania . . . we must conclusively presume . . . has determined that the prohibition of the sale of [oleomargerine] . . . will promote the public health, and prevent frauds in the sale of such articles.[27]

Under this doctrine of judicial toleration the Court had sustained during the years 1867-90 a considerable body of social

24 Slaughter-House Cases, 16 Wall. 36 (1873) at 78.
25 E. S. Corwin, "The Supreme Court and the Fourteenth Amendment" (1909), 7 Mich. L. Rev. 643.
26 127 U.S. 678 (1888). This case involved the constitutionality of a statute regulating the manufacture of oleomargerine.
27 ibid., at 685-6.

legislation. Usury laws, granger legislation, Sunday laws, prohibitions of lotteries and of the liquor traffic, were all upheld as legitimate exercise of the police power.

Although the position taken by the Court in the Powell case grants legislative independence in broad terms, it was conceivable that there might be cases in which "fundamental rights" of the citizen would have to be protected by the courts against the "merely arbitrary" exercise of legislative power. The veering of the Court toward the view that the "due process" clause affords such protection, is evident from the fact that while in 1888 only Justice Field dissented in the Powell case, in 1903 three Justices (Chief Justice Fuller, Justices Peckham and Brewer) all of whom had come onto the bench since that decision, dissented in the similar case of Atkin v. Kansas.[28]

Of even more significance for the fate of social legislation was the ruling in Holden v. Hardy.[29] Proceeding on the theory that "liberty" was fixed and definite, the Court announced that it intended henceforth to require the state to show special justification in support of measures which restricted the right of employers to make economically advantageous contracts with

[28] 191 U.S. 207 (1903). Here the Court's statement of its theory of judicial review in due process cases did not differ essentially from that stated fifteen years earlier. In the first case, however, only one member of the court refused to subscribe to it; whereas in the Atkin Case there were three dissenters.

". . . If it be said that a statute like the one before us is mischievous in its tendencies, the answer is that the responsibility therefor rests upon legislators, not upon the courts. No evils arising from such legislation could be more far-reaching than those that might come to our system of government if the judiciary, abandoning the sphere assigned to it by the fundamental law, should enter the domain of legislation, and upon grounds merely of justice or reason or wisdom annul statutes that had received the sanction of the people's representative. We are reminded by counsel that it is the solemn duty of the courts in cases before them to guard the constitutional rights of the citizens against mere arbitrary power. That is unquestionably true. But it is equally true—indeed, the public interests imperatively demand—that legislative enactments should be recognized and enforced by the courts as embodying the will of the people, unless they are plainly and palpably, beyond all question, in violation of the fundamental law of the Constitution." ibid., at 223.

[29] 169 U.S. 366 (1898).

their employees. This was supposedly permitted and even encouraged by so-called freedom of contract. It is true that special
justification was found, the industry being notoriously a haz-
ardous one, and the eight-hour law for such employments was
sustained. The implication of the doctrine asserted therein
became more clearly defined seven years later in the Lochner
Case, in which the Court, in the absence of any special justification for a ten-hour law for bakers, set aside the New York
statute on this subject. "There is no reasonable ground," the
Court decided, "for interfering with the liberty of person or the
right of free contract, by determining the hours of labor, in the
occupation of a baker."[30] Moreover, Mr. Justice Peckham, who
spoke for the Court, took cognizance of the fact that "this interference on the part of the legislatures of the several States with
the ordinary trades and occupations of the people seems to be on
the increase."[31] He feared that "the legislature in its paternal
wisdom" might extend the regulation of hours of labor to other
fields and he did "not believe in the soundness of the views"
which upheld such legislation.[32]

The course thus indicated is paralleled in rate regulation cases,
the original theory of judicial review being plainly stated in
Munn v. Illinois[33] under the liberal guidance of Chief Justice
Waite. Upholding the reasonableness of rates fixed by the state
of Illinois in the grain elevator business, the Court declared its
purpose to pay deference to legislative findings of fact in determining the reasonableness of such statutes: "For our purposes
we must assume that, if a state of facts could exist that would
justify such legislation, it actually did exist when the statute

---

[30] Lochner v. N.Y., 198 U.S. 45 (1905), at 57.
[31] ibid., at 63.
[32] ibid., at 60-1. It should be pointed out that the foundations for such an extraordinary exercise of judicial power were laid some seventeen years earlier in the
case of Mugler v. Kan. 123 U.S. 623, 662 (1887). See infra, p. 102, Note 1.
[33] 94 U.S. 113 (1876).

now under consideration was passed."[34] And if the particular rates fixed, in a field where rate regulation was held to be permissible, seemed arbitrary and unreasonable, the Court advised that for protection the "people must resort to the polls, not the courts."[35]

After certain misgivings and vehement protest on the part of dissenting justices, this rule was abandoned in a series of cases culminating in Smyth v. Ames[36] where it was definitely held that charges set by public authority must yield what the court finds to be a "fair return" on "property" devoted to a public use. And of this the Court, not the legislature, is the final arbiter since fundamental rights are involved:

> The idea that any legislature, state or federal, can conclusively determine for the people and for the courts that what it enacts in the form of law, or what it authorizes its agents to do, is consistent with the fundamental law, is in opposition to the theory of our institutions. The duty rests upon all courts, federal and state, when their jurisdiction is properly invoked, to see to it that no right secured by the supreme law of the land is impaired or destroyed by legislation.[37]

The gradual abandonment of the *laissez-faire* doctrine by the country at large accounts for this shift of position from that announced in the Slaughter-House Cases and in Munn v. Illinois. The political aspect includes the rise of populism and of Roosevelt's "New Nationalism"; the legal aspect was reflected in the interference of government with business and with labor. As the exponents of these new economic theories gained power and influence in the political branches of state and national government, conservatives invoked the aid of the Court, and by no means in vain. The Court, still imbued with the dogmas of eighteenth century individualism, faithfully performing what

[34] *ibid.,* at 132.
[35] *ibid.,* at 134.
[36] 169 U.S. 466 (1898).
[37] *ibid.,* at 527-8.

it conceived to be its historical function of protecting the individual against arbitrary action of legislative majorities, evolved decisions such as those in the Pollock, E. C. Knight, Debs, and Lochner cases.

New restrictions were fortified against progressive legislative power. Not only was judicial review expanded, especially under the due process clause, but the rights of life, liberty, and property protected by that clause were given broader implications. The common law conceived property as a physical thing held for the owner's use—a narrow view from which the Court has long since departed. In the "Minnesota Rate Cases"[38] it was held that the anticipated earning of revenue was property. In the labor injunction cases, business as a "going concern," the right to do business, was included under the term property; while in the Pollock case all the uses which give value to property were treated by the Court as inseparable from property itself.[39] During the same period liberty came to mean more than the mere absence of physical restraint. It was extended to include the individual's right "to be free in the enjoyment of all his faculties; to be free to use them in all lawful ways; to live and work where he will; to earn his livelihood by any lawful calling; to pursue any livelihood or avocation."[40] New definitions of "lib-

[38] 134 U.S. 418 (1890).

[39] The judicial meaning of the word "property" reached an extreme point in the International News Service v. Associated Press, 248 U.S. 215 (1918), where Justice Brandeis delivered a strong dissenting opinion.

Mr. Justice Stone has stated his view in this interesting language: "Beyond the traditional boundaries of the common law only some imperative justification in policy will lead the courts to recognize in old values new property rights." Reichelderfer v. Quinn, 287 U.S. 315, 319 (1932).

A number of judicial definitions of "property" as it relates to labor are collected in my article "Organized Labor as Party Plaintiff in Injunction Cases" (1930), 30 Col. L. Rev. 466 at 485, n. 70.

[40] Justice Peckham in Allgeyer v. Louisiana, 165 U.S. 578, 589 (1897). These concepts of liberty as connoting essentially freedom of contract, and of property considered as "profits" played a leading rôle in Justice Peckham's opinion in Lochner

erty" and "property" coined by the Court in the 'nineties were thus the means, rather than the cause, of the Judiciary's becoming substantially "a perpetual censor upon all legislation of the states."

This whole period was one fraught with dynamic possibilities, charged with a new restlessness excited by the closing frontier, which urged at once new forms of internal development and external expansion. Under the fostering philosophy of *laissez faire,* with easy access to cheap public lands and seemingly unlimited resources, great railroads were flung across the continent, and an era of intense industrial development set in which opened unbounded opportunities for a luxuriant and greedy individualism. The Supreme Court made the Fourteenth Amendment the vehicle of its meticulous guardianship. "Liberty of contract" flourished. Sound leadership but short-lived was furnished during the tenure of Chief Justice Waite. Sturdy individualists such as Peckham, Brewer, and Field, soon dominated the Court to delay or prevent American legislatures from dealing with pressing social problems in a manner approved by the enlightened experience of other industrial nations of the world. Such was the environment in the midst of which Brandeis lived, and no phase of this conflict, turmoil, and change escaped him. Such was the pattern of ideas, concepts, and forces within which and against which he was compelled to battle as his ideals of public service forced him into collision with the conventional methods and established doctrines of the Supreme Court.

v. New York, 198 U.S. 45 (1905), and Justice Sutherland's opinion in Adkins v. Children's Hospital, 261 U.S. 525 (1923).

For a good discussion of the changing concepts of property, see John R. Commons, *Legal Foundations of Capitalism* (1924), Chap. ii.

See also the stimulating article by Max Lerner, "The Supreme Court and American Capitalism" (1933), 42 *Yale L. J.,* 668.

CHAPTER VI

MORE LIFE IN THE LAW: THE BRANDEIS BRIEF

THE Supreme Court by 1890 abandoned "judicial toleration" and began to interpret the "due process" clause not
only as requiring a particular form of procedure but also as
fixing substantive limitations upon the states' legislative power.[1]
Judicial authority therefore involved enlarged responsibility; our
Supreme Court became final judge of the states' economic and
social policy.[2] With "few scientifically certain criteria of legislation" it was hard "to mark the line where what is called the
police power of the states is limited by the Constitution." What
measures should be taken lest the judges read into the Constitution "a *nolumus mutare* as against the law-making power?"[3]

[1] In Mugler v. Kan. 123 U.S. 623 (1887), a case involving a state prohibition
statute, Justice Harlan observed: "The courts are not bound by mere forms, nor are
they to be misled by mere pretenses. They are at liberty—indeed, are under a solemn
duty—to look at the substance of things, whenever they enter upon the inquiry
whether the legislature has transcended the limits of its authority. If, therefore, a
statute purporting to have been enacted to protect the public health, the public morals,
or the public safety, has no real or substantial relation to those objects, or is a
palpable invasion of rights secured by the fundamental law, it is the duty of the courts
to so adjudge, and thereby give effect to the Constitution" (at 661).

[2] "The task of applying the constitutional test of due process of law to modern
legislation has enormously strengthened the prestige and power of the American
courts and has brought out in sharp relief the unique character of the American
doctrine of the judicial review of legislation. In no other field of the law is there so
complete an absence of concrete tests and standards, so much room for the exercise
of pure discretion by the court. In applying the due process test to police regulations
of the control of public utilities the courts constitute a third chamber, marshaling
their own views of social and economic policy and legal theory in settling the vague
question whether the acts in question are arbitrary or not." Robert E. Cushman, "Due
Process of Law," *Encyclopaedia of the Social Sciences* (1931), Vol. V, pp. 264, 268.
See also J. L. Nesbitt, "Due Process of Law and Opinion" (1926), 26 *Col. L. Rev.* 23.

[3] Language of Mr. Justice Holmes in Noble State Bank v. Haskell, 219 U.S. 104, 110
(1911).

In a new case the judge was free, so far as compelling rules of logic were concerned, to decide much as he pleased; and his choice usually turned upon considerations of political, economic or social policy. If he made this choice intelligently, he had to go beyond the bounds of constitutional exegesis.[4] But our tradition of juridical technique afforded no provision whereby counsel could furnish the Court with essential social and economic statistics. Implicit confidence in the "simple tool of logic" to solve constitutional questions, however novel or complex, had prior to 1908 (as in certain quarters even now), resulted in proscribing any realistic test of legislative-judicial conclusions.

The briefs of counsel as well as the opinions of judges were steeped in the convention that law was to be mastered only by a series of syllogisms. Among jurists and lawyers the supreme qualification was dialectic skill. The best chance to win a case in the court-room lay not with those who appealed to the judges' sense of right and justice. Since this sense was so frequently uninformed as to the facts, success usually came to him who knew how the fill the judges' souls with the logical beauty of that law for which he gained a hearing.[5] Armed with "common understanding" and experience as men and as judges, it was believed that any case, notwithstanding involved tangles of law and economics, could be solved by simple rules of abstract logic. Excursions into fields related to the law, as economics and

[4] H. W. Biklé, "Judicial Determination of Questions of Fact Affecting the Constitutionality of Legislative Action" (1924), 38 *Harv. L. Rev.* 6.

"I do not expect or think it desirable that the judges should undertake to renovate the law. . . . But I think it most important to remember whenever a doubtful case arises . . . that what is really before us is a conflict between two social desires . . . the social question is which desire is stronger at the point of conflict. . . . Where there is doubt the simple tool of logic does not suffice, and even if it is disguised and unconscious, the judges are called on to exercise the sovereign prerogative of choice." "Law in Science and Science in Law" (1899), 12 *Harv. L. Rev.* 443, 460-1. Reprinted in O. W. Holmes, *Collected Legal Papers* (1920), pp. 210, 239.

[5] Compare H. Krabbe, *The Modern Idea of the State* (1922), pp. 128-9 and Roscoe Pound, "Courts and Legislation" (1913), 7 *Am. Pol. Sci. Rev.* 361, 372.

sociology, were not necessary. Nevertheless two questions arose, neither primarily requiring legal knowledge: First, what social consequences or results does the statute in question aim at? Second, how will the decision affect the attainment of such results?[6] The judge is not apt to answer, for to do so he must have recourse to social sciences other than law.

If the Court should have such knowledge, the next question is: Whose business is it to find the facts as to the need for legislation? Is it the function of the legislature passing the statute, of the counsel defending or opposing it, or of the court which passes upon its constitutionality? One may infer from the opinions of certain judges that they think this work should be done by the legislature.

> . . . Questions of fact and public policy . . . belong to the legislative department to determine. . . . It is not a part of their [the Courts'] functions to conduct investigations of facts entering into questions of public policy merely, and to sustain or frustrate the legislative will, embodied in statutes, as they may happen to approve or disapprove its determination of such questions.[7]

The problem of fact-finding, according to the late Professor Ernst Freund, is "one that only the legislature itself can handle

[6] Compare W. W. Cook, "Scientific Method and the Law," 13 *Am. Bar Assoc. Jour.*, 303, 307-9 (1927).

[7] Powell v. Pennsylvania, 127 U.S. 678, 685 (1888).

"The legislature being familiar with local conditions is, primarily, the judge of the necessity of such enactments." Mr. Justice Day in McLean v. Ark., 211 U.S. 539, 547 (1909). Quoted with approval by Mr. Justice Hughes in Chicago, B. and Q. R.R. Co. v. McGuire, 219 U.S. 549, 569 (1911). "Many laws which it would be vain to ask the Court to overthrow could be shown, easily enough, to transgress a scholastic interpretation of one or another of the great guarantees in the Bill of Rights. . . . If . . . the legislature of the state thinks that the public welfare requires the measure under consideration, analogy and principle are in favor of the power to enact it." Mr. Justice Holmes speaking for the Court in Noble State Bank v. Haskell, 219 U.S. 104, 111 (1911).

These quotations, it is true, concern not so much the question of who should ascertain the facts as that of who should exercise a judgment as to the need for the legislation. But one may infer from these that the legislature should know the facts out of which the legislation grew. These could then be brought before the Court for an independent judgment.

adequately."[8] It is, however, a function which American legislatures have not exercised. "The student of the history of legislation has constant occasion to wonder, not merely at the absence of impartial and authoritative statements of facts and conclusions, but at the entire failure on the part of those demanding legislative interference to make an impressive or plausible, or, for that matter, any kind of a presentation of their case."[9]

Here is a striking difference between legislative procedure in this country and in Great Britain. During the past century hardly a piece of important legislation has passed Parliament without investigation by a Royal Commission appointed for the purpose. Felix Frankfurter says that "the history of British democracy might in considerable measure be written in terms of the history of successive Royal Commissions."[10] In the United States work of this sort is almost unknown, despite the fact that "such commissions of investigation ought more and more to be called into use to deflate feeling, define issues, sift evidence, formulate alternative remedies."[11] In this country fact-finding studies tend to follow rather than precede the enactment of legislation.[12]

Certainly if the Court is to accept the findings of the legislature, as Mr. Justice Holmes usually insisted, legislative action should be preceded by careful investigation. So long as the Court followed our traditional policy, "to presume in favor of its validity, until its violation of the Constitution is proved beyond all reasonable doubt,"[13] forward-looking legislation did

[8] *Standards of American Legislation* (1926), p. 98.

[9] *ibid.*, p. 135.

[10] *The Public and Its Government* (1930), p. 162. See also W. H. Moore, "Executive Commissions of Inquiry" (1913), 13 *Col. L. Rev.* 500; J. H. Richardson, "What Has Been Done by British Fact-Finding Bodies in Industrial Relations" (1928), *Proc. Acad. Pol. Sci.*, Vol. XIII.

[11] Felix Frankfurter, *op. cit.*, p. 162.

[12] Silas Bent, "Mr. Hoover's Sins of Commissions," *Scribner's Magazine,* July 1931. See also *Editorial Research Reports,* May 28, 1931.

[13] "It is but a decent respect due to the wisdom, the integrity, and the patriotism of the legislative body, by which any law is passed, to presume in favor of its validity, until

not suffer. But once the Court took the position that the state must show special justification for legislation restrictive of abstract fundamental rights, the need for a new technique in brief-making became imperative. This is abundantly illustrated by the Court's decision in the Lochner Case.[14]

Here the rule applied was that arbitrary restriction of men's activities, unrelated in reason to public welfare, offends due process. This rule holds today. Brandeis cited it as authoritative in his brief in Muller v. Oregon,[15] basing nearly all his constitutional argument upon the Lochner Case. An apparent paradox results from indefiniteness of the rule. What actually constitutes an arbitrary restriction upon fundamental rights? And when does legislation become related, in reason, to the public welfare? That these questions cannot be answered by reason alone is evidenced by the dissent of four justices in the Lochner Case. Nor is common knowledge or understanding a safe guide, for "common understanding" as Professor Ernst Freund has well said, "is often equivalent to popular ignorance and fallacy."[16]

its violation of the constitution is proved beyond all reasonable doubt." Mr. Justice Washington in Ogden v. Saunders, 12 Wheat. 214, 270 (1827).

One notes a revival of this doctrine in O'Gorman and Young v. Hartford Fire Insurance Co., 282 U.S. 251 (1931), where Mr. Justice Brandeis, speaking for the Court, upheld the right of the state to regulate the commissions paid fire insurance agents: ". . . The presumption of constitutionality," Brandeis observed, "must prevail in the absence of some factual foundation of record for overthrowing the statute. It does not appear upon the face of the statute, or from any facts of which the court must take judicial notice, that in New Jersey evils did not exist in the business of fire insurance for which this statutory provision was an appropriate remedy. The action of the legislature and of the highest court of the state indicates that such evils did exist. The record is barren of any allegation of fact tending to show unreasonableness" (at 258).

This doctrine has been followed in a number of recent cases. These are collected in the dissenting opinion of Mr. Justice Brandeis in Liggett v. Lee, 288 U.S. 517 (1933) at 543. See, in this connection, the excellent note, "The Presumption of Constitutionality" (1931), 31 Col. L. Rev., 1136.

[14] 198 U.S. 45 (1905).

[15] 208 U.S. 412 (1908).

[16] "Limitations of Hours of Labor and the Federal Supreme Court" (1905), 17 Green Bag 411, 416.

Scientific scrutiny and critique are required for authoritative interpretation of accredited facts.

Three years after the Lochner decision Brandeis presented to the Supreme Court the first brief ever based upon authoritative extra-legal data.[17] He felt keenly his own responsibility, and that of other counsel, in this particular. ". . . A judge," he later pointed out, "rarely performs his functions adequately unless the case before him is adequately presented. Thus were the blind led by the blind. It is not surprising that under such conditions the laws as administered failed to meet contemporary economic and social demands."[18] In his opinion courts, as compared with counsel and legislatures, are unfitted to investigate those social and economic conditions which modern legislation is designed to regulate. It is not their function, and the courts do not have facilities for examining complex social and economic phenomena.

> Except as counsel furnish material in their printed arguments, the Court has no facilities for obtaining knowledge of social facts comparable to hearings before committees, testimony of specialists who have conducted detailed investigations, and other means of the sort available to the legislature.[19]

Dean Pound goes on to suggest that judicial reference bureaus might well be developed which would aid the courts with their law-making as legislative reference bureaus serve some seventeen of our states today. It is doubtful, however, whether the courts will "be furnished with investigating machinery that

[17] 208 U.S. 412 (1908).

[18] "The Living Law" (1916), 10 *Ill. L. Rev.* 461, 470.

Mr. Justice Holmes has also emphasized the responsibility of counsel in this particular: "It may or may not be that if the facts were called to our attention in a proper way the objection would prove to be real. . . . It rests with counsel to take the proper steps, and if they deliberately omit them, we do not feel called upon to institute inquiries on our own account." Quong Wing v. Kirkendall, 223 U.S. 59 (1912) at 63-4.

[19] Roscoe Pound, "Legislation as a Social Function" (1913), *Pub. Am. Soc. Society,* Vol. VII, 148, 160.

will equal in effectiveness the sources of information at the disposal of a legislative body...."[20]

The legislature of Oregon, before enacting the eight-hour law for women, failed to build up any factual foundation to support that statute. When this legislation was contested Brandeis set himself to give the Court a careful appraisal of the factual situation out of which it had grown. Two pages of his brief cover the legal arguments; approximately one hundred pages are devoted to a new kind of evidence from over ninety reports of committees, bureaus of statistics, commissioners of hygiene, and inspectors of factories, both in this country and in Europe, all bearing witness that long hours are dangerous to women's health. Included in the brief also are extracts from similar reports discussing the general benefits of short hours from the economic point of view.[21] The Court approved his method:

> It may not be amiss, in the present case, before examining the constitutional question to notice the course of legislation as well as expressions of opinion from other than judicial sources. In the brief filed by Mr. Louis D. Brandeis ... is a very copious collection of all these matters.
>
> ... The legislation and opinions referred to in the margin may not be, technically speaking, authorities, and in them is little or no discussion of the constitutional question presented to us for determination, yet they are significant of a widespread belief that woman's physical structure, and the functions she performs in consequence thereof, justify special legislation restricting or qualifying the conditions under which she should be permitted to toil. Constitutional questions, it is true, are not settled by even a consensus of present public opinion. ... At the same time, when a question of fact is debated and debatable, and the extent to which a special constitutional limitation goes is affected by the truth in respect to that fact, a

---

20 Ernst Freund, *Standards of American Legislation* (1926), p. 96.

21 This brief in the preparation of which Mr. Brandeis was assisted by Miss Josephine Goldmark (his sister-in-law) was reprinted by the National Consumers' League under the title, *Women in Industry*. Mr. Brandeis' brief is also reprinted in a volume, Josephine Goldmark, *Fatigue and Efficiency* (1912), Part II.

widespread and long continued belief concerning it is worthy of con- ↙
sideration.[22]

Here for the first time the Supreme Court recognized the need
for supporting legislation by facts which establish its reasonableness or unreasonableness. The Court rejected the freedom-
of-contract fiction as regards working women. And one thinks
the Court assumed at least an implied obligation to insist
upon this new method of dealing with similar cases—certainly before setting legislation aside. Precisely this position
was taken nine years later in Bunting v. Oregon.[23] "There is a
contention made," Mr. Justice McKenna observed, "that the
law, even regarded as regulating hours of service, is not either
necessary or useful 'for preservation of the health of employes
in mills, factories and manufacturing establishments.' The
record contains no facts to support the contention, and against
it is the judgment of the legislature and the [State] Supreme
Court."[24]

Having presumed the constitutionality of the act, the Court
logically proceeded to cast the burden of proof as to invalidity
upon those who attacked the legislative judgment; counsel
were summoned to make some factual foundation of record for
overthrowing the statute. The record being barren of any allegation of facts tending to show unreasonableness, the act was sustained. Such procedure is not followed without exception. When
Mr. Justice Sutherland in the Adkins Case laid down the proposition that "freedom of contract is . . . the general rule and
restraint the exception,"[25] he thereby called upon those who

---

[22] 208 U.S. 412, 419-21 (1908). Language of Mr. Justice Brewer.
[23] 243 U.S. 426 (1917).
[24] *ibid.* at 438.
[25] Adkins v. Children's Hospital, 261 U.S. 525, 546 (1923). Compare with the
position taken by Mr. Justice Brandeis, speaking for the Court, in O'Gorman and
Young v. Hartford Insurance Co., 282 U.S. 251, 257-8 (1931). See also his
dissenting opinions in New State Ice Co. v. Liebmann, 285 U.S. 262, 284-5 (1932),
and Liggett v. Lee, 288 U.S. 517, 543 (1933): "Since the presumption of consti-

favored the restraint to justify the exception in the case at bar. It is obviously impossible to reconcile "the presumption of constitutionality" with such a doctrine. And which of these procedures is followed is a matter of great significance for the fate of the legislation.

"The time may come," Dr. Freund wrote in 1926, "when courts will be justified in demanding that the legislature shall act only upon some evidence somewhere placed on record, but that time has hardly yet arrived . . . and . . . if there have been instances of conclusions reached upon a totally unsatisfactory basis, the courts have sinned in that respect no less than the legislatures."[26] The Court has inherent power to take such measures either by indicating the kind of argument needed to help it reach a just decision, or by calling on members of the bar who are equipped to deal with the case in hand.[27]

Beginning with Muller v. Oregon (in 1908), the chief arguments in several labor cases, state and federal, were thus fully presented by Brandeis, sometimes as *amicus curiae*. In 1909, an Illinois statute similar to that involved in the Muller Case was contested before the supreme court of that state. The manufacturer claimed that a certain woman, thirty-five years in his employment, could not earn a living wage unless she worked over ten hours a day. Brandeis appeared for the defense and won.[28] In 1911 he was invited by the attorney-general of Ohio

tutionality must prevail in the absence of some factual foundation of record for overthrowing the statute [Florida Chain Store Tax] its validity should, in my opinion, be sustained." Liggett v. Lee, *ibid*.

✓ [26] Ernst Freund, *Standards of American Legislation,* p. 99.

[27] Compare Felix Frankfurter, "Hours of Labor and Realism in Constitutional Law" (1916), 29 *Harv. L. Rev.* 353, 371 ff.

[28] Ritchie v. Wayman, 244 Ill. 509, 91 N.E. 695 (1910). This decision, in effect, overruled Ritchie v. People, 155 Ill. 98, 40 N.E. 454 (1895) despite the Court's rather futile effort to distinguish the two cases. "In the first Ritchie case the court, reasoning from abstract conception, held a limitation of working hours to be arbitrary and unreasonable; while in the second Ritchie case, reasoning from life, it held the limitation of hours not to be arbitrary and unreasonable." L. D. Brandeis, "The Living Law" (1916), 10 *Ill. L. Rev.* 461, 465.

to assist in the defense of a statute regulating the hours of labor for women. He prepared the brief and successfully presented it to the Supreme Court.[29]

The legislature of Oregon had established in 1913 an Industrial Welfare Commission and empowered it to provide such regulation of wages, hours of labor, and conditions of work as seemed on investigation necessary for the safety, health, and welfare of employees. The commission at once promulgated a minimum wage requirement for women employed in factories and stores. The validity of the act under which these orders were issued was contested, and at the commission's request Brandeis filed a brief in its support. The statute was unanimously sustained by the Oregon Supreme Court on grounds previously urged in support of hours of labor legislation for women.[30] When the case came before the Supreme Court of the United States in 1916, Brandeis found three pages of his brief enough to state the points of law; but evidence to support his contention that the legislation had reasonable relation to public health, safety and welfare, filled three hundred and ninety pages.[31] The Supreme Court divided equally on the constitutionality of the act, Mr. Justice Brandeis having been appointed to the Court after taking part in the preparation of the brief, not voting.[32] It was generally under-

[29] *Ex parte* Anna Hawley, 85 Ohio 495, 98 N.E. 1125 (1911). Brief of Mr. Brandeis reprinted in Josephine Goldmark, *Fatigue and Efficiency*. This case was carried on appeal to the Supreme Court of the United States. Here Brandeis also filed a brief and took part in the oral argument. The law was sustained without opinion in Hawley v. Walker, 232 U.S. 718 (1914). The Illinois act was again subject to attack in 1912 and Brandeis took part in the defense in the case of People v. Elerding, 254 Ill. 579, 98 N.E. 982 (1912). Brief reprinted in Josephine Goldmark, *Fatigue and Efficiency*.

[30] Stettler v. O'Hara, 69 Ore. 519, 139 Pac. 743 (1914).

For Mr. Brandeis' constitutional argument in support of the minimum wage, see also his article, "The Constitution and the Minimum Wage," *The Survey*, Feb. 6, 1915; Report of the Commission on Industrial Relations, 64th Cong., 1st Sess., Sen. Doc., Vol. XXVI, pp. 7674 ff. (1915); Fourth Report of the New York State Factory Investigating Commission, Vol. V, pp. 2897 ff. (1915).

[31] Reprinted by the National Consumers' League.

[32] Stettler v. O'Hara, 243 U.S. 629 (1916).

stood that this decision established the validity of minimum wage legislation. In Adkins v. Children's Hospital,[33] however, the Court revived the Lochner Case to find precedent for an unfavorable decision.

In 1907 the New York Court of Appeals declared invalid a statute prohibiting night work for women on the ground that the act was "discriminative against female citizens, in denying to them equal rights with men in the same pursuit."[34] "When it is sought," Judge Gray observed, "under the guise of a labor law, arbitrarily, as here, to prevent an adult female citizen from working any time of day that suits her, I think it is time to call a halt."[35]

Prior to enacting a second measure the legislature made a detailed survey of the facts on which the new statute was based. And when, in 1915, the constitutionality of the new act was contested, Brandeis presented a summary of facts against night work for women, covering more than four hundred pages. It required eighteen pages merely to list the sources from which material was drawn. Some of these facts, it is true, were not available in 1907. In the later brief they are presented in detail besides facts available but not produced by counsel in 1907. The New York Court of Appeals, in sustaining the act, indicates the nature of the burden imposed upon the legislature which enacts social legislation as well as upon counsel who defend it:

> While theoretically we may [in 1907] have been able to take judicial notice of some of the facts and of some of the legislation now called to our attention as sustaining the belief and opinion that night work in factories is widely and substantially injurious to the health of women, actually very few of these facts were called to our attention, and the argument to uphold the law on that ground was brief and inconsequential. . . .

[33] 261 U.S. 525 (1923).
[34] People v. Williams, 189 N.Y. 131, 135, 81 N.E. 778 (1907).
[35] ibid.

So, as it seems to me, in view of the incomplete manner in which the important questions underlying this statute—the danger to women of night work in factories—was presented to us in the Williams Case, we ought not to regard its decision as any bar to a consideration of the present statute in the light of all the facts and arguments now presented to us and many of which are in addition to those formerly presented. . . . Particularly do I feel that we should give serious consideration and great weight to the fact that the present legislation is based upon and sustained by an investigation by the legislature deliberately and carefully made through an agency of its own creation, the present factory investigating commission.[36]

Despite the remarkable encouragement received by the Brandeis type of brief from both state and federal courts, it has not influenced judgments as much as was expected. Certain writers saw in the Court's emphasis upon statistics an evidence of increased liberalism.[37] A period of judicial self-abnegation was heralded. The results, however, do not justify such optimism, especially the results during the decade just passed. If social data are furnished by counsel, there is still no assurance that the Court will find these either acceptable or important. Of course the data may be biased, *ex parte* statements advocating particular measures, or other reasons may make such materials unreliable evidence. But, if facts are ignored, it is more than likely because they run counter to cherished economic or political doctrines of the Judiciary. Even in the Lochner Case the Court went into the facts much more carefully than is generally supposed. It was Mr. Justice Peckham's dominant concept of liberty of contract, not merely his ignorance of fact, which invalidated the law. Not until after four of the five judges who prevailed in that case were replaced by others who held different

---

[36] Judge Hiscock in People v. Schweinler Press, 214 N.Y. 395, 411-413, 108 N.E. 83 (1915).

[37] See especially Charles Warren, "The Progressiveness of the United States Supreme Court" (1913), 13 *Col. L. Rev.* 294; Louis M. Greeley, "The Changing Attitude of the Courts Toward Social Legislation" (1910), 5 *Ill. L. Rev.* 222.

ideas regarding liberty of contract, was the Lochner decision modified.

Even in the Muller Case, where this new technique of brief making was first introduced, the influence of facts *per se* has probably been overemphasized. It is true that Mr. Brandeis' brief won favorable comment in the opinion, but one finds language elsewhere to justify the conclusion that an eight-hour law for women would have been sustained even without the support of scientific data.[38] The point deserving special emphasis is that when facts, however stubborn, are confronted by a "stubborn theory," it is the latter that usually wins. When dogmas and doctrines control judges' thought, a formidable barrier is set up against the entrance of facts into the judicial mind. "Facts," as Professor Morris R. Cohen has well said, "are more pliable than stubborn theories. Facts can be ignored, explained away, or denied. But theories are mental habits which cannot be changed at will."[39]

The manner in which a court possessed by preconceived theory regards factual material is shown in the Oregon Minimum Wage Case.[40] Chief Justice White, after examining Felix Frankfurter's elaborate collection of facts, is said to have remarked: "Mr. Frankfurter, I could produce twice as much material to show that private property is wrong and should be abolished."

[38] "That woman's physical structure and the performance of maternal functions place her at a disadvantage in the struggle for subsistence is obvious. . . . History discloses the fact that woman has always been dependent on man. . . . Some legislation to protect her seems necessary to secure a real equality of right. . . . It is impossible to close one's eyes to the fact that she still looks to her brother and depends upon him. . . . A widespread and long-continued belief concerning [a fact] is worthy of consideration. We take judicial cognizance of all matters of general knowledge." 208 U.S. 412, 421-2 (1908). This apparently means that the decision was based on "common knowledge" rather than on the knowledge gained from Mr. Brandeis' brief.

A friend suggests that this may have been "conventional 'window-dressing' for a decision actually induced by the facts in the brief."

[39] "The Process of Judicial Legislation" (1914), 48 *Amer. L. Rev.* 161, 164.

[40] Stettler v. O'Hara, 243 U.S. 629 (1916).

An even better illustration of the judicial mind dominated by "a jurisprudence of concepts," is Mr. Justice Sutherland's opinion in the Adkins Case:

> We have . . . been furnished with a large number of printed opinions approving the policy of the minimum wage, and our own reading has disclosed a large number to the contrary. These are all proper enough for the consideration of the law-making bodies, since their tendency is to establish the desirability or undesirability of the legislation; but they reflect no legitimate light upon the question of its validity, and that is what we are called upon to decide. [Presumably this question can be decided *in vacuo,* so to speak, by recourse to reason and authority and with no regard to relevant facts.] The elucidation of that question cannot be aided by counting heads. . . . It is said that great benefits have resulted from the operation of such statutes, not alone in the District of Columbia but in the several states, where they have been in force. A mass of reports, opinions of special observers and students of the subject, and the like, has been brought before us in support of this statement, all of which we have found interesting but only mildly persuasive.[41]

The truth is Mr. Justice Sutherland has not the slightest sympathy with the sort of social legislation then before him. He sees the people "beset and bedevilled"[42] by it and hence no fact,

---

[41] 261 U.S. 525 at 559-60.

[42] "In the old days it was the liberty of person, the liberty of speech, the freedom of religious worship, which were principally threatened. Today it is the liberty to order the detail of one's daily life for oneself—the liberty to do honest and profitable business —the liberty to seek honest and remunerative investment that are in peril. In my own mind I feel sure that there never has been a time when the business of the country occupied a higher moral plane; never a time when the voluntary code which governs the conduct of the banker, the manufacturer, the merchant, the railway manager, has been finer in tone or more faithfully observed than it is today; and yet never before have the business activities of the people been so beset and bedevilled with vexatious statutes, prying commissions, and governmental intermeddling of all sorts.

". . . In my judgment an extraordinarily large proportion of the statutes which have been passed from time to time in our various legislative bodies might be repealed without the slightest detriment to the general welfare.

"Most of these evils, if left alone, would disappear under the powerful pressure of public sentiment, but we become impatient because the force of the social organism is not sufficiently radical and the demand goes forth for a law which will instantly put an end to the matter." Address by George Sutherland of Utah, president of the

however imposing, is likely to impress him. But as Professor
Corwin pithily says, "there is no sound reason why the Court
should stuff cotton in its ears in this way."[43]

Another case which illustrates what has been termed "a jurisprudence of concepts" is Coppage v. Kansas.[44] Here the question
at issue was decided entirely on reason and authority, and one
sees again the futility of producing facts for a court which holds
the law to be a closed system. Counsel, it is true, failed to attempt
any proof of reasonable relationship between trade union membership and the general welfare, by recourse to facts. But one
is safe in concluding that the legislation would have fared no
better if they had. The Court was frank to say that "no attempt
is made, or could reasonably be made, to sustain the purpose to
strengthen these voluntary organizations, any more than other
voluntary associations of persons, as a legitimate object for the
exercise of the police power."[45] Certainly Brandeis was right
when he described this case as showing "the potency of mental
prepossessions."[46]

Even where a judge furnishes the data upon his own initiative,
it may prove ineffective. This was shown in the Washington
Employment Agency Case[47] where Mr. Justice Brandeis' collection of facts showing the evil practices of employment agencies
proved unacceptable to the Court. Evidently the Court felt that
other facts could have been supplied to show the utility of such
businesses. Thus the Court reserved for itself the right to pass

American Bar Association, September 4, 1917. *Reports of The Am. Bar Assoc.,* Vol.
XLII, pp. 198, 199, 200.

One wonders whether Mr. Justice Sutherland would care to subscribe to these views
today. That he would, seems almost incredible, yet his Adkins opinion stands as a
living embodiment of this philosophy.

[43] *The Supreme Court and Minimum Wage Legislation* (1925), p. 175. (Published by *The New Republic* under the auspices of the National Consumers' League.

[44] 236 U.S. 1 (1915).

[45] *ibid.,* at 16.

[46] L. D. Brandeis, "The Living Law" (1916), 10 *Ill. L. Rev.* 467.

[47] 244 U.S. 590 (1917).

upon means used to carry out a policy which it recognized as justifiable. This reservation reduces the importance of facts in "due process" cases. The standards which the Court has set up to determine when a law is more drastic than necessary, are as vague as those general standards (if any exist) which mark off the police power.

It is evident, therefore, that there are distinct limits to the effectiveness of facts. Direct contact with reality is often lost because of prior concepts, principles, systems, and postulates. "The scrutiny and dissection of social facts may," as Mr. Justice Cardozo has pointed out, "supply the data upon which the creative spirit broods, but in the process of creation something is given out in excess of what is taken in."[48] This explains why the discretionary veto which the Court enjoys over state legislation in due-process cases may be exercised mildly, as between 1910-20, but at other times rigidly, as from 1920 to 1930. Whether it be applied loosely or strictly, depends not so much upon facts brought to the attention of the Court, nor upon any statable rule, but rather upon what social-political philosophy is held by a majority of the justices.

In recent cases counsel as well as Court have tended toward full consideration of underlying facts. The results, however, have not been altogether satisfying to those who regard the factual type of brief as a champion for social legislation. If one may judge from more recent cases, use of such material has rather given the Court but one more weapon to strike down theoretically offensive legislation. Besides those granite concepts of "liberty" and "property" on which pioneer social legislation, like the minimum wage, and the ten-hour law for bakers, were wrecked, the Court can now fortify itself with statistical data to show that a particular exercise of police power is arbitrary and

[48] *The Growth of the Law* (1924), p. 90.

unreasonable, and therefore violative of due process. A case in point is that of Jay Burns Baking Co. v. Bryan.[49]

The statute there in question regulated the size of bread and was designed to prevent fraud by means of underweight loaves. It is doubtful whether so petty a law would ever have reached the Court before the Lochner Case and, if it had, it would probably have been sustained as a local regulation, of the necessity for which the local legislature was the best judge. This law differed from an earlier statute which had been sustained[50] in that it prescribed a maximum as well as a minimum limit for the weight of standard loaves of bread. A group of large bakers, the plaintiffs, presented a mass of evidence and special reports of chemists dealing with technical phases of baking. This tended to show that the two-ounce leeway between the maximum and minimum weights allowed was unreasonable and could only be complied with by wrapping the bread. The professional bakers supporting the act testified they could comply with the law. An official in charge of enforcing the city bread law testified that two ounces was a liberal allowance. He also stated that the chief difficulty arose from selling oversize one-pound loaves for one and one-half pounds. The Court was thus confronted with conflicting expert testimony. Seven judges decided, after exhaustive research, that the evidence sustained the contentions of the plaintiff; two judges, presumably as well versed in bread-making, were convinced that the state had proved its case.

How then can the Court (assuming that it is to continue to apply the due-process clause as a substantive limitation of legislative power) be supplied with the facts? Exhaustive factual investigation by the Judiciary becomes necessary only in case the doctrine of presumption in favor of constitutionality is

---

[49] 264 U.S. 504 (1924). See also Weaver v. Palmer Bros., 270 U.S. 402 (1926).
[50] Schmidinger v. Chicago, 226 U.S. 578 (1913).

rejected, and with the recent revival of this doctrine such whole-sale investigations as the Court undertook in the Jay Burns Case may pass into history.[51] The doctrine of presumption of constitutionality minimizes the need for judicial fact-finding. The Court, relying usually upon briefs of counsel, need examine the facts no further than will enable it to determine whether, considered as a means, the legislation is necessary to achieve a permissible end.

There are sources of information other than the lawyer's brief. The legislature itself may, as in England, conduct preliminary investigation of the conditions supposed to require legislative action. Whenever such a record is available the Court has usually shown disposition to give it weight. In James Everard's Breweries v. Day,[52] reports of committees in charge of the legislative measure were regarded as a proper basis for decision. In Chicago Board of Trade v. Olsen,[53] the Court quoted at length from information collected by the Senate Committee on Agriculture and Forestry to sustain the Grain Futures Act of 1922.[54]

A mere legislative declaration concerning general conditions, however, is not necessarily binding on the Court. It "is entitled at least to great respect," but "may not be held conclusive by the courts."[55] Legislative declarations that certain businesses had

[51] See note 13, *supra*.

[52] 265 U.S. 545, 561 (1924). This case involved the validity of an act of Congress providing that "only spirituous and vinous liquor may be prescribed for medicinal purposes and all permits to prescribe and prescriptions for any other liquor shall be void."

[53] 262 U.S. 1, 10-15 (1923).

[54] "It is clear from the citations, in the statement of the case, of evidence before committees of investigation as to manipulations of the futures market and their effect, that we would be unwarranted in rejecting the findings of Congress as unreasonable." *ibid.* 37-8.

Differences in procedure as between Congress and the state legislatures greatly affect availability of facts as to the work of legislation. Records of debates, committee reports and hearings, are almost wholly lacking in the states, New York being an outstanding exception.

[55] Block v. Hirsh, 256 U.S. 135, 154 (1921). Here the Court upheld a Congressional statute fixing rents in the District of Columbia on the ground that the emergency

become affected with a public interest have in recent years been frequently overthrown.[56]

Another source of facts recognized by the Supreme Court is the findings of the state court of last resort. We have already seen how the Court in the Bunting Case considered the decisions of the Oregon legislature and of the Oregon Supreme Court (in the absence of evidence to the contrary), as furnishing convincing evidence of the necessity of a general ten-hour law. Justice Holmes also emphasized this rôle of the lower court in the Second Emergency Rent Case: "Obviously the facts should be accurately ascertained and carefully weighed, and this can be done more conveniently in the Supreme Court of the District [of Columbia] than here. The evidence should be preserved so that if necessary it can be considered by this Court."[57]

There are, of course, distinct limits to the reliance of the Court upon legislative committee reports and findings of lower courts. Only one party to the suit can, as a rule, depend upon them. It would seem then that the Court's chief reliance for facts must continue to be counsel's briefs. Much of the material presented, however, is likely to be so technical as to require an expert to interpret it. The facts of the Jay Burns Case were not entirely contradictory but so highly technical that each side could use material, which to the layman differed merely in detail, to prove its own points. It is quite apparent then that the Court can reach a just decision only by calling in competent, unbiased technicians

declared by the legislature must be assumed by the Court to exist. Yet a similar law was invalidated three years later on the ground that the emergency had ceased to exist. Chastleton Corp. v. Sinclair, 264 U.S. 543 (1924).

56 Wolff Packing Co. v. Court of Industrial Relations, 262 U.S. 522 (1923); Ribnik v. McBride, 277 U.S. 350 (1928); Tyson and Bro. v. Banton, 273 U.S. 418 (1927); New State Ice Co. v. Liebmann, 285 U.S. 262 (1932).

57 Chastleton Corp. v. Sinclair, 264 U.S. 543, 549 (1924). See also Hairston v. Danville and Western Ry. Co., 208 U.S. 598, 607 (1908) where the Court observed: "The propriety of keeping in view by this Court, while enforcing the Fourteenth Amendment, the diversity of local conditions and of regarding with great respect the judgments of the state courts upon what should be deemed public uses in that state, is expressed, justified, and acted upon in [a number of cases]." Citing cases.

to advise as to what can be properly concluded from technical facts presented.

So whether it be the business of legislature, counsel or court, to ascertain, collect, weigh, and evaluate facts, there is a great and growing need for enlarging and perfecting our agencies for objectively ascertaining social and economic data. "Just as it requires an expert to know where to find the law, so it requires a person no less expert to know where to find statistical data."[58] One writer has suggested that a solution of the problem may "be found in the use of the economist's knowledge as an expert on such subjects as taxation, transportation, finance, statistics, questions of public policy, and the like."[59] This is daring advice since 1929 but it is not enough. The judge himself must have had such training in these subjects as will make him willing to use this knowledge and able to use it understandingly.

What the Court has stood in sore need of, certainly since 1875, has been judges who were not only trained lawyers but also informed as to the conditions which the law was then beginning to regulate so vitally. It is impossible to apply the law to facts unless one knows both law and facts. In all the problems he has tackled Mr. Brandeis has demonstrated that he knew both. He is never content, either as counsel or judge, to make merely a legal argument; nor is this true only in labor cases. He demonstrated in the Ballinger controversy the necessity of knowing not only the laws as to conservation of our natural resources but also the actual practices and conditions as well. His briefs in railroad cases emphasize the economics of railroading no less than legal

---

[58] H. W. Humble, "Economics from a Legal Standpoint" (1908), 42 *Am. L. Rev.*, 379, 385.

[59] *ibid*. "While the training and experience of the judges have qualified them to deal with strict questions of law, the same training and experience have not qualified them to deal in an expert way with such questions of fact." H. W. Biklé, *op. cit.*, p. 21. Mr. Biklé argues that judges ought not undertake this function "except when the relevant facts are properly brought before them either by means of direct evidence or through such presentation as justifies judicial notice." *ibid*.

aspects. Those who feel that the law should be alive, consider such material essential to a proper exercise of the judicial function, whereas those who regard the very essence of law as atrophy, do not share this view.

It is evident from his epoch-making briefs that law for Brandeis is no mere embodiment of *a priori* abstractions in a vacuum. The law operates only within limits set by economic and social conditions and these must be understood. He reaffirms the truth of the old maxim of the Civilians—*ex facto jus oritur*. Contrasting his own method of treating constitutional questions with that generally followed by the Court, he observed: "In the past the courts have reached their conclusions largely deductively from preconceived notions and precedents. The method I have tried to employ in arguing cases before them has been inductive, reasoning from the facts."[60] Whether the issue be workmen's compensation, collective bargaining, employment agencies, or methods of determining depreciation for rate-making purposes, a correct decision, he holds, can be reached only by exhaustive resort to facts. In case after case he compiled data on labor, fatigue, health, economic productivity, bargaining abilities, values, costs, services, and all for the purpose of showing urgent social need for the legislation he was supporting. The masterful fashion in which he brought something of the spirit of modern science to the court-room may be Brandeis' chief claim to fame in the history of our law. He ended the reign of *nolumus mutare.*

[60] Recorded by Ernest Poole from an interview with Mr. Brandeis, *The American Magazine*, February 1911.

CHAPTER VII

MORE LIFE IN THE LAW: THE LOGIC OF REALITIES 'IN SUPREME COURT OPINIONS'

WHEN President Wilson on January 28, 1916, sent Mr. Brandeis' name to the Senate he precipitated the most extraordinary publicity campaign in the history of the Court. Austen G. Fox, a New York lawyer retained by Boston attorneys and capitalists, mailed *ex parte* statements in the form of briefs, as news and as raw materials for editorials, to every state in the Union, opposing Brandeis' confirmation. The drive against Brandeis took on threatening proportions but collapsed completely under the searching investigation of the Senate Judiciary Committee. The precise and coldly logical Senator Thomas J. Walsh in summarizing the weight of objections, said:

> The real crime of which this man is guilty is that he has exposed the iniquities of men in high places in our financial system. He has not stood in awe of the majesty of wealth. He has, indeed, often represented litigants, corporate and individual, whose commercial rating was high, but his clients have not been exclusively of that class. . . . He has been an iconoclast. He has written about and expressed views on "social justice" to which vague term are referred movements and measures to obtain greater security, greater comfort, and better health for the industrial workers. . . . They all contemplate that a man's a man and not a machine.[1]

To the clamorous alarm of eminent lawyers a man had been appointed to our highest court who was thoroughly versed in

[1] Hearings before the Sub-Committee of the Senate Committee on the Judiciary, on the Nomination of Louis D. Brandeis to be an Associate Justice of the Supreme Court of the United States. 64th Cong., 1st Sess., Sen. Doc., No. 409, Vol. II (1916), p. 234. Mr. Brandeis was confirmed on June 1, 1916, by a vote of 47 to 22.

modern business, who looked at industrial problems from the standpoint of both public and employee; one, moreover, who would certainly continue to press far beyond the bounds of legal technicality and judicial precedent, to the realms of fact and reality. The fears of those who opposed his appointment on these grounds were proved to be well founded.

1. *Ex facto jus oritur*

Shortly after his accession, the Court considered the now famous Employment Agency Case,[2] in which a five-to-four decision overturned the Washington state statute prohibiting employment agencies from taking workers' fees. The state had argued that the private employment agency is "economically ... non-useful, if not vicious, because it compels the needy and unfortunate to pay for that which they are entitled to without fee or price, that is, the right to work."[3] Although personal placement costs can well be met by the employer, the Court speaking through Mr. Justice McReynolds demurred, setting forth the doctrine that legitimate and useful businesses, when attended by abuses, may be regulated, but that only obnoxious and vicious businesses can be prohibited and destroyed. The Court's conclusion that private employment agencies are of the former type was reached by resort to judicial precedent, with no examination whatever into the evils attending this business in Washington or anywhere else.

In a strong dissenting opinion, Mr. Justice Brandeis demonstrated the inadequacy of the Court's treatment of the question at issue. Little space is given to precedents, and much devoted to showing that no correct decision can be reached by reasoning from past cases. Mr. Justice Brandeis absolutely denied the authority of the courts to set aside social legislation "unless, in looking at the matter, they can see that it 'is a clear, unmistak-

[2] Adams v. Tanner, 244 U.S. 590 (1917).
[3] *ibid.* at 594.

able infringement of rights secured by the fundamental law.' . . . Whether a measure relating to the public welfare," he continues, "is arbitrary or unreasonable, whether it has no substantial relation to the end proposed, is obviously not to be determined by assumptions or by *a priori* reasoning. The judgment should be based upon a consideration of relevant facts, actual or possible —*ex facto jus oritur*. That ancient rule must prevail in order that we may have a system of living law."[4]

Using the technique developed ten years earlier in arguments before the Supreme Court, he made the following inquiries: "What was the evil which the people of Washington sought to correct? Why was the particular remedy embodied in the statute adopted? And, incidentally, what has been the experience, if any, of other states or countries in this connection?"[5]

None of these questions is raised by Mr. Justice McReynolds and, so far as one can judge from his opinion, no official investigation of these matters might ever have been made. But Mr. Justice Brandeis gathered his materials from official reports of the United States Bureau of Labor, the United States Commission on Industrial Relations, and writings of acknowledged experts. Such pertinent and easily available sources revealed evils of far-reaching effect—extortionate fees, discrimination, misrepresentation as to conditions of work and as to terms of employment, fee-splitting with foremen, almost a rascal's litany of wrongs against workers.

The report to Congress of the United States Commission on Industrial Relations showed that many private employment agencies were quite unable to meet the needs for which they were supposed to exist. These agencies were operated not to relieve unemployment and secure jobs for men out of work, but actually to congest the labor market and increase irregularity of

---

[4] *ibid.* at 599. This view is reiterated in New State Ice Co. v. Liebmann, 285 U.S. 262, 285 (1932), and Liggett v. Lee, 288 U.S. 517, 542-3 (1933).
[5] Adams v. Tanner, 244 U.S. 590 at 600.

employment. The peculiar defects of these agencies and the pressing need for their regulation in the state of Washington, were fully demonstrated in a published report of the State Bureau of Labor.

Nor had the abuses of employment agencies been accepted as inevitable and unavoidable. Twenty-four states had attempted direct regulation by statute and by municipal ordinances; nineteen had undertaken indirect control by establishing municipal employment offices. This extensive experience in regulating employment agencies had developed the conviction "that the evils of private agencies were inherent and ineradicable, so long as they were permitted to charge fees to the workers seeking employment."[6]

Furthermore, Mr. Justice Brandeis saw in the Washington statute a purpose not appreciated at all by Mr. Justice McReynolds. The purpose behind the act was not merely negative, it was also positive: to strike at that paramount evil in the workingman's life—irregularity of employment.

> The problem which confronted the people of Washington was far more comprehensive and fundamental than that of protecting workers applying to the private agencies. It was the chronic problem of unemployment—perhaps the gravest and most difficult problem of modern industry. . . . Students of the larger problem of unemployment appear to agree that establishment of an adequate system of employment offices or labor exchanges is an indispensable first step toward its solution. There is reason to believe that the people of Washington not only considered the collection by the private employment offices of fees from employees a social injustice; but that they considered the elimination of the practice a necessary preliminary to the establishment of a constructive policy for dealing with the subject of unemployment.[7]

[6] Adams v. Tanner, 244 U.S. 590 at 606.

[7] ibid. at 613-14. Compare New State Ice Co. v. Liebmann, 285 U.S. 262, 308: "All agree that irregularity in employment—the greatest of our evils—cannot be overcome unless production and consumption are more nearly balanced."

Brandeis has long insisted that "the greatest need of the working man is regularity

This opinion is typical of Mr. Justice Brandeis' research into social and economic problems dealt with by the Supreme Court during the last seventeen years. It also illustrates his ideas as to the nature and scope of the judicial function.

How is the Court to judge of the constitutionality of legislation such as that concerning unemployment? Certainly not by merely examining legal precedents. Nor would the test of "common knowledge," or what a "reasonable man" considers necessary to promote the general welfare, be a safe guide. Nothing is clearer to Mr. Justice Brandeis than that questions of social and economic policy can be decided only with the help of accumulated empirical data on actual conditions. Counsel, as a rule, had not assisted courts in making such data available. Thus the judge was obliged to investigate fields not otherwise cultivated by him. Just what the exercise of the judicial function in "due process" cases demands, Mr. Justice Brandeis states as follows:

> Whether a law enacted in the exercise of the police power is justly subject to the charge of being unreasonable or arbitrary, can ordinarily be determined only by a consideration of the contemporary conditions, social, industrial and political, of the community to be affected thereby. Resort to such facts is necessary, among other things, in order to appreciate the evils sought to be remedied and the possible effects of the remedy proposed. Nearly all legislation involves a weighing of public needs as against private desires; and likewise a weighing of relative social values. Since government is not an exact science, prevailing public opinion concerning the evil and the remedy is among the important facts deserving consideration.[8]

of employment. Irregularity of employment creates hardships and demoralization of every kind. It is the most sinful waste." L. D. Brandeis, "Organized Labor and Efficiency" (1911), *The Survey*, Vol. XXVI, p. 150. Reprinted in *Business—A Profession*, p. 38. See also L. D. Brandeis, "The Road to Social Efficiency" (1911), *The Outlook*, Vol. XCVIII, pp. 291-2. Reprinted in Brandeis, *op. cit.*, p. 57. Ample evidence of the truth of this observation is to be found today on the streets of every city in the United States.

[8] Mr. Justice Brandeis dissenting in Truax v. Corrigan, 257 U.S. 312 at 356-7 (1921).

For many years Brandeis had been taking cognizance of our revolution in social and economic life, and therefore in institutions. He had observed that every change in the law governing economic relationships must, if liberty and property be judged by eighteenth century legal standards, necessarily abridge both liberty and property for the contending parties. But changed conditions, he thought, demanded ever-increasing regulation of individual rights, and the Court should not declare that a statute violates the "due process" clause, unless it appears that such interference is arbitrary or unreasonable, or that, considered as a means, the measure has no real or substantial relation of cause to a permissible end.[9]

Put at its highest, our function is to determine, in the light of all facts which may enrich our knowledge and enlarge our understanding, whether the measure, enacted in the exercise of an unquestioned police power and of a character inherently unobjectionable, transcends the bounds of reason. That is, whether the provision as applied is so clearly arbitrary or capricious that legislators acting reasonably could not have believed it to be necessary or appropriate for the public welfare.[10]

[9] Truax v. Corrigan, 257 U.S. 312 at 355. The position here taken as to the scope of judicial review in cases involving social legislation is essentially that stated by Brandeis in 1911:

"The real test, as I conceive it is: . . . If there is an evil, is the remedy, this particular device introduced by the legislature, directed to remove that evil which threatens health, morals, and welfare? Does it bear a reasonable relation to it? And in applying it, is there anything discriminatory, which looks like a purpose to injure and not a purpose to aid? Has there been an arbitrary exercise of power . . . ?" L. D. Brandeis, "The Constitution and the Minimum Wage," *The Survey*, February 6, 1915.

"Some may doubt whether this particular remedy is the best remedy, or whether its adoption may not lead to some other evils which later legislatures may have to deal with, possibly by a repeal of this law. Even if you entertained a doubt well founded, you cannot interfere because you have doubts as to the wisdom of an act, provided that act is of such a character that it may conceivably produce results sought to be attained. . . . The legislature must be given latitude in experimentation." *ibid.* at 521. Compare with the statement of Mr. Justice Hughes in C. B. & Q. R.R. Co. v. McGuire, 219 U.S. 549 at 569 (1911).

[10] Jay Burns Baking Co. v. Bryan, 264 U.S. 504 at 534 (1924).

The question to be asked is this: In view of facts and conditions can rational opinion support the statute? That criterion
calls for insight, for knowledge of the broad currents of legislation and of the conditions from which they rise. The problem
is to find what lies back of the opinion that has manifested
itself in legislation. In performing this delicate task Mr. Justice
Brandeis believes it dangerous to rely upon rationalistic concepts,
for these cannot be accurately measured. Individuals differ,
depending upon the particular environmental influences to
which they have been subjected. Therefore, he insists, the Court
must know the facts. He has comparatively little faith in uninformed reason: "Knowledge is essential to understanding; and
understanding should precede judging. Sometimes, if we would
guide by the light of reason, we must let our minds be bold."[11]

In evaluating the use of facts by Mr. Justice Brandeis, one is
bound to note that his most elaborate opinions are in dissent,
where he uses facts to smash what he holds to be obsolete conceptions. When he leads the Court, he is content to rely, if he favors
the legislation, on the constitutional presumption. This doctrine,
however, is not always consistently followed and hence his use
of it, especially in cases in which he disagrees with the constitutionality of legislation, may be challenged on the score of
consistency.[12] The chief significance of Brandeis' influence, in
this connection, is that he has forced a consideration of the facts
and has greatly weakened, even in professional esteem, purely
abstract conceptualist arguments and opinions.

2. Founding Trade Unionism on the Facts and the Law

While at the bar Mr. Brandeis frankly stated his particular
concern for the workingman. He saw in the growth of the

---

[11] *ibid*. at 520. Compare New State Ice Co. v. Liebmann, 285 U.S. 263, 311.

[12] Compare Meyer v. Neb., 262 U.S. 390 (1923); Near v. Minn., 283 U.S. 697
(1931); Wolff Packing Co. v. Court of Industrial Relations, 262 U.S. 522 (1923), where
Mr. Justice Brandeis joined with the Court in denying the constitutionality of legislation. See also his dissenting opinion in Olmstead v. U.S., 277 U.S. 438 (1928).

employer's economic power a serious threat to the general welfare and to the worker's liberty. He felt, moreover, that there would be but "little probability [in most trades] of attaining the best conceivable conditions unless in some form a union of the employees exists."[13] For this reason he believed that peace and prosperity could not be achieved by weakening trade unions and by lessening collective bargaining. "Our hope lies rather in their growing strength and stability."[14]

This point of view is maintained in his labor opinions. The first and perhaps most famous is his dissent in the Hitchman Case[15] where the plaintiff had employed miners for indefinite periods, having with each a separate understanding that he would not, while in plaintiff's employment, become a member of the United Mine Workers of America. In alleged violation of this agreement representatives of the union sought to induce men to agree to join in such numbers that the plaintiff might be coerced into recognizing the union. These anti-union promises, or "yellow dog" contracts, were the barriers to labor activity which the Hitchman Company successfully called upon equity to maintain and preserve.

Practically the entire opinion of Mr. Justice Pitney, who spoke for the Court, is devoted to the technical question whether there had been a breach of contract. Mr. Justice Brandeis by no means neglected this question, but one is impressed particularly with his emphasis upon the need of strengthening bargaining power among workers. For Mr. Justice Pitney, the right "to make non-membership in a union a condition of employment . . . is

13 L. D. Brandeis, *Business—A Profession* (1933), p. 18.

14 *ibid.*, p. 20. See also Hearings before the Committee on Investigation of the United States Steel Corporation, January 30, 1912, p. 2862. "Of course, there isn't any such thing as a law of supply and demand as an inexorable rule. . . . One reason why the trades union had to come into existence was because the law of supply and demand did not work properly between the opposing forces of the powerful employer and the individual worker." Hearings of the New York State Factory Investigating Commission, Vol. V, p. 2881 (1915).

15 Hitchman Coal and Coke Co. v. Mitchell, 245 U.S. 229 (1917).

a part of the constitutional rights of personal liberty and private property, not to be taken away even by legislation. . . ."[16] He saw in the activity of the union organizers no purpose other than an illegal one: to compel the company to change its method of operation. To Mr. Justice Brandeis' mind such activity was motivated by a *bona fide* desire to increase membership, and hence the bargaining power, of the union. His opinion reveals realistic evaluation of the trade union as an agency for promoting economic security among workers; whereas equitable protection of a "yellow dog" contract (such contract being rooted in disparity of bargaining power, and utterly lacking in reciprocal obligation) would seriously jeopardize trade union growth. What to him was necessary to equalize bargaining power between employer and employee, and "to establish the equality of position between the parties in which liberty of contract begins,"[17] was denounced by the majority of the Court as an unconstitutional infringement of that very liberty.

Although the Supreme Court has not since spoken definitely on the question in the Hitchman Case, there is reason to think the Court has come around to Mr. Justice Brandeis' view.[18] Today the Court would probably refuse to aid enforcement of a "yellow dog" contract. There is growing recognition of a need for wider unionization, which need justifies interference by those not parties to the immediate controversy. In certain quarters Mr. Justice Brandeis' position has already received more than verbal recognition. Since the Hitchman Case, the "yellow dog" contract appears to have been hounded out of the juris-

[16] *ibid.*, 251.

[17] Mr. Justice Holmes, dissenting in Coppage v. Kansas, 236 U.S. 1 at 27 (1915).

[18] See Texas and New Orleans Ry. Co. v. Brotherhood of Railway and Steamship Clerks, 281 U.S. 548 (1930), where Chief Justice Hughes, speaking for a unanimous Court, sustained an injunction to protect the integrity of collective bargaining against the establishment of a company union. Compare Coppage v. Kansas 236 U.S. 1 (1915), where Mr. Justice Hughes joined in the dissenting opinion of Mr. Justice Holmes. See also H. F. Carey and Herman Oliphant, "The Present Status of the Hitchman Case" (1929), 29 *Col. L. Rev.* 441, and "Rival Unions" (1932), 46 *Harv. L. Rev.* 125.

diction of New York,[19] in the statutory enactments of certain
states it has been declared against public policy;[20] a nomination
to the Supreme Court has been rejected largely because the
candidate refused to follow Mr. Justice Brandeis' dissent in the
Hitchman Case.[21] So today it is almost inconceivable that equity
would sanction the "yellow dog" contract.[22]

[19] Exchange Bakery and Restaurant v. Rifkin, 216 App. Div. 663, 215 N.Y. Supp.
753 (1926); Interborough Rapid Transit Co. v. Green, 131 Misc. 682, 227 N.Y. Supp.
258 (1928). In the former case the Court of Appeals took a position entirely opposed
to that of Mr. Justice Pitney in the Hitchman Case: "All engaged in a trade are
affected by the prevailing rate of wages. All, by the principle of collective bargaining. Economic organization today is not based on a single shop." 245 N.Y. 260,
262, 157 N.E. 130, 132. The Court disposed of the "yellow dog" contract in this case
as an agreement unsupported by consideration. In International Rapid Transit Co. v.
Lavin, 247 N.Y. 65, 159 N.E. 863 (1928), the Court confined its decision to the case
at bar in which it was held that no contract of non-association existed between the
plaintiff and its employees. Thus the "yellow dog" contract issue was sidestepped.

[20] Wisconsin recently enacted a statute declaring "yellow dog" contracts "to be
contrary to public policy, and wholly void and shall not afford any basis for the
granting of legal or equitable relief by any court." Wis. Laws 1929, c. 123. Similar
measures were passed in 1931 in the following states: Arizona (C. 19), Colorado (C.
112), Ohio (S.B. 108) and Oregon (C. 247).

For a discussion of the constitutionality of the Wisconsin act, see Donald Mac-
Donald, "The Constitutionality of Wisconsin's Statute Invalidating 'Yellow Dog' Contracts" (1931), 6 Wis. L. Rev. 86.

A dissenting voice among the states is that of the Supreme Judicial Court of
Massachusetts, which in an advisory opinion (In re Opinion of the Justices, 171 N.E.
294 (1931)) held unconstitutional a provision denying legal or equitable protection
to the "yellow dog" contract.

A Congressional bill approved on March 23, 1932, declares the "yellow dog"
contract "to be contrary to public policy of the United States, shall not be enforceable
and shall not afford any basis for the granting of legal or equitable relief by any court
of the United States." 47 Stat. 70, c. 90 (1932).

The "yellow dog" contract is dealt still another legislative blow under the National
Industrial Recovery Act, approved June 16, 1933. One of the minimum requirements
for codes of fair competition is "that no employee and no one seeking employment
shall be required as a condition of employment to join any company union or to
refrain from joining, organizing, or assisting a labor organization of his own choos-
ing." P.L. No. 67, 73rd Cong., Title 1, sec. 7 (a).

[21] The Hitchman precedent was followed by Judge Parker in International Organization v. Red Jacket Consolidated Coal and Coke Co., 18 F. (2nd) 839 (C.C.A. 4th,
1927), and this was certainly instrumental in barring him from the Supreme Court.

[22] A close reading of the Court's opinion in the Hitchman Case might conceivably
lead to the conclusion that the decision was confined to cases of breach of "yellow
dog" contracts where the means employed by the union involved deception and mis-

The divergence of judicial views in the Hitchman Case occurs also in the Duplex Printing Case.[23] Here the employer asked for an order to restrain labor activities in unionizing his shop. The defendants claimed immunity from injunctive relief under the labor clauses of the Clayton Act.[24] Mr. Justice Pitney for the Court, construed the labor clauses of that statute narrowly, closing his eyes to trade union program and policy. He saw in labor's activities no motive other than malicious injury to the employer. The federal courts, he held, were denied equity jurisdiction under section twenty of the Clayton Act, only in cases where the parties to the dispute were employer and employee, or persons employed and those seeking employment. The defendants "standing in no relation of employment under complainant, past, present or prospective . . ." therefore have no right "to make that dispute their own and proceed to instigate sympathetic strikes, picketing, and boycotting against employers wholly unconnected with complainant's factory. . . ."[25]

Moreover, in order to enjoy equity exemption, the dispute in question, Mr. Justice Pitney said, must arise out of "terms or conditions of their own employment, past, present or prospective. . . ."[26] Congress had in mind particular industrial controversies, not a general class war; . . . and it would do violence to the guarded language employed were the exemption extended beyond the parties affected in a proximate and substantial, not

representation; that the injunction was sustained as a protection against these abuses rather than as a protection of the "yellow dog" contract itself. In other words, if the solicitations of labor's representatives are not accompanied by threats, intimidation, or deceit, they are within their right, and cannot be restrained. These latter facts were present in the Tri-City Case, 257 U.S. 184 (1921), and here Mr. Justice Brandeis concurred in the majority opinion.

[23] Duplex Printing Co. v. Deering, 254 U.S. 443 (1921).

[24] 38 Stat. 730 (1914), 15 U.S.C.A. 12 (1927). The principal reliance of the defendants was upon sections 6 and 20.

[25] Duplex Printing Co. v. Deering, 254 U.S. 443 at 471.

[26] ibid. at 472.

merely a sentimental or sympathetic, sense by the cause of dispute."[27]

Only when one reads Mr. Justice Brandeis' dissent, does one discover the facts that underlie such industrial controversies. There are only four manufacturers of printing presses in the country, all in active competition. All had been unionized save the Duplex Company. Finally two of the unionized manufacturers notified the union that they would be obliged to end their agreement unless the Duplex Company raised its standard of labor. The local machinists' union thereupon called a strike against the Duplex factory in Battle Creek to compel the Duplex Company to unionize. The strike order was ineffective; only eleven union machinists actually quit work. Representatives of the International Machinists' Association then boycotted Duplex products in and around New York City, by threatening customers, and intimidating haulers and installers of Duplex presses.

Mr. Justice Brandeis held that the defendants "injured the plaintiff, not maliciously, but in self-defense . . . that the contest between the company and the machinists' union involves vitally the interest of every person whose cooperation is sought. May not all," he asks, "with a common interest join in refusing to expend their labor upon articles whose very production constitutes an attack upon their standard of living and the institutions which they are convinced supports it?"[28] Mr. Justice Pitney's opinion harks back to a common law rule of handicraft days, while for Mr. Justice Brandeis the problem is that of the legal limits of group activity in an industrial society:

> When centralization in the control of business brought its corresponding centralization in the organization of workingmen, new facts had to be appraised. A single employer might, as in this case,

[27] Duplex Printing Co. v. Deering, 254 U.S. 443 at 472.
[28] ibid. at 481.

threaten the standing of the whole organization and the standards of all its members.[29]

Thus he recognized the unity of interest throughout the union. In refusing to work on materials which threatened it, the union was only refusing to aid in destroying itself. For Mr. Justice Brandeis the Court's ruling (that the controversy was not one "involving, or growing out of, a dispute concerning terms or conditions of employment")[30] was "founded upon a misconception of the facts." Mr. Justice Pitney regarded the case simply as a dispute between two litigants; Mr. Justice Brandeis saw an issue of far-reaching social consequence.

The essential point in the Duplex Case was whether the Clayton Act had forbidden federal courts to issue an injunction in that type of case; the question of reasonable or unreasonable restraint was not involved. The latter point came before the Court in the more recent Bedford Cut Stone Case.[31] The significance of this decision is in the analysis by Mr. Justice Brandeis—an analysis unchallenged by the majority:

> The combination complained of is the cooperation of persons wholly of the same craft, united in a national union, solely for self-protection. No outsider—be he quarrier, dealer, builder or laborer—was a party to the combination. No purpose was to be subserved except to promote the trade interests of members of the Journeymens' Association.[32]

Therefore the facts in this case differed essentially from those in the Duplex Case:

[29] *ibid.* at 482.

[30] Language of § 20 of the Clayton Act.

[31] Bedford Cut Stone Co. v. Journeymen Cutters' Ass'n., 274 U.S. 37 (1927).

[32] *ibid.* at 60. Mr. Justice Brandeis pointed out that the union consisted of approximately 5,000 workers, divided into 150 locals. Standing alone these locals were weak. The average employer could destroy a local over night by importing scabs from other cities. It was only through combining 5,000 organized stonecutters in a national union and developing loyalty to it, that the individual stonecutter anywhere could protect his own job.

There was no attempt by the unions to boycott the plaintiffs. There was no attempt to seek the aid of members of any other craft, by a sympathetic strike or otherwise. The contest was not a class struggle. It was a struggle between particular employers and their employees. But the controversy out of which it arose, related, not to specific grievances, but to fundamental matters of union policy of general application throughout the country.[33]

To protect their interests, the union had begun to enforce their constitutional provision that " 'no member of this Association shall cut, carve or fit any material that has been cut by men working in opposition to this Association.' "[34] It was against union effort to enforce this order that the Bedford Cut Stone Company sought an injunction. After Judge Anderson of the Indiana District Court and Judges Alschuler, Evans, and Page of the Circuit Court of Appeals had refused to grant the order, the Supreme Court, arguing that the Duplex opinion "might serve as an opinion in this case," reversed the two lower courts and granted an injunction. The restraining order was issued despite the fact that the conduct of the union was admittedly innocent unless, in the Sherman Act, Congress had declared it illegal, as a restraint upon the plaintiff's interstate trade, for union officials to urge members not to work on stone cut by men opposed to the union. According to Mr. Justice Sutherland's decision the activities of the union had precisely the effect of contravening the Sherman Act. He held that although the union was lawful and had a lawful end in view, its operations "necessarily threatened to destroy or narrow petitioners' interstate trade by taking from them their customers."[35]

Such a ruling was extraordinary; Chief Justice Taft, usually regarded by labor as unsympathetic, had recognized the social

---

[33] Bedford Cut Stone Co. v. Journeymen Cutters' Ass'n., 274 U.S. 37 (1927) at 60.
[34] ibid. at 56.
[35] ibid. at 55. Compare with Chief Justice Taft's opinion in United Leather Workers v. Herkert and Meisel Trunk Co., 265 U.S. 457 (1924).

advantages of trade unions, the necessity of extending the combination beyond one shop, and the right of laborers to refuse to work on the product of employers who sought destruction of the union. The decision ignored, moreover, the "rule of reason" which the Court had held applicable in interpreting the Sherman Act as regards cases involving capitalist interests. Mr. Justice Brandeis' reaction to the extraordinary situation thus created is expressed in these words:

> Members of the Journeymen Stone Cutters' Association could not work anywhere on stone which had been cut at the quarries by "men working in opposition" to it, without aiding and abetting the enemy. Observance by each member of the provision of their constitution which forbids such action was essential to his own self-protection. . . . If, on the undisputed facts of this case, refusal to work can be enjoined, Congress created by the Sherman Law and the Clayton Act an instrument for imposing restraints upon labor which reminds of involuntary servitude.[36]

It was settled in the Standard Oil[37] and American Tobacco[38] Cases that only unreasonable restraints of trade are forbidden by the Sherman Act. But this statute set up no standard of reasonableness. The judges must supply one, and they are by no means in agreement. Their judgment is likely to turn not upon law but upon views severally held as to economic policy, or upon ideas as to the freedom allowed economic forces.

To Mr. Justice Sutherland "the Anti-Trust Act had a broader application than the prohibition of restraints of trade unlawful at common law."[39] Reading the act strictly, he held its effect was to declare illegal " 'every contract, combination or conspiracy, in whatever form, of whatever nature, and whoever may be the parties to it, which directly or necessarily operates in

[36] Bedford Cut Stone Co. v. Journeymen Cutters' Ass'n., 274 U.S. 37 at 64-5.
[37] Standard Oil Co. v. United States, 221 U.S. 1 (1911).
[38] United States v. American Tobacco Co., 221 U.S. 106 (1911).
[39] Bedford Cut Stone Co. v. Journeymen Cutters' Ass'n., 274 U.S. 37 at 52.

restraint of trade or commerce among the several States.' "[40]
It was easy then to bring the activities of the union within its
provisions. But to Mr. Justice Brandeis, "the propriety of the
union's conduct can hardly be doubted by one who believes in
organization of labor." He insisted, moreover, that the "rule of
reason" is as applicable in construing the Sherman Act in labor
cases as it is in capital cases:

> The Sherman Law was held in United States v. United States Steel
> Corporation, 251 U.S. 417, to permit capitalists to combine in a
> single corporation fifty per cent of the steel industry of the United
> States dominating the trade through its vast resources. The Sherman
> Law was held in United States v. United Shoe Machinery Co., 247
> U.S. 32, to permit capitalists to combine in another corporation
> practically the whole shoe machinery industry of the country, neces-
> sarily giving it a position of dominance over shoe-manufacturing in
> America. It would, indeed, be strange if Congress had by the same
> act willed to deny to members of a small craft of workingmen the
> right to cooperate in simply refraining from work, when that course
> was the only means of self-protection against a combination of militant
> and powerful employers. I cannot believe that Congress did so.[41]

Mr. Justice Stone evidently appreciated the force of this conclusion, for as "an original proposition" he would "have doubted
whether the Sherman Act prohibited a labor union from peace-
ably refusing to work upon material produced by non-union

---

[40] 274 U.S. 37 at 52. The Court's conception of the scope of the act clearly belies the
intentions of the framers as expressed by Senator Sherman: "It does not announce a new
principle of law, but applies old and well recognized principles of the common law to the
complicated jurisdiction of our state and federal government. . . . The purpose of this
bill is to enable the courts of the United States to apply the same remedies against
combinations which injuriously affect the interests of the United States that have
been applied in the several states to protect local interests." J. Sherman, *Recollections
of Forty Years* (1895), p. 1072. See also Senator Sherman's speech in the Senate, March
21, 1890. 21 Cong. Rec., 2456 ff.

[41] Bedford Cut Stone Co. v. Journeymen Cutters' Ass'n, 274 U.S. 37 at 65.
Compare Justice Sutherland's opinion in Levering and Garrigues Co. v. Morrin, 289
U.S. 103 (1933). See, in this connection, E. S. Corwin, "The Anti-Trust Acts and the
Constitution" (1932), 18 *Va. L. Rev.* 355 at 372 ff., and E. S. Corwin, "Congress's
Power to Prohibit Commerce" (1933), 18 *Cornell L. Quart.* 477.

labor or by a rival union even though interstate commerce were affected."[42] In view of the policy as to organized labor adopted by Congress in the Clayton Act, and in view of the Court's decisions in the Standard Oil and American Tobacco Cases, he would not have thought "that such action as is now complained of was to be regarded as an unreasonable and therefore prohibited restraint of trade."[43] And yet he concurred. Views he should not have hesitated to apply, were rejected because of the Duplex Printing Case. "For that reason alone," he agreed with the majority. Mr. Justice Brandeis pays no such respect to past cases. Rather he thinks, "it behooves us to reject, as guides, the decisions . . . which prove to have been mistaken."[44]

English policy defines the rights of labor primarily by legislative enactment. In this country such definition has been largely the work of the courts. Our legislatures, both federal and state, have been signally unsuccessful in ameliorating the harshness of judge-made labor law. Both have tried repeatedly to rid labor of the injunction incubus. But the courts have either construed immunity clauses narrowly, and held the statute largely declaratory of existing law (as with the labor clauses of the Clayton Act), or have held the statute defective on constitutional grounds. Even if the Clayton Act had exempted labor from the injunction in such disputes as the Duplex Case, the exemption would have had to run the gauntlet of constitutional objections such as were used to overturn the Arizona anti-injunction law in Truax v. Corrigan.[45]

[42] 274 U.S. 37 at 55.
[43] ibid. at 56.
[44] Di Santo v. Pennsylvania, 273 U.S. 34 at 42 (1927). See infra, pp. 179-80.
[45] 257 U.S. 312 (1921).
Important distinctions are to be noted between the Truax Case and one involving a federal statute, such as the recently enacted Norris-La Guardia Act (47 Stat. 70, c. 90, 1932). The basic theory of this legislation is that Congress has authority to prescribe the jurisdiction of the inferior federal courts, and this seems firmly established. (The cases on this point are collected by Mr. Justice Brandeis in his dissenting opinion in Crowell v. Benson 285 U.S. 22 (1932) at 87 n. 22.) The act prescribes the

This case involved an Arizona statute which placed much the same limitations on state courts of equity as were imposed upon federal courts of equity by sections six and twenty of the Clayton Act. Chief Justice Taft found the statute wanting under both the "equal protection" clause and the "due process" clause of the Fourteenth Amendment. He held that persons may be as effectively denied equal protection of the laws by conferring a favor as by imposing a penalty; that even in the absence of violence an employer may not be deprived of the only effective protection he has against such tactics of labor, namely the injunction. Chief Justice Taft's argument boils down to the proposition that there is a minimum of protection to which a property or business owner is entitled, and of which he may not be deprived, by denial of equitable relief, without invading those fundamental rights guaranteed by the Fourteenth Amendment.

Mr. Justice Brandeis felt that this decision was reached without adequate appreciation of modern industrial life. "The divergence of opinion," he observed, "in this difficult field of gov-

conditions under which injunctions may be issued by the federal courts in cases involving or growing out of labor disputes. The conditions proposed relate to both jurisdiction and procedure. It does not prohibit all injunctions in labor disputes and does not affect damage suits and criminal prosecutions. An exception is provided in the case of "yellow dog" contracts, which are denied all legal and equitable protection in the federal courts. The limited scope of the act would seem to be a point in favor of its constitutionality, as compared with the Arizona statute, since Chief Justice Taft apparently assumed that denial to the employer of injunctive relief was tantamount to denial of all protection. Another point in favor of the constitutionality of the federal act is that it does not have to meet the requirements of the "equal protection" clause which Chief Justice Taft found especially exacting in the Truax Case. The "due process" clause of the Fifth Amendment remains as a source of objection, and this is perhaps a less formidable constitutional barrier than the same clause of the Fourteenth Amendment. See, in this connection, "Dissimilarities in Content between the Two Due Process Clauses of the Federal Constitution," (1929), 29 *Col. L. Rev.* 624, where it is maintained that the Supreme Court has construed the due process clause of the Fifth Amendment more narrowly than the same clause of the Fourteenth Amendment.

For a discussion of the constitutionality of the Norris-La Guardia Act, see Felix Frankfurter and N. Greene, "Congressional Control Over the Labor Injunction" (1931), 31 *Col. L. Rev.* 385, and J. F. Christ, "The Federal Anti-Injunction Bill" (1932), 26 *Ill. L. Rev.* 516.

ernmental action should admonish us not to declare a rule arbitrary and unreasonable merely because we are convinced that it is fraught with danger to the public weal, and thus to close the door to experiment within the law."[46] He also discussed the consideration the case in hand demanded:

What, at any particular time, is the paramount public need is, necessarily, largely a matter of judgment. Hence, in passing upon the validity of a law challenged as being unreasonable, aid may be derived from the experience of other countries and of the several states of our Union in which the common law and its conceptions of liberty and property prevail.[47]

Therefore he made, in brief compass, a thorough investigation of the development of labor law in English-speaking countries, showing that in England the emancipation and improvement of the condition of workingmen was deemed the paramount public need; that resort to the injunction has been infrequent; that it has played no appreciable part in conflicts between capital and labor; that history of the rules governing contests between employer and employee in English-speaking countries illustrates changing rules and a variety of opinion as to what rules best serve the public interest.[48]

But in the United States it was felt that:

The equitable remedy, although applied in accordance with established practice, involved incidents which . . . endangered the personal liberty of wage-earners . . . that the real motive in seeking the injunction *was not ordinarily to prevent property from being injured nor to protect the owner in its use, but to endow property with active, militant power which would make it dominant over men.* In other words, that, *under the guise of protecting property rights, the employer was seeking sovereign power.* And many disinterested men, solicitous only for the public welfare, believed that *the law of property was not appropriate for dealing with the forces beneath social*

[46] 257 U.S. 312 at 357.
[47] *ibid.*
[48] *ibid.*

unrest; that in this vast struggle it was *unwise to throw the power of the state on one side or the other according to principles deduced from that law;* that the *problem of the control and conduct of industry demanded a solution of its own; and that, pending the ascertainment of new principles to govern industry, it was wiser for the state not to interfere in industrial struggles by the issuance of an injunction.*[49]

Anti-injunction proposals, Mr. Justice Brandeis pointed out, occupied the attention of Congress during every session but one between 1894 and 1914. These efforts culminated finally in the Norris-La Guardia Bill which became law on March 23, 1932. Several states had earlier passed such legislation.[50] Nor, as Mr. Justice Brandeis contends, does the Constitution stand in the way:

> States are free since the adoption of the Fourteenth Amendment as they were before, either to expand or to contract their equity jurisdiction. The denial of the more adequate equitable remedy for private wrongs is in essence an exercise of the police power, by which in the interest of the public and in order to preserve the liberty and the property of the great majority of the citizens of a state, rights of property and the liberty of the individual must be remoulded, from time to time, to meet the changing needs of society.[51]

Here, as elsewhere, Mr. Justice Brandeis looks beyond the immediate dispute to its underlying social implications: "it is of the nature of our law that it has dealt not with man in general, but with him in relationships."[52] He understands that a rela-

---

[49] 257 U.S. 312 at 366, 368. The italics are the author's.

[50] For list of citations to these statutes see A. T. Mason, "Organized Labor as Party Plaintiff in Injunction Cases" (1930), 30 *Col. L. Rev.* 466, n. 2.

[51] Truax v. Corrigan, 257 U.S. 312 at 376.

[52] *ibid.* at 355. Mr. Justice Brandeis paid this same deference to legislative discretion in his dissenting opinion in the Duplex Case: "The conditions developed in industry may be such that those engaged in it cannot continue their struggle without danger to the community. But it is not for judges to determine whether such conditions exist, nor is it their function to set the limits of permissible contests and to declare the duties which the new situation demands. This is the function of the legislature which, while limiting individual and group rights of aggression and defense, may substitute processes

tionship classification such as employer and employee satisfies the equal protection requirement of the Fourteenth Amendment; further, he holds that the law is " 'forced to adapt itself to new conditions of society, and, particularly, to the new relations between employers and employees as they arise.' "[53]

Though he advocates collective bargaining, Mr. Justice Brandeis has never condoned trade union abuses, their hasty and ill-considered actions, their ignoring laws which restrict their efforts.[54] On the Supreme Court he follows the principle he announced while at bar, that "industrial liberty, like civil liberty, must rest upon the solid foundation of law."[55] Thus it was easy for him to join Chief Justice Taft, in the Coronado Case,[56] in ruling that a trade union, an unincorporated association, is suable and liable to treble damages under sections seven and eight of the Sherman Act. Indeed, he had anticipated the Coronado ruling twenty years previously in an address delivered at a meeting of the Economic Club of Boston. Although it was

---

of justice for the more primitive method of trial by combat." Duplex Printing Co. v. Deering, 254 U.S. 443 at 488.

[53] Quoted from Holden v. Hardy, 169 U.S. 366 at 387 (1898) in his dissenting opinion in Adams v. Tanner, 244 U.S. 590 at 616.

[54] L. D. Brandeis, *Business—A Profession* (1933), p. 26. See also statement of Mr. Brandeis before the House Committee Hearings on Investigations of the United States Steel Corporation, January 30, 1912, p. 2862.

[55] L. D. Brandeis, *Business—A Profession* (1933), p. 26.

[56] United Mine Workers v. Coronado Coal Co., 259 U.S. 344 (1922). In an address delivered in 1902, Mr. Brandeis had this to say on the suability of trade unions: "The rules of law established by the courts of this country afford . . . no justification for this opinion [that trade unions cannot be made legally responsible for their acts]. A union, although a voluntary unincorporated association, is legally responsible for its acts in much the same way that an individual, a partnership or a corporation is responsible. If a union, through its constituted agents, commits a wrong or is guilty of violence or of illegal oppression, the union, and not merely the individuals who are the direct instruments of the wrong, can be enjoined or made liable for damages to the same extent that the union could be if it were incorporated; and the funds belonging to the unincorporated union can be reached to satisfy any damages which might be recovered for the wrong done." L. D. Brandeis, *Business—A Profession* (1933), p. 93.

denounced on all sides by labor as a "blow to human freedom,"[57] Mr. Justice Brandeis saw the decision rather as a gain for labor. He understood that immunity from suit and legal responsibility, so much cherished by labor, had really built foundations for the greatest grievance labor has suffered from the courts— "government by injunction." In his opinion, "If the courts had been dealing with a responsible union instead of with irresponsible defendants, they would doubtless in many of the cases, have refused to interfere by injunction."[58]

Now, with legal capacity bestowed upon trade unions by judicial decision, making them suable and their funds subject to execution in suits for torts, the chief ground on which appeals to equity courts have succeeded is seriously undermined. In the Coronado decision he could see the partial attainment of that for which labor had been working since the Debs Case,[59] namely, limitation upon the use of injunctions in labor disputes. More than that, he believed incorporation would tend to correct trade union abuses.[60] And not least of the reasons for incorporating

[57] *American Federationist*, official organ of the American Federation of Labor, commented on the decision as follows: "The Supreme Court has not only rendered a decision which goes beyond any previous decision of that tribunal in its antagonism and opposition to labor but it has rendered such a decision when under the law of the land and under practices hitherto obtaining its decision should have been exactly the reverse." *American Federationist*, Vol. XXIX (1922), p. 509.

[58] L. D. Brandeis, *Business—A Profession* (1933), pp. 95-6. "While the rules of legal liability apply fully to the unions, though unincorporated, it is, as a practical matter, more difficult for the plaintiff to conduct the litigation, and it is particularly difficult to reach the funds of the union with which to satisfy any judgment that may be recovered. There has consequently arisen, not a legal, but a practical immunity of the unions, as such, for most wrongs committed." *ibid.*, p. 94.

"This practical immunity of the unions from legal liability is deemed by many labor leaders a great advantage. To me it appears to be just the reverse. It tends to make officers and members reckless and lawless, and thereby to alienate public sympathy and bring failure upon their efforts." *ibid.*

[59] *In re* Debs, 158 U.S. 564 (1895).

[60] "For these defects [hasty, ill-considered and lawless action among trade unionists], being but human, no complete remedy can be found; but the incorporation of labor unions would . . . tend in some measure to correct them." L. D. Brandeis, *op. cit.*, p. 91.

trade unions is that it would remove the groundless fears of employers of such corporations.[61]

Another decision which labor considered a blow almost equal to the Coronado decision was Dorchy v. Kansas.[62] "Neither the common law nor the Fourteenth Amendment confers the absolute right to strike," is the declaration of the Supreme Court. And these are the words not of Mr. Justice Sutherland but of Mr. Justice Brandeis.[63]

Dorchy, a trade union officer, called a strike to compel payment of an ex-employee's disputed wage claim. Convicted under sections seventeen and nineteen of the Kansas Industrial Court Act,[64] Dorchy brought the case before the Supreme Court on a writ of error, his chief contention being that these sections of the act, in prohibiting the right to strike, contravened the Fourteenth Amendment. Mr. Justice Brandeis disposed of the case in few words:

> The right to carry on business—be it called liberty or property—has value. To interfere with this right without just cause is unlawful. The fact that the injury was inflicted by a strike is sometimes a justification. But a strike may be illegal because of its purpose, however orderly the manner in which it is conducted. To collect a stale claim

[61] Statement before the Commission on Industrial Relations, 64th Cong., 1st Sess., Sen. Doc., Vol. XXVI, 7671 (1915).

[62] 272 U.S. 306 (1926).

[63] The legal information bureau of the American Federation of Labor made this quite submissive comment on the decision: "It now seems clear that our various state legislatures may declare strikes for certain objects to be unlawful, and any one urging such a strike may be deemed guilty of a felony and be subject to fine and imprisonment. This decision in the Dorchy Case will undoubtedly be the forerunner of several attempts to curtail the right of labor unions to strike." *American Federationist*, Vol. XXXIII (1926), pp. 1501, 1502. One finds little or nothing in the opinion to warrant any such prediction. The Court expressly pointed out that the decision was of limited scope. 272 U.S. 306 at 309.

[64] *Kan. Rev. Stat. Ann.* (1923), §44-617, §44-619. Section 617 makes it unlawful to conspire to induce others to quit their employment "for the purpose and with the intent to hinder, delay, limit or suspend the operation" of any business affected with a public interest. Section 619 makes it a felony for an officer of a labor union to use the power or influence incident to his office to induce another person to violate any provision of the act.

due to a fellow member of the union who was formerly employed
in the business is not a permissible purpose. . . . To enforce payment
by a strike is clearly coercion. The legislature may make such action
punishable criminally, as extortion or otherwise.[65]

In this decision Mr. Justice Brandeis was invoking a rule he
deemed applicable in considering the legality of trade union
practices.[66] Nor is his opinion so far-reaching as may appear at
first glance. Without the statute, the strike might well have been
condemned as illegal, as a conspiracy at common law.[67] And
lest erroneous implications be drawn, Mr. Justice Brandeis adds
that "the question requiring decision is not . . . the broad one
whether the legislature has power to prohibit strikes."[68]

Believing, as he does, that trade-unions have accomplished
much, that "their fundamental principle is noble,"[69] Mr. Justice
Brandeis' labor decisions naturally incline toward increasing the
power of unions and toward limiting any use of injunctions
in industrial disputes. He believes in trade unions because he
knows that society as a whole depends upon higher wages,
reasonable hours of work and better working conditions.[70]

Yet despite his desire to protect workers from the tyranny
and oppression of their employers, his decisions do not purpose
to exchange tyranny of capital for that of labor. He still insists
that lawless methods of trade unions, whether violence or intimidation or less warlike infringements of legal rights, "must be
put down at once and at any cost."[71]

[65] Dorchy v. Kansas, 272 U.S. 306 at 311.
[66] "If unions are lawless, restrain and punish their lawlessness; if they are
arbitrary, repress their arbitrariness; if their demands are unreasonable or unjust,
resist them; but do not oppose the unions as such." L. D. Brandeis, *op. cit.*, p. 90.
[67] See, in this connection, A. T. Mason, "The Right to Strike" (1928), 77 *U. of Pa.
L. Rev.* 52.
[68] Dorchy v. Kansas, 272 U.S. 306 at 309.
[69] L. D. Brandeis, *op. cit.*, p. 90.
[70] *ibid.*, p. 88.
[71] L. D. Brandeis, *Business—A Profession*, p. 26.

3. *The Stable Rate Base and Fair Rate of Return*

The Supreme Court long since ceased to be only a legal tribunal. Today it decides great social and economic issues. This has not always been the case. In Munn v. Illinois,[72] decided in 1876, the Court adopted a position of non-interference in rate-making, claiming that fixing public utility rates was a legislative matter which should remain free from judicial interference. Ten years later the Court shifted its position,[73] to recognize that this power of the legislature was not without limit; that utility rates must yield a fair return upon a fair valuation of the property devoted to such a public service. Although the Court two years later[74] retreated somewhat from this position, when it suddenly recognized that it was without a basis upon which to question legislative control over public utility prices, all misgivings on the latter score had vanished by 1890, when the Court held judicial review applicable in public utility cases, and maintained that due process of law requires the rate to be reasonable, and that of this the Court is final judge.[75] The right of judicial review in this field was more boldly stated in Smyth v. Ames,[76] and this despite the prior protest of a minority which had held that judges are not equipped to decide social and economic issues.[77] Certainly judges, passing upon such questions, can find precious little guidance in the Constitution.

Interpretations of "due process of law," "just compensation," "deprivation of liberty and property" are susceptible of flexibility, to say the least. By these the Supreme Court can give in large measure its own definitions of social and economic relationship. What is there, for instance, in the phrase "due process"

---

[72] 94 U.S. 113 (1876).
[73] Railroad Commission Cases, 116 U.S. 307 at 331 (1886).
[74] Dow v. Beidelman, 125 U.S. 680 at 691-2 (1888).
[75] Chicago, Milwaukee and St. Paul R.R. Co. v. Minnesota, 134 U.S. 418 (1890).
[76] 169 U.S. 466 at 527-8 (1898).
[77] See the dissenting opinion of Mr. Justice Bradley with whom Justices Gray and Lamar concurred in Chicago, etc. Ry. v. Minnesota, 134 U.S. 418 at 461.

that hints whether five, six or eight per cent be a fair return on public utility property? What is there that sheds light on whether utilities should be valued for rate-making purposes at original cost, or at reproduction cost new? What indication is there of the measure of return needed for computing fair and reasonable rates? Absolutely none. These questions must be settled in Court by applying highly controversial accounting measurements and economic theories. Without enjoying rate-making power as such, the courts have come to exercise power of tremendous importance in rate-making.

It was in Smyth v. Ames[78] that the Supreme Court constituted itself the final judge of "fair return" within the meaning of the "due process" clause of the Fourteenth Amendment. The case is especially significant for its enumeration of the elements to be taken into account in determining the value of the property on which a fair return is guaranteed.

> We hold . . . that the basis of all calculations as to the reasonableness of rates to be charged by a corporation maintaining a highway under legislative sanction must be the fair value of the property being used by it for the convenience of the public. And in order to ascertain that value, the original cost of construction, the amount expended in permanent improvements, the amount and market value of its [the company's] bonds and stock, the present as compared with the original cost of construction, the probable earning capacity of the property under particular rates prescribed by statute, and the sum required to meet operating expenses, are all matters for consideration, and are to be given such weight as may be just and right in each case.[79]

This judicial rule of rate-making combines three theories of valuation: (1) Historical cost of tangible property plus that of permanent improvements. (2) Capitalization and commercial value of the business, as determined by current market prices of

[78] 169 U.S. 466 (1898).
[79] ibid. at 546-7.

the company's stocks and bonds. (3) Cost of reproduction new, less depreciation.

Mr. Justice Brandeis has denounced this rule as "legally and economically unsound." His reasoning follows:

> The rule does not measure the present value either by what the utility cost to produce; or by what it should have cost; or by what it would cost to reproduce, or to replace, it. Under that rule the tribunal is directed, in forming its judgment, to take into consideration all those and also, other elements, called relevant facts.
>
> Obviously, "value" cannot be a composite of all these elements. Nor can it be arrived at on all these bases. They are very different; and must, when applied in a particular case, lead to widely different results. The rule of *Smyth* v. *Ames,* as interpreted and applied, means merely that all must be considered. What, if any, weight shall be given any one, must practically rest in the judicial discretion of the tribunal which makes the determination.[80]

Since then the Court has divided, in a long line of important decisions, regarding the relative weight to be given the various factors in rate base determination. The theory of reproduction cost is, in Mr. Justice Brandeis' opinion, particularly faulty. It is vague, delusive and leaves room for wide divergence of opinion.

Reproduction cost has had a varied and curious history. It was urged in 1893 in behalf of the community. William Jennings Bryan appeared in the Smyth Case and argued in favor of present value based on reproduction cost, as protection against inflated claims based on past high prices. The long depression after 1893 brought prices to the lowest level of the nineteenth century. Insistence upon reproduction cost was the shipper's protest against watered stock, reckless finance, and racketeering contracts. During the rising prices of the World War, railroads and other public utilities promptly adopted the position once taken by Bryan on behalf of the consumers. Today the way is paved for another shift back to Bryan by those who favor the public inter-

[80] Southwestern Bell Tel. Co. v. Public Serv. Comm., 262 U.S. 276 at 294-5 (1923).

est. The vagueness and uncertainty of the rule has prompted Mr. Justice Brandeis to make a detailed study of public utility valuation. He proposes a substitute:

> The experience of the twenty-five years since [Smyth v. Ames] ... was decided has demonstrated that the rule there enunciated is delusive. In the attempt to apply it insuperable obstacles have been encountered. It has failed to afford adequate protection either to capital or to the public. It leaves open the door to grave injustice. . . .[81]
>
> The rule of Smyth v. Ames sets the laborious and baffling task of finding the present value of the utility. It is impossible to find an exchange value for a utility, since utilities, unlike merchandise or land, are not commonly bought and sold in the market. Nor can the present value of the utility be determined by capitalizing its net earnings, since the earnings are determined, in large measure, by the rate which the company will be permitted to charge; and, thus, the vicious circle would be encountered.[82]

To give public utility capital its due constitutional protection, Mr. Justice Brandeis argues that the rate base be definite, stable and readily ascertainable; that the percentage to be earned on the rate base be measured by the cost, or charge, of the capital employed in the enterprise. The rule announced in the Smyth Case, he insisted, was signally faulty on this very score. "Under it the value for rate-making purposes must ever be an unstable factor."[83] Mr. Justice Brandeis felt, moreover, that there was a widespread conviction regarding the inadequacy of the existing rule; a feeling that "actual value of a utility is not to be reached by a meticulous study of conflicting estimates of the cost of reproducing new the congeries of old machinery and equipment, called the new plant, and the still more fanciful estimates con-

[81] Southwestern Bell Tel. Co. v. Public Serv. Comm., 262 U.S. 276 at 292 (1923).

[82] *ibid.* Compare Chief Justice Hughes' opinion in Los Angeles G. & E. Corp. v. Railroad Comm. 289 U.S. 287 (1933). "In determining that basis [established in Smyth v. Ames], the criteria at hand for ascertaining market value, or what is called exchange value, are not commonly available. The property is not ordinarily the subject of barter and sale and, when rates themselves are in dispute, earnings produced by rates do not afford a standard for decision" (at 305).

[83] 262 U.S. 276 at 308.

cerning the value of the intangible elements of an established business."[84]

Mr. Justice Brandeis proceeded therefore to offer what he believed "a definite, stable and readily ascertainable" rate base, and also a measure of fair rate of return. As to the first, he sponsored a theory of valuation followed by many commissions, especially that of Massachusetts: " 'Capital honestly and prudently invested must, under normal conditions, be taken as the controlling factor in fixing the basis for computing fair and reasonable rates.' "[85] In support of this rule he argued as follows:

> The adoption of the amount prudently invested as the rate base and the amount of the capital charge as the measure of the rate of return would give definiteness to these two factors involved in rate controversies which are now shifting and treacherous, and which render the proceedings peculiarly burdensome and largely futile. Such measures offer a basis for decision which is certain and stable. The rate base would be ascertained as a fact, not determined as a matter of opinion. It would not fluctuate with the market price of labor, or materials, or money. It would not change with hard times or shifting populations. It would not be distorted by the fickle and varying judgments of appraisers, commissions, or courts. It would, when once made in respect to any utility, be fixed, for all time, subject only to increases to represent additions to plant, after allowance for the depreciation included in the annual operating charges. The wild uncertainties of the present method of fixing the rate base under the so-called rule of Smyth v. Ames would be avoided; and likewise the fluctuations which introduce into the enterprise unnecessary elements of speculation, create useless expense, and impose upon the public a heavy, unnecessary burden.[86]

As to the measure of a reasonable rate of return, he argued for "the cost to the utility of the capital, required to construct, equip and operate its plant."[87] "Cost includes not only operating expenses, but also capital charges. Capital charges cover the allowance, by way of interest, for the use of the capital, whatever

[84] *ibid.* at 301.
[85] *ibid.*
[86] *ibid.* at 306-7.
[87] *ibid.* at 306.

the nature of the security issued therefor; the allowance for risk incurred; and enough more to attract capital."[88]

It is conceded that the actual prudent investment rule would have been difficult or impossible to apply when Smyth v. Ames was decided. It was then impossible to ascertain, Mr. Justice Brandeis admits, what it cost in money to establish the utility; or what the money cost with which the utility was established, or what income had been earned by it; or how the income had been expended. Now, the situation, he thinks, is different: "These amounts are, now, readily ascertainable in respect to a large, and rapidly increasing, proportion of the utilities. . . . It is, therefore, feasible now to adopt as the measure of a compensatory rate—the annual cost, or charge, of the capital prudently invested in the utility. And, hence, it should be done."[89] Regulated accounting had done its work.

Much dicta in the majority opinion in the Southwestern Bell Telephone Case make strongly for the reproduction cost theory. But the rates there involved were so inadequate that they did not bring a fair return even on the actual cost of the properties, much less on the reproduction cost. This explains why Mr. Justice Brandeis concurred in reversing the state court. He joined in declaring the rates confiscatory, but did so because they did not bring a fair return on the actual investment.

The same observations may be made with reference to the Bluefield Case.[90] Here the rates were held to be confiscatory. Mr. Justice Butler, speaking for the Court, used *dicta* which indicated the Court's leaning toward reproduction cost. Again Mr. Justice Brandeis concurred in holding that the rates were confiscatory. He considered the rates invalid because they did not yield a fair return on the actual investment. In both the

[88] 262 U.S. 276 at 291.
[89] *ibid.* at 309-10.
[90] Bluefield Water Works and Improvement Co. v. Public Serv. Comm., 262 U.S. 679 (1923).

Southwestern Bell Telephone and Bluefield Cases Mr. Justice Brandeis concurred in the decisions but not in the *dicta* in favor of reproduction cost.

In the Georgia Railway Case,[91] where Mr. Justice Brandeis spoke for the Court, the rates were sustained, because unlike the Southwestern Bell Telephone and Bluefield Cases, the rates set by the commission did yield a fair return upon actual investment of about 7¼ per cent, though only four per cent on reproduction value as shown by the company.

Considering these cases together, the conclusion is that although a majority of the Court leans toward the reproduction theory of public utility valuation, the Court will hesitate to declare specific rates confiscatory and unconstitutional if they bring a fair return on actual investment, notwithstanding a much higher reproduction cost.

The clearest indication, prior to the Baltimore Street Railways Case, and the O'Fallon Case, of the Court's preference for the reproduction theory of valuation, is Mr. Justice Butler's opinion in McCardle v. Indianapolis Water Company.[92] And the Court's opinion in that case evoked from Mr. Justice Brandeis a flat denial that any statement had been made by the Court to the effect "that value is tantamount to reproduction cost."[93]

[91] Georgia Ry. and Power Co. v. Railroad Commission, 262 U.S. 625 (1923).

[92] 272 U.S. 400 (1926).

[93] *ibid.* at 423. "Nor do I find," Mr. Justice Brandeis continues, "in the decisions of this Court any support for the view that a peculiar sanction attaches to 'spot' reproduction cost, as distinguished from the amount that it would actually cost to reproduce the plant if that task were undertaken at the date of the hearing. 'Spot' reproduction would be impossible of accomplishment without the aid of Aladdin's lamp. The actual cost of a plant may conceivably indicate its actual value at the time of completion or at some time thereafter. Estimates of cost may conceivably approximate what the cost of reproduction would be at a given time. But where a plant would require years for completion, the estimate would be necessarily delusive if it were based on 'spot' prices of labor, materials and money. The estimate, to be in any way worthy of trust, must be based on a consideration of the varying costs of labor, materials, and money for a period at least as long as would be required to construct the plant and put it into operation. Moreover, the estimate must be made in the light of a longer experience and with due allowances for the hazards which attend

One of the main points on which the Court divided in the Baltimore Street Railways Case[94] was depreciation. The Maryland Public Service Commission, in fixing a rate of fare, agreed that depreciation be reckoned on the cost of the thing depreciated and not on present value. The Maryland Court of Appeals held this erroneous, contending that depreciation should have been reckoned on present value. This decision, the Supreme Court held, was "plainly right"; that "It is the settled rule of this Court that the rate base is present value, and it would be wholly illogical to adopt a different rule for depreciation."[95]

To this ruling Mr. Justice Brandeis made vigorous dissent. He thought "A net return of 6.26 per cent upon the present value of the property of a street railway enjoying a monopoly in one of the oldest, largest, and richest cities on the Atlantic seaboard would seem to be compensatory."[96] The difference between the depreciation charges originally allowed by the commission and those computed on the basis of present value, amounted to $755,166 annually, and if this item were eliminated from the operating costs of the company and applied against the rate base of $70,000,000 it would add 1.08 per cent to the estimated return. He insisted that this should have been done.

> . . . Acceptance of the doctrine of Smyth v. Ames does not require that the depreciation charge be based on present value of plant. For, an annual depreciation charge is not a measure of the actual consumption of plant during the year. No such measure has yet been invented. There is no regularity in the development of depreciation. It does not proceed in accordance with any mathematical law. There is nothing in business experience, or in the training of experts, which enables man to say to what extent service life will be impaired by the

all prophesies in respect to prices. The search for value can hardly be aided by a hypothetical estimate of the cost of replacing the plant at a particular moment, when actual reproduction would require a period that must be measured by years." *ibid.* at 423-4.

[94] United Railways and Elec. Co. v. West, 280 U.S. 234 (1930).

[95] *ibid.* at 254.

[96] *ibid.* at 255.

operations of a single year, or of a series of years less than the service life.[97]

Mr. Justice Brandeis' study of the economics of insurance had shown him how legal science could solve this intricate economic problem of depreciation:

> The depreciation charge is frequently likened to the annual premium in legal reserve life insurance. The life insurance premium is calculated on an agreed value of the human life—comparable to the known cost of plant—not on a fluctuating value, unknown and unknowable. . . . Because every attempt to approximate more nearly the amount of premium required proved futile, justice was sought and found in the system of strictly mutual insurance. Under that system the premium charged is made clearly ample; and the part which proves not to have been needed enures in some form of benefit to him who paid it.

> Similarly, if, instead of applying the rule of Smyth v. Ames, the rate base of a utility were fixed at the amount prudently invested, the inevitable errors incident to estimating service life and net expense in plant consumption could never result in injustice either to the utility or to the community. For, if the amount set aside for depreciation proved inadequate and investment of new capital became necessary, the utility would be permitted to earn a return on the new capital. And if the amount set aside for depreciation proved to be excessive, the income from the surplus reserve would operate as a credit to reduce the capital charge which the rates must earn. If the railway should ever suffer injustice from adopting cost of plant as the basis for calculating the depreciation charge, it will be an unavoidable incident of applying in valuation the rule of Smyth v. Ames.[98]

Nor does his claim that the depreciation charge should be based upon the cost of the property, rather than upon present value, rest upon reason alone. This is the method adopted by the United States Chamber of Commerce;[99] it is the practice of

[97] *ibid*. at 262.

[98] *ibid*. at 278-9. See also his dissenting opinion in Pacific Gas and Elec. Co. v. San Francisco, 265 U.S. 403 (1924).

[99] "Wherever adopted, the depreciation charge is based on the original cost of the plant to the owner. When the great changes in price levels incident to the World War led some to question the wisdom of the practice of basing the charge on original

public accountants;[100] it is supported by leading business institutions;[101] it conforms to the policy of utility commissions.[102] On these points Mr. Justice Brandeis cites in footnotes covering several pages, references to hundreds of authorities—studies in economics and in political science, studies of the practice of administrative bodies, of trade associations and private corporations, works on accountancy, and more. As an expert in accountancy, he understands that Courts are ill-equipped to deal with the technique of valuation, rate-fixing and monopoly. Therefore he generally defers to findings of the Interstate Commerce Commission,[103] the Federal Trade Commission,[104] and various

cost, the Chamber of Commerce of the United States warned business men against the fallacy of departing from the accepted basis. And that warning has been recently repeated." United Railways and Elec. Co. v. West, 280 U.S. 234 at 265-6.

100 "Such is today, and ever has been, the practice of public accountants. . . . By those accustomed to read the language of accounting a depreciation charge is understood as meaning the appropriate contribution for that year to the amount required to make good the cost of the plant which ultimately must be retired." ibid. at 267-8.

101 "Business men naturally took the plant at cost, as that is how they treat other articles consumed in operation. The plant, undepreciated, is commonly carried on the books at cost; and it is retired at cost . . . they realized also that to attempt to make the depreciation account reflect economic conditions and changes would entail entry upon new fields of conjecture and prophecy which would defeat its purposes. . . . In 1927 the business men's practice of basing the depreciation charge on cost was applied by this Court in United States v. Ludey, 274 U.S. 295, 300-301." ibid. at 269-70, 274.

102 "A depreciation charge based on original cost has been uniformly applied by the public utility commissions of the several states when determining net income, past or expected, for rate-making purposes." ibid. at 273.

103 See United States v. Los Angeles and Salt Lake R.R. Co., 273 U.S. 299 (1927); Great Northern Ry. v. Merchants Elevator Co., 259 U.S. 285 (1922). In both of these cases Mr. Justice Brandeis spoke for the Court.

The first case to come before the Court under the valuation clause of the Transportation Act of 1920 is St. Louis and O'Fallon Ry. v. United States, 279 U.S. 461 (1929). Under paragraph four, section 15a, Congress had directed the Interstate Commerce Commission to give due consideration to all the elements of value recognized by the law of the land for rate-making purposes. The commission itself was divided as to the weight to be given to reproduction cost. Without following any particular rule of valuation, the majority of the commission found that "the value of the property of railroads for rate-making purposes . . . approaches more nearly the reasonable and necessary investment in property than the cost of reproducing it at a particular time." Quoted by Mr. Justice Brandeis, ibid. at 541. The majority of the Court speaking through Mr. Justice McReynolds sided with the minority of the commission, on the score that insufficient weight had been given to the principle of reproduction cost.

state public service commissions.[105] Nevertheless he holds the Courts responsible for adjudicating the relation of all these problems to the general welfare.[106]

Until Chief Justice Hughes' opinion in the recent Los Angeles Gas Case, which is considered on a later page, it seemed to be established that the rule for determining the rate base is "present value"; that original cost is not present value nor an approximation thereof; that substantial weight must be given to present costs of labor and materials, and hence to increased reproduction cost. Mr. Justice Brandeis has never been willing to admit that the rule enunciated in the Smyth Case justifies any such conclusions. He still insists that if the Court allowed actual cost as the rate base, much of the difficulty with reference to the determination of reasonable rates and depreciation allowances, would be avoided. He sees in the adoption of "original cost" the only

Mr. Justice Brandeis voted to sustain the findings of the commission. He argued that "the commission was clearly authorized to determine for itself to what extent, if any, weight should be given to the evidence; and its findings should not be disturbed by the Court, unless it appears that there was an abuse of discretion" (at 494).

[104] In Federal Trade Commission v. Gratz, 253 U.S. 421 (1920), the Court affirmed the judgment of the Circuit Court annulling an order of the Commission that a company desist from the practice of imposing upon purchasers a so-called "tying clause." Arguing that the judgment of the Circuit Court should be overruled and that the order of the Commission be sustained, Mr. Justice Brandeis observed:

"The proceeding is . . . a novelty. It is a new device in administrative machinery, introduced by Congress in the year 1914, in the hope thereby of remedying conditions in business which a great majority of the American people regarded as menacing the general welfare, and which for more than a generation they had vainly attempted to remedy by the ordinary processes of law . . ." (at 432).

"Instead of undertaking to define what practices should be deemed unfair, as had been done in earlier legislation, the act left the determination to the Commission. . . . Recognizing that the question whether a method of competitive practice was unfair would ordinarily depend upon special facts, Congress imposed upon the Commission the duty of finding the facts; and it declared that findings of fact so made (if duly supported by evidence) were to be taken as final" (at 436-7).

See, in this connection, Louis L. Jaffe, "The Contributions of Mr. Justice Brandeis to Administrative Law" (1933), 18 *Iowa L. Rev.* 213.

[105] United Railway and Elec. Co. v. West, 280 U.S. 234 (dissenting).

[106] Mr. Justice Brandeis' contribution to the law of railroad regulation is ably treated by Henry Wolf Biklé in "Mr. Justice Brandeis and the Regulation of Railroads" (1931), 45 *Harv. L. Rev.* 4. Reprinted in Felix Frankfurter, ed., *Mr. Justice Brandeis* (1932).

means of securing a stable and practicable base for steady use in rate case adjudications. He urges this rule because he understands that the use of either reproduction cost or present value is quite as likely, through the fluctuation of values, to operate at one period against the public and in favor of the utilities, at another period against the utilities and in favor of the public.[107]

4. This Tangled Web of Freedom

The high value which Mr. Justice Brandeis places upon human rights has already been emphasized. These he regards as basically more important to society than property rights. It necessarily follows, as to the political aspect, that the state exists for man, man does not exist for the state. The worth of the state is in what it wins for man:

> Those who won our independence believed that the final end of the state was to make men free to develop their faculties; and that in its government the deliberative forces should prevail over the arbitrary. They valued liberty both as an end and as a means. They believed liberty to be the secret of happiness and courage to be the secret of liberty. They believed that freedom to think as you will and to speak as you think are means indispensable to the discovery and spread of political truth.[108]

> The makers of our Constitution undertook to secure conditions favorable to the pursuit of happiness. They recognized the significance of man's spiritual nature, of his feelings and of his intellect. They knew that only a part of the pain, pleasure, and satisfactions of life are to be found in material things. They sought to protect Americans in their beliefs, their thoughts, their emotions, and their sensations. They conferred, as against the gov-

---

[107] For illustrations of the effect of using reproduction cost among the "relevant facts" to be taken into account in determining fair value, see M. G. Glaeser, *Outlines of Public Utility Economics* (1927), pp. 462 ff., and authorities cited. See also "Utility Rates in the Slump," *The New Republic,* July 12, 1933, and the recent volume by W. E. Mosher and F. G. Crawford, *Public Utility Regulation* (1933).

[108] Whitney v. California, 274 U.S. 357 at 375 (1927).

ernment, the right to be let alone—the most comprehensive of rights and the right most valued by civilized men.[109]

The political system, as well as the industrial and social should be directed not so much toward material progress as for the development of men. "Our business is not to make goods, but to make men."[110] "I cannot believe," Mr. Justice Brandeis observed, "that the liberty guaranteed by the Fourteenth Amendment includes only liberty to acquire and to enjoy property."[111] The reason he feels such an interest in scientific management is that it does tend to make men.[112] He opposes long hours of labor and big industrial combinations,[113] restrictions on freedom of speech and assembly, because these dwarf the individual. He objects to the use of injunctions in labor disputes because of its tendency "to endow property with active militant power which would make it dominant over man."[114] He favors trade unions, the minimum wage, the Volstead Act, workmen's compensation and unemployment insurance chiefly on the score of their tendency to favor individual development. His implicit faith in democracy,[115] industrial and political, is rooted in the belief that

[109] Olmstead v. United States, 277 U.S. 438 at 478 (1928).

[110] Statement before Commission on Industrial Relations, 64th Cong., 1st Sess., Sen. Doc., Vol. XIX, 1003 (1914).

[111] Gilbert v. Minnesota, 254 U.S. 325 at 343 (1920).

[112] "Conserving human effort, and the man, is a fundamental tenet of scientific management." L. D. Brandeis, Business—A Profession (1933), p. 41.

"To my mind the best game that there is is the game of work, and I want to see men in it for all the joys that come with working effectively." Statement before Commission on Industrial Relations, loc. cit., p. 1003.

[113] For a discussion of the incompatibility between big business and industrial democracy, see Statement before the Commission on Industrial Relations, 64th Cong., 1st Sess., Sen. Doc., Vol. XXVI, 7659 (1915).

[114] 257 U.S. 312 at 366, 368.

[115] ". . . I have such a faith in democracy and such a distrust of the absence of it that I have felt a grave apprehension as to what might ultimately be the effect of these foundations [Rockefeller, and Russell Sage] when the control shall have passed out of the hands of those who at present are administering them to those who may not be governed by the excellent intent of the creators." Statement before the Commission on Industrial Relations, 64th Cong., 1st Sess., Sen. Doc., Vol. XXVI, 7664 (1915).

it alone affords the conditions under which an individual is free to develop his power.

Mr. Justice Brandeis, like John Stuart Mill, knows that unless men talk and write freely they are less than men. Therefore a state cannot prohibit unpopular doctrine merely because a majority hates such views as false and dangerous: "To justify suppression of free speech there must be reasonable ground to fear that serious evil will result if free speech is practised. There must be reasonable ground to believe that the danger apprehended is imminent. There must be reasonable ground to believe that the evil to be prevented is a serious one."[116] The rights of others alone can justifiably restrict liberty: "All rights are derived from the purposes of the society in which they exist, above all rights rises duty to the community."[117]

Urging *laissez faire* in politics, Mr. Justice Brandeis is an ardent advocate of government regulation in industry. Indeed his principles exhibit an element of collectivism so strong as somewhat to embarrass those who endorse his libertarian doctrines. Both liberty and democracy are seriously threatened by the growth of big business. Today the need is not so much for freedom from physical restraint as for freedom from economic oppression:

> Already the displacement of the small independent business man by the huge corporation with its myriad of employees, its absentee

[116] Whitney v. California, 274 U.S. 357 at 376.

"The fundamental right of free men to strive for better conditions through new legislation and new institutions will not be preserved, if efforts to secure it by argument to fellow citizens may be construed as criminal incitement to disobey the existing law —merely, because the argument presented seems to those exercising judicial power to be unfair in its portrayal of existing evils, mistaken in its assumptions, unsound in reasoning or intemperate in language." Pierce v. United States, 252 U.S. 239 at 273.

[117] Duplex Printing Co. v. Deering, 254 U.S. 443 at 488.

". . . The liberty of each individual must be limited in such a way that it leaves to others the possibility of individual liberty; the right to develop must be subject to that limitation which gives to everybody else the right to develop; the restriction is merely an adjustment of the relations of one individual to another." Statement before New York State Factory Investigating Commission, January 22, 1915, p. 2881.

ownership, and its financier control, presents a grave danger to our democracy. The social loss is great; and there is no economic gain.[118]

Political liberty, then, is not enough; it must be attended by economic and industrial liberty. Trade unions have done much, but if the individual is to be free from modern economic oppression, government itself must intervene[119] to reduce large business combinations and to maintain fair competition between these smaller units.

Mr. Justice Brandeis' preference for small cooperating business units rather than the crushing power of combined capital, is shown by his dissent in the Quaker City Cab Case. Philadelphia cab corporations objected to a Pennsylvania taxing statute on the ground that competing individuals and partnerships were not subject to the tax. The Court, in a six-to-three decision, declared the statute unconstitutional under the "equal protection" clause. The classification, the Court held, to be legitimate, "must be based on a real and substantial difference having reasonable relation to the subject of the legislation." The Court felt there was no such difference. Mr. Justice Brandeis wrote:

> In Pennsylvania the practice of imposing heavier burdens upon corporations dates from a time when there, as elsewhere in America, the fear of growing corporate power was common. The present heavier imposition may be a survival of an early effort to discourage the resort to that form of organization. The apprehension is now less common. But there are still intelligent, informed, just-minded and civilized persons who believe that the rapidly growing aggregation of capital through corporations constitutes an insidious menace to the liberty of the citizen . . . that the evils incident to the accelerating absorption of business by corporations outweigh the benefits thereby secured; and that the process of absorption should be retarded.[120]

[118] "Cutthroat Prices, The Competition that Kills," *Harper's Weekly*, November 15, 1913.
[119] Statement before the Commission on Industrial Relations, 64th Cong., 1st Sess., Sen. Doc., Vol. XXVI, 7662 *ff*. (1915).
[120] Quaker City Cab Co. v. Pennsylvania, 277 U.S. 389 at 410-11 (1928).

The social and economic desirability of the small business enterprise is an enduring principle with Brandeis. Its advantages are even more obvious to him today than twenty years ago. This is decisively shown by his dissenting opinion in the Florida Chain Stores Case,[121] decided March 13, 1933. Here one finds detailed and scholarly analysis of the corporation as a form of business activity. He points out that the early use of the corporate mechanism was attended by grave apprehension.

> Fear of encroachment upon the liberties and opportunities of the individual. Fear of the subjection of labor to capital. Fear that the absorption of capital by corporations, and their perpetual life, might bring evils similar to those which attended mortmain.[122]

Such reasoning had neither meaning nor effect during "Coolidge prosperity." The original legal restrictions so carefully thrown around corporations had been removed almost without trace. "The states joined in advertising their wares [corporate charters]. The race was one not of diligence but of laxity."[123] Indeed the prevalence of the corporation in America "led men of this generation to act, at times, as if the privilege of doing business in corporate form were inherent in the citizen; and has led them to accept the evils attendant upon the free and unrestricted use of the corporate mechanism as if these evils were the inescapable price of civilized life and, hence, to be borne with resignation."[124]

The economic depression has already stimulated considerable research into modern corporate enterprise, and the recent findings are those made by Mr. Brandeis before 1908.

> They show that size alone gives to giant corporations a social significance not attached ordinarily to smaller units of private enterprise. Through size, corporations . . . are sometimes able to dominate

[121] Liggett v. Lee, 288 U. S. 517, 541 (1933).
[122] ibid., 548.
[123] ibid., 558-9.
[124] ibid., 548.

the state. The typical business corporation of the last century, owned by a small group of individuals, managed by their owners, and limited in size by their personal wealth, is being supplanted by huge concerns in which the lives of tens or hundreds of thousands of employees and the property of tens or hundreds of thousands of investors are subjected, through the corporate mechanism, to the control of a few men. Ownership has been separated from control; and this separation has removed many of the checks which formerly operated to curb the misuse of wealth and power. And as ownership of the shares is becoming continually more dispersed, the power which formerly accompanied ownership is becoming increasingly concentrated in the hands of a few. The changes thereby wrought in the lives of the workers, of the owners, and of the general public, are so fundamental and far-reaching as to lead these scholars to compare the evolving "corporate system" with the feudal system; and to lead other men of insight and experience to assert that this "master institution of civilised life" is committing it to the rule of a plutocracy."[125]

The depression, Mr. Justice Brandeis believes, has proved anew other economic and social evils of "bigness."

There is a widespread belief that the existing unemployment is the result, in large part, of the gross inequality in the distribution of wealth and income which giant corporations have fostered; that by the control which the few have exerted through giant corporations, individual initiative and effort are being paralyzed, creative power impaired and human happiness lessened; that the true prosperity of our past came not from big business, but through the courage, the energy and the resourcefulness of small men; that only by releasing from corporate control the faculties of the unknown many, only by reopening to them the opportunities for leadership, can confidence in our future be restored and the existing misery be overcome; and that only through participation by the many in the responsibilities and determinations of business, can Americans secure the moral and intellectual development which is essential to the maintenance of liberty. If the citizens of Florida share that belief, I know of nothing in the Federal Constitution which precludes the state from endeav-

[125] ibid., 565.

oring to give it effect and prevent domination in intrastate commerce by subjecting corporate chains to discriminatory license fees. To that extent, the citizens of each state are still masters of their destiny.[126]

For all these reasons, he is convinced that business may become dangerous to the community by size alone. And if the state should conclude that bigness in retail merchandising by corporate chain stores, menaces the public welfare, he maintains that the state can prohibit that excessive "bigness" just as it prohibits excessive size or weight in motor trucks, and excessive height in city buildings.[127] But the state might, as in this case, "first try the more temperate remedy of curbing the chain by imposing the handicap of discriminatory license fees."[128] And it does not follow that because independently owned stores are overcoming by cooperation the advantages once possessed by chain stores, there is no taxable difference between corporate and cooperative chains. The state's power to apply discriminatory taxation is not conditioned upon the existence of economic need but flows from the broader right of Americans to preserve and to establish such institutions, social and economic, as seem to them desirable, and, likewise, to end those which they consider undesirable. The state might even subject giant corporations to a control similar to that now exerted over public utilities, or escape the domination of giant corporations by itself engaging in business. But there is open to Americans another form of economic and social control, and one more in keeping with our traditions.

They may prefer the way of cooperation, which leads directly to the freedom and the equality of opportunity which the Fourteenth Amendment aims to secure. That way is clearly open. For the fundamental difference between capitalistic enterprise and the cooperative

[126] Liggett v. Lee, 288 U.S. 580 (1933).
[127] *ibid.*, 574.
[128] *ibid.*

—between economic absolutism and industrial democracy—is one which has been commonly accepted by legislatures and the courts as justifying discrimination in both regulation and taxation.[129]

Since certain untoward events in 1929 many competent observers are disposed to agree with Mr. Justice Brandeis in the position he has held so long: that size, *per se,* is a threat to the well-being of the modern economic community against which government must ever be on its guard. Property has a social function to perform; it is a means, not an end in itself. It may interfere "with that fundamental freedom of life for which property is *only a means."* When it does, Mr. Justice Brandeis insists that it should be controlled. "This applies to the regulation of trusts and railroads, public utilities, and all the big industries that control the necessities of life. Laws regulating them, far from being infringements on liberty, are in reality protections against infringements on liberty."[130]

This view does not, however, commit him to such a strict interpretation of the anti-trust laws as would prevent business from rationalizing its methods of competition. "The Sherman Law," he maintains, "does not prohibit every lessening of competition; and it certainly does not command that competition shall be pursued bindly, that business rivals shall remain ignorant of trade facts or be denied aid in weighing their significance."[131] Just as the trade union is a necessary instrument for securing higher wages, shorter hours and better working conditions among workers, so the trade association is a "commendable effort by concerns engaged in a chaotic industry to make possible its intelligent conduct under competitive conditions."[132]

[129] *ibid.,* 579.
[130] Ernest Poole, "Brandeis," *The American Magazine,* Vol. LXXI, pp. 481, 492 (1911). Reprinted as an introduction to L. D. Brandeis, *Business—A Profession* (1933), p. liii.
[131] American Column and Lumber Co. v. United States, 257 U.S. 377 at 415 (1921).
[132] *ibid.* at 418.

The first trade association agreement to come before the Court appeared in the famous Hardwood Case. Here an association of some four hundred lumber producers was responsible for about thirty per cent of the total annual production of hardwood lumber in the country. A large majority of these firms agreed to send to the manager of statistics of the association information regarding past sales, production, and stock on hand. As a part of his informational service, the manager also sent to the members market letters advising the hardwood producers to curtail production and to wait for higher prices. Prices rose considerably during the life of the association and the Court held that since "the united action of this large and influential membership of dealers contributed greatly to the extraordinary price increase"[133] it contravened the anti-trust laws. Mr. Justice Brandeis, however, saw in this "open competition plan" enormous possibilities for improving conditions in the industry. At the same time he feared that frustrating this association of producers might lead to consolidation and monopoly. Thus when the Sherman Act (originally intended to secure free competition) becomes an instrument by which the small competitor is destroyed, he dissents:

> The cooperation which is incident to this plan ["open competition"] does not suppress competition. On the contrary it tends to promote all in competition which is desirable. By substituting knowledge for ignorance, rumor, guess, and suspicion, it tends also to substitute research and reasoning for gambling and piracy, without closing the door to adventure or lessening the value of prophetic wisdom. In making such knowledge available to the smallest concern it creates among producers equality of opportunity. In making it available also to purchasers and the general public, it does all that can actually be done to protect the community from extortion. . . . The evidence in this case, far from establishing an illegal restraint of trade, presents, in my opinion, an instance of commendable effort by concerns engaged in chaotic industry to make possible its intel-

[133] American Column and Lumber Co. v. United States, 257 U.S. 377 at 409 (1921).

ligent conduct under competitive conditions. . . . May not these hardwood lumber concerns, frustrated in their efforts to rationalize competition, be led to enter the inviting field of consolidation? And if they do, may not another huge trust with highly centralized control over vast resources, natural, manufacturing and financial, become so powerful as to dominate competitors, wholesalers, retailers, consumers, employees and, in large measure, the community?[134]

As a result of the Court's decisions in these cases, the opinion gained currency among both lawyers and laymen that the mere collection and dissemination of statistical information is unlawful. But by the time the Cement[135] and Maple Flooring[136] Cases came on for decision, the personnel of the Court had changed. The most significant addition was that of Mr. Justice Stone, an able lawyer and a trained economist. So in these cases we find Justices Brandeis and Holmes on the side of the majority, with Mr. Justice McReynolds, who had spoken for the Court in the American Lumber Case, in the minority. Elaborating the economic viewpoint, so strongly insisted upon by Mr. Justice Brandeis in the latter case, Mr. Justice Stone observed:

It is the consensus of opinion of economists and of many of the most important agencies of government that the public interest is served by the gathering and dissemination, in the widest possible manner, of information with respect to the production and distribution, cost and prices in actual sales, of market commodities, because the making available of such information tends to stabilize trade and industry, to produce fairer price levels and to avoid the waste which inevitably attends the unintelligent conduct of economic enterprise.[137]

[134] ibid. at 418-19. See also United States v. American Linseed Oil Co., 262 U.S. 371 (1923).

[135] Cement Mf'rs. Protective Ass'n. v. United States, 268 U.S. 588 (1925).

[136] Maple Flooring Ass'n. v. United States, 268 U.S. 563 (1925).

[137] ibid. at 582-3.

Price-fixing agreements, however, contravene the Sherman Act. "Whether the prices actually agreed upon were reasonable or unreasonable was immaterial." Mr. Justice Stone in U.S. v. Trenton Potteries Co., 273 U.S. 392 at 401 (1927). Mr. Justice Brandeis long ago subscribed to this point of view. See his article, "Shall We Abandon the Policy of Competition?" (1912), 18 Case and Comment, p. 494.

Mr. Justice Brandeis understands that if the common man is to have any sort of bargaining power equally with capital, he must cooperate with his fellows. Every encouragement should be given to cooperatives among farmers and industrial workers. So when the Oklahoma Act for organizing cooperatives among farmers was found wanting as a denial of equal protection of the laws, Mr. Justice Brandeis dissented. He saw the statute as purposing economic democracy:

> The assertion is that cooperatives organized under the law of 1919, being stock companies, do business with the general public for the sole purpose of making money, as do individual or other corporate competitors; whereas cooperatives organized under the law of 1917 are "for mutual help, without capital stock, not conducted for profit, and restricted to the business of their own members." The fact is that these two types of cooperative corporations—the stock and the non-stock—differ from one another only in a few details, which are without significance in this connection; that both are instrumentalities commonly employed to promote and effect cooperation among farmers; that the two serve the same purpose; and that both differ vitally from commercial corporations. . . . Their aim is economic democracy on lines of liberty, equality and fraternity. To accomplish these objectives, both types of cooperative corporations provide for excluding capitalist control.[138]

Strong advocate of competition that he is, Mr. Justice Brandeis is not blind to the fact that, under certain conditions, competition might lead to abuses. He does not subscribe to it under any and all circumstances. Changed conditions may even force the establishment of monopoly by legislation. This flexibility of his mind was shown in New State Ice Company v. Liebmann,[139] concerning an Oklahoma statute which had provided that any one planning to manufacture, sell or distribute ice must first secure a certifi-

---

[138] Frost v. Corporation Commission, 278 U.S. 515 at 536 (1929). In Corporation Commission of Okla. v. Lowe, 281 U.S. 431 (1930), a case involving facts very similar to those in the Frost Case, a unanimous Court reached a decision in conformity with the views of Mr. Justice Brandeis.

[139] 285 U.S. 262 (1932).

cate of convenience and necessity from the State Corporation
Commission. The New State Ice Company obtained such a cer-
tificate, erected a plant and invested about $500,000. Liebmann,
a free-lance dealer, set up a plant and began doing business in
competition with the New State Ice Company. The authorized
company sued to restrain him, but the state courts sustained
Liebmann's plea on the ground that the Oklahoma statute contravened the Fourteenth Amendment, abridged privileges and
immunities of citizens of the United States, and deprived persons
of their property without due process of law. The Supreme
Court, speaking through Mr. Justice Sutherland, affirmed this,
holding:

> The control here asserted does not protect against monopoly, but
> tends to foster it. The aim is not to encourage competition, but to
> prevent it; not to regulate the business, but to preclude persons from
> engaging in it.[140]

To all this Mr. Justice Brandeis would agree, but as he points
out:

> ... Rightly or wrongly, many persons think that one of the major
> contributing causes [of the depression] has been unbridled com-
> petition. Increasingly, doubt is expressed whether it is economically
> wise, or morally right, that men should be permitted to add to the
> producing facilities of an industry which is already suffering from
> over-capacity.[141]

Accordingly the Justice defends the right of the states to meet
changing economic conditions of the machine age by experi-
mental state legislation. A wide degree of experimentation
should be allowed in thus attempting to protect the people.

> There must be power in the states and the nation to remould,
> through experimentation, our economic practices and institutions
> to meet changing social and economic needs. I cannot believe that
> the framers of the Fourteenth Amendment, or the states which

140 *ibid.*, 279.
141 *ibid.*, 307-8.

ratified it, intended to deprive us of the power to correct the evils of
technological unemployment and excess productive capacity which
have attended progress in the useful arts.[142]

Strangely enough, Mr. Justice Brandeis' liberalism as to
economic and political rights, is wanting in his opinions on
"moral" issues. This contrast is even more puzzling in view of the
ideas on prohibition which he expressed as early as 1891. Here
one finds an appreciation of, an insight into the limits of government regulation in the realm of morals, that is lacking in his
latter-day opinions on the Volstead Act. Absolute prohibition,
Mr. Brandeis argued, was bound to fail. He would "make the
liquor business respectable" by limiting liquor dispensing to
men of standing in the community.

> . . . The use of liquor is not a wrong. It is the abuse and not the
> use which is wrong. . . . Remember the weaknesses of men and
> endeavor to protect them but do not forget that even the weak are
> strong enough to resist too severe restrictions. Remember that any
> regulations which you may adopt will, at best, *reduce* the evil which
> is sure to flow from the appetite of men for stimulating liquors. . . .
> No law can be effective which does not take into consideration the
> conditions of the community for which it is designed; no law can be
> a good law—every law must be a bad law—that remains unen-
> forced.[143]

But despite his realistic insight into prohibition problems, he
has proved himself an authoritarian and even a paternalist in

[142] 285 U.S. 311 (1932).
[143] "The Anti-Bar Law." Argument of L. D. Brandeis before the Joint Committee
on Liquor Law of the Massachusetts Legislature, February 27, 1891. Therein Brandeis
summarized his views on the liquor problem as follows:

"Liquor drinking is not a wrong; but excessive drinking is.
"Liquor will be sold; hence the sale should be licensed.
"Liquor is dangerous; hence the business should be regulated.
"No regulation can be enforced which is not reasonable.

"The better the men who sell liquor, the less the harm done by it.
"Hence, strive to secure for the business those who are respectable.
"Self-respect and prosperity are the most effective guardians of morals.
"Unenforceable or harassing laws tend to make criminals."

his interpretation of the Eighteenth Amendment and the Volstead Act. When the "experiment noble in motive" was attacked, the kind of support he had given pacifists, socialists, and other radical liberals, when restrained by regulatory legislation, was not forthcoming. In the case which enabled the federal government to close breweries and distilleries without any compensation whatever for their losses, he delivered the opinion of the Court;[144] further, he held that one conviction for possessing liquor and another conviction for selling the same liquor did not violate the constitutional protection against double jeopardy;[145] the year before he upheld the government's right to confiscate an innocent owner's motor car simply because a guest-passenger had a small flask of whiskey on his person.[146] Later in the same year he sustained that section of the Volstead Act which prohibits, *inter alia,* physicians from prescribing more than one pint of liquor to the same patient within a period of ten days.[147]

One sees in these cases a breakdown of his individualism (perhaps also of his practice of fact finding), so complete that one may wonder whether he had not forgotten his own warnings:

> . . . In every extension of governmental functions lurks a new danger to civil liberty.[148]

> Experience should teach us to be most on our guard to protect liberty when the government's purposes are beneficent. Men born to freedom are naturally alert to repel invasion of their liberty by evil-minded rulers. The greatest dangers to liberty lurk in insidious

[144] Ruppert v. Caffey, 251 U.S. 264 (1920) (Justices McReynolds, Day, and Van Devanter dissenting).

[145] Albrecht v. United States, 273 U.S. 1 (1927).

[146] United States v. One Ford Coupe, 272 U.S. 321 (1926) (Justices Butler, McReynolds, and Sutherland dissenting). Compare Van Oster v. Kansas, 272 U.S. 465 (1926).

[147] Lambert v. Yellowley, 272 U.S. 581 (1926).

[148] United States *ex. rel.* Democratic Pub. Co. v. Burleson, 255 U.S. 407 at 436 (1921).

encroachment by men of zeal, well-meaning but without under-standing.[149]

When one notes that these objections were made, respectively, one year before and two years after the liquor cases cited above, the mystery deepens. The latter observation appears in Mr. Justice Brandeis' dissenting opinion in the famous wire-tapping case. Although generally sustaining government regulations to enforce the Volstead Act, he could not subscribe to the means employed in this case. If, in enforcing moral legislation, such as the Volstead Act, government encroaches upon men's rights to their beliefs, their thoughts, their emotions, and their sensa-tions, or "the right to be alone—the most comprehensive of rights and the right most valued by civilized men,"[150] he dissents. For Brandeis, as for J. S. Mill, liberty comprises freedom of thought and feeling. But that additional tenet in Mill's individ-ualism which held that each person "is the proper guardian of his own health, whether bodily *or* mental and spiritual,"[151] finds only partial support in Mr. Justice Brandeis' philosophy. He does not subscribe to the doctrine that "mankind are greater gainers by suffering each other to live as seems good to themselves, than by compelling each to live as seems good to the rest";[152] that human nature is "a tree which requires to develop itself on all sides."[153] Rather he believes that no small part of the law's function is to make men good. The question for him is one of

149 Olmstead v. United States, 277 U.S. 438 at 479 (1928).

150 *ibid*. at 478.

Mr. Brandeis' early writings on "The Right of Privacy" doubtless influenced his decision in this case. See *supra*, Chap. v, n. 2.

151 J. S. Mill, *On Liberty and Other Essays* (Everyman ed.), p. 75. Even John Stuart Mill admits that "despotism is a legitimate mode of government in dealing with barbarians, provided the end be their improvement, and the means justified by actually effecting that end" (!) *ibid*., p. 73.

152 *ibid*., pp. 75-6.

153 *ibid*., p. 117.

specific fact and not of broad theory.[154] It may be said perhaps that in the cases cited above he was following a rule which in his opinion would procure liberty through law;[155] he was adhering to the principle voiced in earlier cases:

> ... In order to preserve the liberty and the property of the great majority of the citizens of a state, rights of property and the liberty of the individual must be remoulded, from time to time, to meet the changing needs of society.[156]

Thus his zeal for social justice and his belief in the genuine worth of the individual sometimes cause him to favor even drastic regulation of those very liberties which many consider it the primary purpose of the Bill of Rights to protect, as it is the primary purpose of industrial freedom to make these liberties possible.

5. Holmes and Brandeis: Skeptic and Crusader

Although usually coupled with Mr. Justice Holmes in any discussion of Supreme Court personnel, Mr. Justice Brandeis differs singularly in his judicial technique and approach to questions of social policy. The former is generally called a liberal although he himself never pretended to be anything other than a constitutional skeptic.

In terms of political theory, Mr. Justice Holmes believes that whether "wise or not, the proximate test of a good government

---

[154] See Report of Commission on Industrial Relations, 64th Cong., 1st Sess., Sen. Doc., Vol. XXVI, p. 7674 (1915).

Conditions, Mr. Justice Brandeis believes, are such in many of our industrial communities that this necessity exists. He sees individual liberty and rights imperilled by the economic and social conditions of modern life. For this reason any legislation designed to relieve or to better these basic conditions may gain his approval.

His views stand here in bold contrast to those of Mr. Justice Sutherland. For the latter our chief menace to individual liberty flows not from economic conditions but from social legislation that interferes with the right of a "free" individual to do as he wills with his own.

[155] "The great achievement of the English-speaking people is the attainment of liberty through law." L. D. Brandeis, op. cit. supra, note 13 at 330.

[156] Dissenting in Truax v. Corrigan, supra, note 45 at 376.

is that the dominant power has its way";[157] that the sovereign people, speaking through their authorized agent—the legislature—can, in general, embody their opinions in law; that there is nothing in the Constitution to prevent their doing so. Therein he follows Thomas Hobbes of 1651. Mr. Justice Brandeis, no less than he, advocates the right of the legislature to experiment in things social and economic, yet believes that the legislature can embody popular opinion in law only when such enactments conform with certain standards of social justice. This revives "higher law" doctrine, and recalls a predecessor of Hobbes, Sir Edward Coke. To Mr. Justice Brandeis, judicial review of legislation involves "weighing public needs as against private desires," and also "weighing relative social values." Consequently he claims for the Judiciary a larger share in the exercise of sovereignty than his former colleague seems disposed to allow.

That the two men should have reached so frequently the same goal in considering constitutional issues is by no means conclusive evidence that they travelled the same route. If Mr. Justice Brandeis sustains social legislation, it is because he believes it desirable and expedient as well as constitutional; whereas Mr. Justice Holmes' fundamental belief in the right of states to make social experiments would lead him to uphold legislation even though the particular experiment seem "futile or even noxious."[158] A good illustration of their divergent lines of thought and method occurs in Meyer v. Nebraska.[159] When the

[157] O. W. Holmes, *Collected Legal Papers* (1920), p. 258.

For evidence of Hobbes' influence, see Mr. Justice Holmes' reference to the *Leviathan* in Heard v. Sturgis, 146 Mass. 545, 548-9, 16 N.E. 437, 441 (1888); *In re* Opinion of the Justices, 160 Mass. 586 at 595, 36 N.E. 488 at 492 (1894); Kawananakoa v. Polyblank, 205 U.S. 349 at 353 (1907). See also the very pertinent observations of Elizabeth S. Sergeant, "Justice Touched with Fire," reprinted in Felix Frankfurter, *Mr. Justice Holmes* (1931), p. 186.

[158] Dissenting in Truax v. Corrigan, 257 U.S. 312 at 344 (1921).

[159] 262 U.S. 390 (1923). See also Bartels v. Iowa, 262 U.S. 404 (1923).

In Pennsylvania Coal Co. v. Mahon, 260 U.S. 393 (1922), involving the constitutionality of a Pennsylvania statute (the Kohler Act), which prohibited the mining of

state legislature prohibited teaching German in Nebraska's public schools, Mr. Justice Holmes' brand of liberalism, his willingness to allow the state to experiment even though he did not agree, prompted him to uphold the legislation; Mr. Justice Brandeis, on the other hand, believing in liberty as an end, as well as a means, of achieving that which is most valuable in human life, voted with the Court to overthrow the statute. The former's dissenting opinion, interestingly enough, was concurred in by Mr. Justice Sutherland—a strange judicial bedfellow for one reputed to be a genuine liberal!

It follows that Mr. Justice Holmes' liberalism (if it may be so styled) differs fundamentally from that of Mr. Justice Brandeis. The latter becomes deeply concerned with economic and social maladjustments, with means of correction by legislative action, while Mr. Justice Holmes remains cold and un-

anthracite coal so as to cause subsidence of, *inter alia,* any structure used for human habitation, Mr. Justice Holmes, speaking for the Court, held the statute an unconstitutional infringement upon private property. His decision was based on the assumption that in order to justify such exercise of police power there must be "an average reciprocity of advantage" as between the property owner and the community. Mr. Justice Brandeis, apparently less mindful of the sacredness of the property rights involved, and more willing to allow legislative experimentation, reasoned thus: ". . . Where the police power is exercised, not to confer benefits upon property owners, but to protect the public from detriment and danger, there is, in my opinion, no room for considering reciprocity of advantage." *ibid.* at 422.

In Truax v. Corrigan, 257 U.S. 312, after reviewing the application of the common law to the struggle between employers and employees in England and the United States, and after full "consideration of the contemporary conditions, social, industrial, and political, of the community to be affected," Mr. Justice Brandeis reached the conclusion that an Arizona statute limiting the equitable remedy in disputes between capital and labor is necessary and expedient as well as constitutional.

Taking the same position, in a much briefer opinion, Mr. Justice Holmes, with no consideration of the points stressed by Mr. Justice Brandeis, stated his reaction thus:

"There is nothing that I more deprecate than the use of the Fourteenth Amendment beyond the absolute compulsion of its words to prevent the making of social experiments that an important part of the community desires, in the insulated chambers afforded by the several states, even though the experiments may seem futile or even noxious to me and to those whose judgment I most respect" (at 344).

moved toward legislative and other panaceas.[160] Mr. Justice
Brandeis is an avowed partisan of the common man; his special
concern is for those economically and financially dependent; he
prefers human welfare to property rights.[161] Highly sensitive
to present-day economic and social ills, he could never remain
aloof and indifferent as was the habit of Mr. Justice Holmes. He
seeks the causes of each abuse and examines the merit of proposed remedies.

Counsel seldom succeed in presenting a case in a manner
satisfactory to Mr. Justice Brandeis. He uses fact-finding agencies
on his own account. He feels called upon to make such investi-

[160] The following is a typical statement of Mr. Justice Holmes' position: "I am far
from saying that I think this particular law a wise and rational provision. That is
not my affair. But if the people of the state of New York speaking by their authorized
voice say that they want it, I see nothing in the Constitution of the United States
to prevent their having their will." Mr. Justice Holmes dissenting in Tyson and
Brother v. Banton, 273 U.S. 418 at 447 (1927). Dissenting in Lochner v. New
York, 198 U.S. 45 at 75 (1905) Mr. Justice Holmes wrote: "I strongly believe that
my agreement or disagreement [with any particular economic theory] has nothing
to do with the right of a majority to embody their opinions in law."

For similar utterances, see his opinion in Noble State Bank v. Haskell, 219 U.S. 104
at 111 (1911); Mo., Kan. and Tex. Ry. Co. v. May, 194 U.S. 267 at 270 (1904); Block
v. Hirsh, 256 U.S. 135 at 155 (1921); Otis v. Parker, 187 U.S. 606 at 609 (1903);
Louisville and Nashville R.R. v. Barber Asphalt Paving Co., 197 U.S. 430 at 435 (1905).

The position taken by Mr. Justice Holmes in these cases, regarding the leeway that
should be allowed the legislature, is entirely in accord with his earlier views:

"The first requirement of a sound body of law is, that it should correspond with
actual feelings and demands of the community, whether right or wrong." O. W.
Holmes, *The Common Law* (1881), p. 41.

"Of course, such conformity may lead to destruction, and it is desirable that the
dominant power should be wise." O. W. Holmes, *Collected Legal Papers* (1920), p. 258.

[161] Brandeis' protest against the tendency of the Court to accord property greater
protection than liberty is expressed as follows: "I have difficulty in believing that the
liberty guaranteed by the Constitution, which has been held to protect against state
denial, the right of an employer to discriminate against a workman because he is
a member of a trade union, Coppage v. Kansas, 236 U.S. 1 at 27 (1915); the right
of a business man to conduct a private employment agency, Adams v. Tanner, 244
U.S. 590 (1917), or to contract outside the state for insurance of his property, Allgeyer
v. Louisiana, 165 U.S. 578, 589, although the legislature deems it inimical to the public
welfare, does not include liberty to teach, either in the privacy of the home or pub-
licly, the doctrine of pacifism; so long, at least, as Congress has not declared that
public safety demands its suppression." Gilbert v. Minnesota, 254 U.S. 325 at 343. See
also his dissenting opinion in the Bedford Cut Stone Case, 274 U.S. 37 (1927).

gation of the facts as will enable him to decide whether the provision in question is so clearly arbitrary or capricious that legislators acting reasonably could not have believed it to be necessary or appropriate for the public welfare.[162] Mr. Justice Holmes feels no such responsibility. "It rests with counsel to take the proper steps [to furnish the Court with relevant facts], and if they deliberately omit them, we do not feel called upon to institute inquiries on our own account."[163]

Silas Bent relates a story which illustrates Mr. Justice Holmes' distaste for such research as delights Mr. Justice Brandeis. Soon after taking his seat on the Supreme Court, Mr. Justice Brandeis impressed Mr. Justice Holmes with the idea that "a study of statistics would be good for him." Mr. Justice Holmes was then leaving for his summer home at Beverly Farms and so instructed Mr. Justice Brandeis to "pick out the right books and send them up." The box of books arrived in due course. An examination of the titles revealed a formidable array of monographs and books on the eight-hour day, the textile industry, the employment of women, employers' liability, and so on. Gazing at the box in unaffected dismay, Mr. Justice Holmes is said to have instructed a servant: "Just nail it up and send it back to him." And then with a sigh of relief the Justice immersed himself in

---

[162] Jay Burns Baking Co. v. Bryan, 264 U.S. 504 at 520.

[163] Mr. Justice Holmes speaking for the Court in Quong Wing v. Kirkendall, 223 U.S. 59, 64 (1912). "It may or may not be that if the facts were called to our attention in a proper way the objection would prove to be real. But even if when called to our attention the facts should be taken notice of judicially, whether because they are only the premise for a general proposition of law [citing cases], or for any other reason, still there are many things that courts would notice if brought before them that beforehand they do not know." *ibid*.

Mr. Justice Brandeis has stated his point of view as follows: "Much evidence referred to by me is not in the record. Nor could it have been included. It is the history of the experience gained under similar legislation, and the result of scientific experiments made, since the entry of the judgment below. Of such events in our history, whether occurring before or after the enactment of the statute or of the entry of the judgment, the Court should acquire knowledge, and must, in my opinion, take judicial notice, whenever required to perform the delicate judicial task here involved." Dissenting in Jay Burns Baking Co. v. Bryan, 264 U.S. 504 at 533 (1924).

Plato.[164] The reason perhaps may be his conviction that "the social reformers of today seem . . . so far to forget that we . . . can [not] get something for nothing by legislation. . . . The notion that with socialized property we should have women free and a piano for everybody seems to me an empty humbug."[165]

Mr. Justice Brandeis might well share this skepticism but he has great faith that men, by taking thought, *can* solve our social and economic problems and create the world we all would like to have. Whether writing a brief or a judicial opinion he is at heart a crusader. He has been accused by Mr. Justice Holmes of having "the crusading spirit," of talking "like one of those upward-and-onward fellows."[166] His reason for supporting any social enactment may be, and usually is, "partly legal, partly sentimental, and partly a recognition of economic rights and a sound social policy."[167] Never has he been able to see social and economic life as built on the logical fictions so carefully framed by jurists.

[164] Silas Bent, *Justice Oliver Wendell Homes* (1932), pp. 280-1.

[165] O. W. Holmes, *Collected Legal Papers* (1920), pp. 305-6.

[166] Observation of Mr. Justice Holmes after discussing informally with Mr. Justice Brandeis the constitutional issues involved in the California Criminal Syndicalism Statute of 1919. Related by Silas Bent, *loc. cit.,* p. 281.

[167] Statement before the Commission on Industrial Relations, 64th Cong., 1st Sess., Sen. Doc., Vol. XXVI, p. 7681 (1915).

CHAPTER VIII

CONCLUSIONS

FOR Mr. Justice Brandeis law is essentially an instrument of social policy. Adequate grasp of it does not proceed out of mastery of the rules of logic. "No law, written or unwritten, can be understood without a full knowledge of the facts out of which it arises and to which it is to be applied."[1] He has only slight regard for that "jurisprudence of concepts" which would keep both society and the law rigid and unchangeable. The idea that law can be found but not made forms no part of his philosophy. Although reordering the law to bring it in accord with life, is partly the work of the courts, it is more truly the function of the legislature.[2]

It follows that Mr. Justice Brandeis does not pay *stare decisis* the deference customary among certain of his colleagues. Unlike more conservative brethren, he has insisted that the law must look outside itself if it is to cope adequately with a rapidly changing civilization. "*Stare decisis,*" he believes, "is ordinarily a wise rule of action. But it is not a universal, inexorable com-

---

[1] L. D. Brandeis, "The Living Law" (1916), 10 *Ill. L. Rev.* 461 at 467.

[2] ". . . With the increasing complexity of society, the public interest tends to become omnipresent; and the problems presented by new demands for justice cease to be simple. Then the creation or recognition by courts of a new private right may work serious injury to the general public, unless the boundaries of the right are definitely established and wisely guarded. In order to reconcile the new private right with the public interest, it may be necessary to prescribe limitations and rules for its enjoyment; and also to provide administrative machinery for enforcing the rules. It is largely for this reason that, in the effort to meet the many new demands for justice incident to a rapidly changing civilization, resort to legislation has latterly been had with increasing frequency." International News Service v. Associated Press, 248 U.S. 215 at 262-263 (1918). See also Duplex Printing Co. v. Deering, 254 U.S. 443, 488 (1921). See, in this connection, the excellent article by J. M. Landis, "The Study of Legislation in the Law Schools," *The Harvard Graduate Magazine,* June 1931.

mand."[3] It "does not command that we err again when we have
occasion to pass upon a different statute;"[4] a proposition which
would, perhaps, be equally applicable in interpreting the same
statute. "The logic of words should yield to the logic of realities."[5] In short, he feels that the peculiar virtue of our legal system
lies in the fact "that the process of inclusion and exclusion, so
often employed in developing a rule, is not allowed to end with
its enunciation."[6] "The rule as announced must be deemed tentative. For the many and varying facts to which it will be applied
cannot be foreseen."[7]

Thus Mr. Justice Brandeis brings to his consideration of the
legislative product, not merely judicial precedents and decisions
but also committee reports, legislative debates and authoritative
treatises of various sorts, hitherto almost entirely neglected by
judges. No significant contribution, legal, social or economic,
escapes his attention.[8] Elaborate documentation of such material
is made not solely to reach judicial solution of the problem in
hand; he is equally eager to make his opinion instructive. Instructive to whom? Certainly not merely to his colleagues; nor
to lawyers and judges. It is more than likely that the Justice has
long since lost hope of instilling even elementary economics into
certain of the learned jurists who are his colleagues. One feels

---

[3] Washington v. Dawson and Co., 264 U.S. 219, 238 (1924). For citation of
cases in which the Court has disregarded the principle of *stare decisis,* see *ibid.,* foot-
note 21 at p. 238. For a more recent collection of such cases, see Mr. Justice Brandeis'
dissenting opinion in Burnet v. Coronado Oil and Gas Co., 285 U.S. 393, 406 n. 1
(1932).

[4] Di Santo v. Pennsylvania, 273 U.S. 34 at 42 (1927).

[5] *ibid.* at 43.

[6] Jaybird Mining Co. v. Weir, 271 U.S. 609 at 619 (1926).

[7] Washington v. Dawson and Co., 264 U.S. 219 at 236.

[8] See especially his opinions in the following cases: Adams v. Tanner, 244 U.S. 590
(1917); Truax v. Corrigan, 257 U.S. 312 (1921); Southwestern Bell Tel. Co. v.
Public Serv. Comm., 262 U.S. 276; New York Central R.R. v. Winfield, 244 U.S. 147
(1917); United Railways and Electric Co. v. West, 280 U.S. 234 (1930); Jay Burns
Baking Co. v. Bryan, 264 U.S. 504; St. Louis and O'Fallon Ry. v. United States, 279
U.S. 461 (1929); New State Ice Co. v. Liebmann, 285 U.S. 262 (1932); Liggett v.
Lee, 288 U.S. 517 (1933).

that some of his more recent opinions, especially in the New Ice Company and Florida Chain Stores Cases, were addressed not so much to lawyers and judges as to legislators and others active in creating public opinion. His researches in social science, both as counsel and as judge, not only have bared the falsity of numerous assumptions "upon which many American judges and lawyers had rested comfortably,"[9] but also have furnished abundant material for social planners and present-day legislators. His conviction that eighteenth century individualistic philosophy of rights and property is no longer a creed adequate for modern life, is now generally recognized. It is increasingly evident that society has to have protection against the dragging plague of sweatshop wages, unemployment, industrial accidents, ruthless competition, planless production and distribution, and other social and economic maladjustments, because society must ultimately bear the cost. An official spokesman for the Roosevelt administration observed recently that "our economic life is too complicated to be run without an all-embracing plan and that government must play an important part in formulating such a plan."[10] In launching its plan the administration disclaims any purpose to destroy or to lessen individual initiative or to lessen the opportunity for voluntary action; rather the objective is to establish those conditions wherein every deserving person can have the opportunity to earn a comfortable living.[11] This is essentially the position of Mr. Justice Brandeis. By attempting to enforce individual justice, he endeavors to lay the foundations of social justice.

Though preeminently a factualist, a stickler for statistics, he never lets himself be buried under the facts of industrialism. Particular emphasis should be given to the coherent and pur-

[9] New York Central R.R. v. Winfield, 244 U.S. 147 at 164.
[10] Language of Henry Morgenthau, Jr., *The New York Times,* May 22, 1933.
[11] See Senator Wagner's speech on the Industrial Recovery Bill, 77 Cong. Rec., 525 ff., June 7, 1933.

poseful social-political philosophy which underlies his profound factual knowledge. It is one thing to collect masses of complicated data and statistics; it is quite a different thing to be able to give such material a social interpretation—to see concrete facts in terms of life.[12] Brandeis' unusual capacity for the social interpretation of fact is not denied even by those who consider his conclusions dangerous to their own stake in the established order. For him the result is that he is never forced "to improvise a theory, a philosophy, when confronted over night by the exigencies of the case before him." With insight into the "universal element" involved, his decisions are quickened "with the inspiration of a principle."[13]

[12] "The man of science in the law is not merely a bookworm. To a microscopic eye for detail he must unite an insight which tells him what details are significant. Not every maker of exact investigation counts, but only he who directs his investigation to a crucial point." O. W. Holmes, *Collected Legal Papers* (1920), p. 224.

[13] B. N. Cardozo, *The Growth of the Law* (1924), p. 102. Mr. Justice Brandeis possesses to an unusual degree that peculiar quality of mind which, in the opinion of Mr. Justice Cardozo, judges so frequently lack:

". . . The judge is often left to improvise . . . a theory, . . . a philosophy, when confronted overnight by the exigencies of the case before him. Often he fumbles about, feeling in a vague way that some such problem is involved, but missing the universal element which would have quickened his decision with the inspiration of a principle. If he lacks an adequate philosophy, he either goes astray altogether, or at best does not rise above the empiricism that pronounces judgment upon particulars.

"An avalanche of decisions by tribunals great and small is producing a situation where citation of precedent is tending to count for less, and appeal to an informing principle is tending to count for more. . . . We shall be caught in the tentacles of the web, unless some superintending mind imparts the secret of the structure, lifting us to a height, where the unity of the circle will be visible as it lies below." *ibid.*, pp. 5, 6.

In an address on December 17, 1931, Judge Cardozo again made a strong plea for a "new philosophy in law that will guide the thought of our successors when those of us in place today shall have vanished from the scene." *The New York Times,* December 18, 1931.

Mr. Justice Holmes has emphasized the same point: "Theory is the most important part of the dogma of the law, as the architect is the most important man who takes part in the building of a house. The most important improvements of the last twenty-five years are improvements in theory. It is not to be feared as unpractical, for, to the competent it simply means going to the bottom of the subject." O. W. Holmes, *Collected Legal Papers* (1920), p. 200. See also Holmes' introduction to *The Continental Legal History Series* (1911), p. xlvi.

Judicial interpretation cannot eliminate the personal bias of the interpreter. All men are more or less partisan. Emotions, great and small, compel the judge to choose his side. When once that choice is made, historical events, social and economic facts, judicial precedents and philosophy, are marshalled and emphasized to confirm his stand. These observations are as applicable to Mr. Justice Brandeis as to any other judge. Years of study and of close contact with affairs have developed in him certain emotional preferences. He has shown himself unable to regard constitutional-social issues with the Brahmin detachment that uniquely characterized Mr. Justice Holmes. Nor is this reason for surprise. As Mr. Justice Cardozo wrote while a member of the New York Court of Appeals: "Deep below consciousness are . . . the likes and the dislikes, the predilections and the prejudices, the complex of instincts and emotions and habits and convictions, which make the man, whether he be litigant or judge. . . . The great tides and currents which engulf the rest of men, do not turn aside in their course, and pass the judges by."[14]

Noting the continuity of Mr. Justice Brandeis' views, one may feel that the picture of an ideal society predetermines his position in many decisions. And yet his contention that he has "no rigid social philosophy," is logical enough because he is a social scientist, for whom problems are never solved but are always in process of solution. He remembers "that progress is necessarily slow; that remedies are necessarily tentative."[15] New inventions, great emergencies and the like, give rise to new difficulties. A rule of law once settled may have to yield later on to the impact of factors unforeseen. "Modification implies growth. It is the life of the law."[16] The Constitution itself does not block that growth except when interpreted by minds too rigid and in an

[14] B. N. Cardozo, *The Nature of the Judicial Process* (1928), pp. 167-8.
[15] Letter to Robert W. Bruère, February 25, 1922.
[16] Washington v. Dawson and Co., 264 U.S. 219 at 236.

age of change.[17] Then only does our fundamental law prevent legislation from achieving the social and economic ideal. Mr. Justice Brandeis understands that the Constitution must be given liberal construction, if as John Marshall once said, it is "to endure for all ages to come, and, consequently, to be adapted to the various *crises* in human affairs."[18]

Time works changes, brings into existence new conditions and purposes. Therefore a principle to be vital must be capable of wider application than the mischief which gave it birth. This is peculiarly true of constitutions. They are not ephemeral enactments, designed to meet passing occasions.[19]

. . . Our social and industrial welfare demands that ample scope should be given for social as well as mechanical invention. It is a condition not only of progress but of conserving that which we have. Nothing could be more revolutionary than to close the door to social experimentation. . . . And surely the federal constitution—itself perhaps the greatest of human experiments—does not prohibit [legislation reconciling] the existing industrial system with our striving for social justice and the preservation of the race.[20]

These observations were made in 1911. Twenty-one years later in his famous disagreement with the Court on its construction of the Fourteenth Amendment to restrict the states in their efforts to deal with "an emergency more serious than war," he said:

[17] Such obstacles as there are exist not in the Constitution, but in the minds of those who expound it:

"It [the Constitution] has not lost its capacity for expansion to meet new conditions, unless it be interpreted by rigid minds which have no such capacity." Ernest Poole, "Brandeis . . . ," *The American Magazine,* February 1911.

What Mr. Brandeis said in 1915 with particular reference to minimum wage legislation is applicable to social legislation generally. See L. D. Brandeis, "The Constitution and the Minimum Wage," February 6, 1915.

[18] McCulloch v. Maryland, 4 Wheat. 316 at 415 (1819).

[19] Olmstead v. United States, 277 U.S. 438 at 472 (quoted from Weems v. United States, 217 U.S. 349 at 373 (1910).

[20] L. D. Brandeis, "The Constitution and the Minimum Wage," *The Survey,* February 6, 1915.

Economists are searching for the causes of this disorder and are reexamining the bases of our industrial structure. Business men are seeking possible remedies. Most of them realize that failure to distribute widely the profits of industry has been a prime cause of our present plight. But rightly or wrongly, many persons think that one of the major contributing causes has been unbridled competition. Increasingly, doubt is expressed whether it is economically wise, or morally right, that men should be permitted to add to the producing facilities of an industry which is already suffering from over-capacity. . . .

All agree that irregularity in employment—the greatest of our evils—cannot be overcome unless production and consumption are more nearly balanced. Many insist there must be some form of economic control. . . .

To stay experimentation in things social and economic is a grave responsibility.[21]

Students of Mr. Justice Brandeis' work have been accustomed, heretofore, to lay special stress upon his mastery of figures and statistics.[22] This emphasis is not misplaced, but such analysis may lose sight of the fact that Mr. Justice Brandeis is social scientist and philosopher as well as technician. He has seen, as have few of his generation, the perils of the industrial revolution; he understands that the development of the machine and of the business corporation are threats to liberty and to the general welfare. It is clear to him we have "passed to a subtler civiliza-

[21] New State Ice Co. v. Liebmann, 285 U.S. 262 at 307-8, 311.

[22] Norman Hapgood in his preface to *Other People's Money* (1914), attributes Brandeis' success in various fields largely to his mastery of arithmetic and of the technical details of accounting. Most of Brandeis' contributions to economic statecraft have, it is true, involved arithmetic. When he succeeded in preventing a rise in freight rates, it was through an exact analysis of cost. When he got Savings Bank Insurance started in Massachusetts it was by being able to figure what insurance ought to cost. Thus one can hardly overemphasize the part that mastery of figures has played in his success. As he himself has said: "Cuvier, the great French naturalist, could take a single bone of a prehistoric animal and construct the complete skeleton. He could do this because of his special knowledge of anatomy.

"My special field of knowledge is figures. And so I was able to take a few published figures of the New Haven, and, working backward, build up their complete system of bookkeeping." Robert F. Wilson in the *Boston Traveler*, June 10, 1910.

tion" which requires that the law "protect a man from things
that rob him of his freedom, whether the oppressing force be
physical or of a subtler kind."[23] The Justice emphasized long
ago the need for social intelligence. But he did more. He studied
some of the outstanding social and economic ills from which
society increasingly suffers. In these novel and creative activities
Mr. Justice Brandeis has been dominated by a philosophy, an
ideal, the vision of a social and political community within
which the individual may best develop.

Views based on this philosophy, long propounded in dissent,
are now winning acceptance. As spokesman for the Court in the
New Jersey Insurance Case, he held that the presumption of
constitutionality in favor of legislation, clearly within the police
power, must prevail "in the absence of some factual foundation
of record for overthrowing the statute."[24] The burden of proof,
therefore, is placed squarely on those who oppose the statute,
not on the state that upholds it. This recalls the rule the Court
followed in the famous Munn Case[25] more than fifty years
earlier—a rule from which the Court has departed in important
instances. Either placing the burden of proof upon the state[26]

23 Recorded by Ernest Poole in his interview with Brandeis, *The American
Magazine,* February 1911.

24 O'Gorman and Young v. Hartford Ins. Co., 282 U.S. 251 at 258 (1931).
The same position is taken by Chief Justice Hughes (Justice Brandeis concurring)
in Corporation Commission of Okla. v. Lowe, 281 U.S. 431 at 438.

"It was incumbent upon the appellee in invoking the protection of the Fourteenth
Amendment to show with convincing clarity that the law of the state created
against him the discrimination of which he complained. An infraction of the constitutional provision is not to be assumed. On the contrary, it is to be presumed that the
state in enforcing its local policies will conform its requirements to the federal
guarantees. Doubts on this point are to be resolved in favor of and not against, the
state." Compare with Mr. Justice Hughes' opinion in Price v. Illinois, 238 U.S. 446,
452 (1915).

25 Munn v. Illinois, 94 U.S. 113 at 132, 135. See also, Mr. Justice Harlan's opinion
in Powell v. Pennsylvania, 127 U.S. 678, 685 (1888); Atkin v. Kansas, 191 U.S. 207,
222 (1903).

26 As Mr. Justice Sutherland held in Adkins v. Children's Hospital, 261 U.S. 525
(1923): ". . . Freedom of contract is . . . the general rule and restraint the exception;
and the exercise of legislative authority to abridge it can be justified only by the

for the justification of social legislation, or by making judicial investigation of facts such as is proper only for the legislature, and by substituting its own findings for those of the legislature (as more conservative judges sometimes do),[27] the Court has hitherto found it possible to set aside legislation of social and economic significance. The decision noted may correct this drift.

In the Railway Clerks' Case[28] the Supreme Court went far toward accepting Mr. Justice Brandeis' view that a labor union is entitled to extend its operations beyond the bounds of a single enterprise. The Railway Clerks' Union, to preserve its integrity, had secured an injunction against the formation of a company union. A unanimous Court sustained that order. The case is noteworthy in that, for the first time in a Supreme Court decision, we see the injunction effectively used by labor against capital, thus equalizing somewhat their disparate powers.

In the first Chain Store Case,[29] the claims of industrial liberty, the rights of independent merchants and manufacturers against oppression by monopolistic combinations, prevailed on the basis of the principles of Mr. Justice Brandeis' dissent in the Quaker City Cab Case.[30] During the same term of Court, his conclusion that "in frank expression of conflicting opinion lies the greatest promise of wisdom in governmental action; and in suppression lies ordinarily the greatest peril,"[31] at last obtained a majority in

existence of exceptional circumstances. Whether these circumstances exist in the present case constitutes the question to be answered" (at 546).

Continuing, he wrote: "The feature of this statute which, perhaps more than any other, puts upon it the stamp of invalidity is that it exacts from the employer an arbitrary payment for a purpose and upon a basis having no causal connection with his business, or the contract or the work the employee engages to do" (at 558).

[27] As in Mr. Justice Butler's opinion in Jay Burns Baking Co. v. Bryan, 264 U.S. 504 at 534 (1924).

[28] Texas and New Orleans Ry. Co. v. Brotherhood of Railway and Steamship Clerks, 281 U.S. 548 (1930).

[29] State Board of Tax Commissioners v. Jackson, 283 U.S. 527 (1931).

[30] Quaker City Cab Co. v. Pennsylvania, 277 U.S. 389 at 410-11 (1928).

[31] Gilbert v. Minnesota, 254 U.S. 325 at 388.

the California Red Flag Case.[32] Delivering the opinion of the
Court, Chief Justice Hughes wrote:

> The maintenance of the opportunity for free political discussion
> to the end that government may be responsive to the will of the
> people and that changes may be obtained by lawful means, an oppor-
> tunity essential to the security of the Republic is a fundamental
> principle of our constitutional system.[33]

Public utility events have confirmed his actual prudent-invest-
ment theory of valuation as against reproduction cost which the
Court has usually tended to favor. With deep insight into
economic cause and effect Mr. Justice Brandeis wrote in 1923:
"The present price level may fall to that of 1914 within a decade;
and . . . later, it may fall much lower."[34] In the first major
valuation case to reflect depression conditions, Chief Justice
Hughes uses language strikingly similar to that in which Mr.
Justice Brandeis ten years ago described the practical and theoretical difficulties that attend using *present value* as the rate base:
"It is apparent," the Chief Justice concludes, "that the estimates
of cost of reproduction new of 1929, or 1930, upon which the
Company relies, afforded no secure foundation for prediction of
future values, and the rate base as fixed by the Commission is
not to be invalidated as involving confiscation by reason of these
estimates which the course of events deprived of credit as trust-
worthy prophecies."[35]

Another recent triumph for Mr. Justice Brandeis' views is Chief
Justice Hughes' opinion in Appalachian Coals, Inc. v. United

[32] Stromberg v. California, 283 U.S. 359 (1931). See also Near v. Minnesota, 283
U.S. 697 (1931) where the Court in a five-to-four decision held unconstitutional
the Minnesota "Gag Law" which made possible enjoining any publication which,
in the opinion of a single judge, was contrary to public morals.

[33] 283 U.S. 359 at 369.

[34] Southwestern Bell Tel. Co. v. Public Serv. Comm., 262 U.S. 276 at 303, foot-
note 16.

[35] Los Angeles G. & E. Corp. v. Railroad Co., 289 U.S. 287 at 312 (1933). See, in
this connection, the suggestive editorial "Utility Rates in the Slump," *The New
Republic*, July 12, 1933.

States, decided March 13, 1933.[36] Here, along the line of reasoning followed by Mr. Justice Brandeis, dissenting in the American Column and Lumber Case, the Court (Mr. Justice McReynolds *contra*) upheld under the anti-trust laws an exclusive selling agency for sixty-four per cent of the bituminous mines in the Appalachian territory. The case is all the more significant in view of the fact that it involved more than an "open competition plan," and such mere exchange of information as was brought under the ban of the Sherman Act in the American Column and Lumber Case. The function of the selling agency was not only better methods of distribution, intensive advertising and research, economy of marketing and the elimination of abnormal, deceptive, and destructive trade practices, but also the sale of all the coal at the best available price upon an agreed classification and the apportionment of orders if all the coal could not be sold. The Chief Justice upheld this sort of cooperation among competitors on the theory propounded by Mr. Brandeis before he was a Supreme Court Justice, and since, namely, that by substituting rational competition for ruinous warfare, the flow of commerce is not restrained but immeasurably increased.[37]

As a member of the Supreme Court, Mr. Justice Brandeis has been and is significant because certain preeminent qualities of mind enable him to bring the law into vital relationship with the social possibilities of industry in our own day. He sees beyond the recorded mass of economic and statistical fact, to the basic social and economic consequences, to philosophic implications for the future. Methods of legal technique are not idols but tools —tools serving at once the arts of juristic philosophy and of

[36] 288 U.S. 344 (1933).

[37] The Chief Justice took pains to point out, however, that the judgment in this case was not to be regarded as sanctioning any future activities of the selling agency. Rather the decree directed the District Court to dismiss the bill without prejudice, but to retain jurisdiction, to the end that should results of the cooperative plan in actual operation prove contrary to the Anti-Trust Act, the case might be reopened by that Court for further proceedings by the government. 288 U.S. 344 at 378.

statesmanship. Vast learning in the social sciences and a well-nigh unique mastery of current data are used as instruments of juristic thought. Thus it is that Mr. Justice Brandeis builds for our law of days to come. The recently enacted program of the Roosevelt administration embodies several philosophic principles and practical devices which were urged by him years ago. With a Supreme Court dominated by his doctrines of constitutional law, it would be within the power of government to lay the foundation of a society which offers more security as well as more leisure, broader social responsibilities as well as greater social privileges—in short, a nearer approach than men have ever thought possible to the ideal of liberty through law.

TABLE OF CASES*

* For a complete list of cases (to June 1, 1931) involving constitutional questions and other issues of public law, see Felix Frankfurter, ed., *Mr. Justice Brandeis* (1932), pp. 225 *ff.*

INDEX